Praise for *Butterfl*

"Meg brings you on her journey through her dark night of the soul with such honest, passionate writing you feel you are there. Her beautiful vulnerability opens the door for all of us to peer into our heart and pay attention to its stirrings, inviting us in to discover our bliss. Meg reminds us that we all have the power to transform our lives and the lives of others by following our dreams and becoming the person we were intended to be."

—AMY BUTLER, Editor-in-Chief / *Blossom*

"Meg's memoir is a must-read for anyone dealing with loss. Who knew when Meg and my path crossed that she would end up helping me with my own grief? I am grateful for Meg and all the magic she brings."

—PAM GROUT, #1 *New York Times* bestselling author of *E-Squared, The Course in Miracles for Badasses* and 18 other books

"In *Butterfly Awaken*s Meg Nocero takes us on a quest that is physical, intellectual, emotional and spiritual. We join her as she journeys through fear and despair, with courage and hope. Meg's metamorphosis becomes ours, as it inspires us to transform our lives."

—TAL BEN-SHAHAR, PH.D, *New York Times* bestselling author, *Happier, No Matter What*

"As I read Meg's beautiful words, just beautiful things came up. . . . I appreciate Meg's courage to be transparent and real and vulnerable to the benefit of us all. I appreciate Meg's candor in not holding back, and more than anything, I really appreciate Meg's eloquence in writing. Meg *is* among the best of the best, and I'm honored that I got a sneak peek at this beautiful artistic magnum opus (or one of her many anyway). I TOTALLY LOVE THIS."

—BERTA MEDINA-GARCIA, keynote speaker, adventure coach, and founder of Dreamers Succeed

"Meg takes us on her deeply personal journey of transformation that ultimately serves as profoundly hopeful encouragement for finding one's own true path. Her story truly moved me to tears in some places, to giddy joy in others."

—JESSICA CIOSEK, author of *Sometimes a Soldier Comes Home*

"*Butterfly Awakens* celebrates a woman's journey to her authentic self as it illuminates the enduring bond between mother and daughter. . . . With this life-affirming memoir, Meg Nocero will become your soul-sister, enthusiastically welcoming you into her world, as she lays her heart wide open on her journey to wholeness. She bravely reveals her own dark night of the soul, offering her readers permission to be beautifully and imperfectly human: to stumble, fall apart, grieve and ultimately awaken to boundless self-love."

—TANYA MIKAELA, author of *The Circle, A Woman's Guide to Joy, Passion, and Authenticity*

"This book is wonderful. It is such a different look upon life and how to navigate your way through grief or pain and come out the other end on top of it. This is a story of resilience and transformation. . . . Meg's vulnerability and rawness reminds you not to give up. It is not only a beautiful tribute to her mother but a reminder that you can always find your way back home: to you."

—PAULINA DE REGIL, employee relations specialist at Cushman and Wakefield

"Meg's words carry you into her world. You find yourself sighing with sadness or smiling as she takes you on her journey from grief through fulfillment. I wanted to call the author to dig deep into her experiences and explore the emotions that are so raw and on the table. May your metamorphosis take off as you read through the pages of this memoir."

—GRISSEL SEIJO, ESQ.

"Reading *Butterfly Awakens*, you'll feel that Meg is an old friend you'll be rooting for. We can all relate to her story of overcoming grief and loss and emerging stronger for it."

—DAVID LANDAU, ESQ., editor

"Relatable and emotional. A must read for anyone going through a transformative life experience."

—KELLIE SANTOS-DE JESUS, ESQ.

"Meg drew me into her pain and her struggle. Meg's vulnerability and rawness of emotion keeps her story pure. And those who have been through that depth of pain—those who are in it right now—will understand the incomprehensible and all-consuming effects of a broken heart. She had me laughing, crying, holding my breath, and cheering her on. Even in the midst of the thick, stinking mud-hurricane that is depression, Meg knew there had to be more. Her story serves as a guide, lighting a path out of darkness."

—TAMAIRA RIVERA, ESQ.

"Meg gave me a true glimpse into her honest and true personal life journey from the pain and awkwardness of childhood through the downward spiral of unspeakable mourning that continued through recovery, self-empowerment, then true growth. Her daring to undergo the metamorphosis has her arriving at a more bliss-filled life. . . I highly recommend the inspiring writings of *Butterfly Awakens* to anyone seeking to better understand the process of healing and growth."

—ANDREW DEUTSCH, global marketing and sales executive, Fangled Tech International

"At one time or another, we all experience adversities that challenge us to the core. In reading this book, you'll share her journey and may start to ask those difficult questions we all must ask to 'transform'—you don't have to agree with all the decisions she took, but you will see the courage and love expended to go from cocoon to butterfly."

—THOMAS AYZE, ESQ., lieutenant colonel, USAFR (retired)

"Through her warm and vivid story about love, life and loss, Meg Nocero reminds us that vulnerability is a form of strength. Like the butterflies that guide her on her journey to acceptance and healing, she helps us find beauty in unexpected places, inspiration at unexpected moments, and connectivity in seemingly unrelated events. Meg's is a generous, empathetic and important voice for anyone seeking self-healing."

—WENDY SHANKER, author, *Are You My Guru?: How Medicine, Meditation & Madonna Saved My Life*

Butterfly Awakens

Butterfly Awakens

A MEMOIR OF TRANSFORMATION THROUGH GRIEF

Meg Nocero

SHE WRITES PRESS

Published 2021
Printed in the United States of America
Print ISBN: 978-1-64742-175-5
E-ISBN: 978-1-64742-176-2
Library of Congress Control Number: 2021907906

For information, address:
She Writes Press
1569 Solano Ave #546
Berkeley, CA 94707

Interior design by Tabitha Lahr

She Writes Press is a division of SparkPoint Studio, LLC.

All company and/or product names may be trade names, logos, trademarks, and/or registered trademarks and are the property of their respective owners.

Names and identifying characteristics have been changed to protect the privacy of certain individuals.

There are as many versions of every family's history as there are family members. This is mine. I have changed some names, places, and recognizable details to protect the privacy of friends and family members mentioned in the book.

Love Is Our Mission

Souls transform when they connect with others
on this magic carpet ride we call life.
Seeing all the beautiful faces on this journey, knowing that
divinity has dealt a beautiful hand. Standing on the edge of
the passage of time, looking out over the horizon. One sunset
giving way to the sunrise of hope, possibility, and even bliss.
Praying that we are brave enough to walk into and embrace the
unknown so we can fully become the hero of our own journey.
The next part shall be where we will not apologize for ourselves.

Holding our hands over our hearts,
connecting with our center of balance, of brilliance, of light.
Exhaling into the moment, inhaling all that it has to offer—
Exhaling gratitude, inhaling wonder—
Exhaling love, inhaling life.

For it has taken this long to truly realize that we are not lost.
We are finding direction in the chaos, finding purpose in
the pain, finding our voice, finding our way.
We wander together side by side, love is our mission!

For my Nocero Tribe and my Butterflies

In loving memory of my mother, Mary Jo Nocero
and my Camino amigo, Paulina Gutierrez-Tawil

Contents

Foreword

We first met Meg when she reached out to us with regard to helping with our nonprofit organization, the Love Button Global Movement (Love Button). We founded Love Button in 2013 to inspire people to reach out to others in loving ways both big and small in order to overcome differences and foster social cohesion. When we extend our love to someone in an act of kindness, there's an instant connection, a moment where we realize we all have the same needs in which we recognize our shared humanity and interconnectedness. We were not surprised that someone like Meg wanted to be part of Love Button, and since then, she's been one of our greatest ambassadors.

Of course, letting love lead us through life is easy when things are going well. When our personal world is turned upside down, when we're angry, sad, confused, and scared, that's when the real challenge begins. Can we remain in our loving with others, as well as ourselves, as we stand in the eye of a storm where everything seems to be coming apart? Can we resist the urge to become resentful or bitter while seeing our challenges as what they really are—opportunities for personal growth?

Love is what keeps us grounded in the stillness when everything else is spinning out of control around us. It's only in that neutral space where the answers can be found and we're able to see that in every loss there is always the chance to gain in some other way if we're willing to remain open to it. This is what the poet John Keats called negative capability or the ability to be okay with things not being okay . . . until they're okay again. Only living from love can do that.

As Meg takes you through her extraordinary journey, you'll be inspired by seeing how living from a loving consciousness brought healing, reconciliation, and resolution to her life after moments of great loss and struggle. She's really someone who walks her talk and did so literally when she walked part of the famous El Camino del Santiago in Spain, an ancient pathway stretching from the northern border with France to the northwest corner of the country ending at the Cathedral of Santiago de Compostela in Galicia where Saint James is buried. Since the ninth century, the path has attracted hundreds of thousands of travelers to take the pilgrimage that is said to lead to spiritual growth. Most make the journey on foot; Meg walked over 111 km in six days, completing the final part of the pilgrimage on a sprained ankle.

Even during this immense challenge, Meg remained dedicated to love, handing out our trademark Love Buttons for people to wear all along the way, while listening to an MP3 player of inspirational songs we sent to keep her spirits up and motivation high. As she checked in with us from time to time during the walk, what impressed us even more about Meg was her determination to keep going day after day, even in spite of the weather, fatigue, and those pesky blisters.

In the end, we're not surprised that Meg accomplished such an incredible task because in a very real way El Camino de Santiago is symbolic of how she approaches her entire life with perseverance, belief in her own inner strength, and of course, love. Both her pilgrimage and her personal story are inspirational examples that prove reaching a better place in life has nothing to do with how many times we stop because the burden is too heavy, but how many times we choose to start again.

—DR. HABIB SADEGHI & DR. SHERRY SAMI
Founders of the Love Button Global Movement,
a 501 (c)(3) that cultivates a culture of love
Los Angeles, 2020

Prologue

*"I dreamed I was a butterfly, flying in the sky; then I awoke.
Now I wonder, am I a man who dreamt of being a butterfly, or
am I a butterfly dreaming that I am a man?"*
—**CHUANG TZU**, c. 369 BC–c. 286 BC, Tao dream master

Call me Butterfly—this may not be my real name, but its symbolism aligns with my soul. You see, the soul story is so much bigger than just a given name anyway. And, daring to share my story of transformation, I hope my soul story will outlast me and my name. For we all need to awaken to question who we are, why we are here, and perhaps why we go through what we do.

One thing is certain. Whether we think so or not, we all have a story to tell. Maybe my story will resonate with you. Maybe it won't. But something within me beckoned to share, nonetheless. My life has shown me that everything does have a purpose. And my hope is that by being open with my journey through personal loss, health challenges, and professional struggles—and overcoming these adversities—my story will serve as a ray of hope for anyone struggling to find their own light at the end of the tunnel.

What I know for sure is that we will always find extraordinary in the ordinary if we are paying attention. And we all have amazing dreams that will astonish us if we let them. Once upon a time, I dreamt about a beautiful butterfly flying free. It just took me half my life to realize that the extraordinary, beautiful butterfly I dreamt about could actually be me.

When I was a kid, especially during those awkward, formative years, I used to live in closets, both the literal kind and the ones in my mind. Even before I retreated to protect myself from the constant ridicule and harassment of my young peers, I preferred to live in my imagination. When I was five or six, I pretended I was a magical fairy granting wishes to anyone who sought my assistance. Other days, I set out to discover the world, taking journeys to the far corners of the globe. Free to create, my active imagination opened magical doors where incredible stories were about to unfold. Other imaginary friends would greet me there, welcoming and joining me in celebration. With eyes wide open, I stepped into possibility and felt incredibly lucky.

But my imagination didn't prepare me for the unwelcoming world to come. When I turned ten years old, others brought to my attention how unappealing they thought I was. I saw the disdain for my appearance on the faces of some of my classmates when I walked into a room. In fifth grade, on the first day of school, it was as though others had nominated me as a focus for humiliation and judgment. With thick eyeglasses, a mouth full of metal, slicked-back hair pulled tightly by two Goody barrettes, accompanied by a round face and a thick waist, my changing body and sense of self took a giant hit. While I dreamt of being the belle of the ball, their incessant snickering and ugly name-calling blew up my fantasy. As I grew more and more uncomfortable in my own skin, I looked around at the other awkward children and wondered why I was the one who was constantly belittled. I had no earthly idea what I had done to deserve such nastiness from my peers. Why was I made to feel I needed to apologize daily for my existence?

Elementary school was not a kind place for me. I never even had a chance to defend myself when the deciding votes against me were cast. Showing up in other children's estimation as a blend of ugly and insecure, I was a perfect target. With no idea how to respond, I concluded that their opinion must have been right, even though my mother would tell me how beautiful I was. Almost every day, in this tale, those who declared themselves the fairest of them all harassed me. I so desperately wanted to be liked, so desperately wanted to be a part of something that I thought being kind would shift the tides. *Be nice to them, Meg . . . Be a good girl,*

Meg . . . Move along quickly, Meg, they will go away . . . Ignore them and don't pay attention, Meggie, the little voice in my head desperately advised. Unfortunately, the bullying did not stop. Yet I kept smiling, even though the joyful, carefree part of me started to die.

After school, I returned to the safety of my home. I would glom on as the third wheel to my younger sister Aimee and her best friend as we rode our beat-up bicycles up and down the cul-de-sac, arguing over who got to play the glamorous Farrah Fawcett's Jill, Jaclyn Smith's Kelly, or Cheryl Ladd's Chrissie of *Charlie's Angels.*

When I wanted to be alone, I went to the room I shared with my older sister Mary where my Shetland sheepdog, Fred, awaited me. He, like me, was sure to be labeled less than perfect by others. He had mange, a disease that had caused infections of the skin since Fred was two years old, and my father would painstakingly bathe him to relieve the itching and sores when a flareup attacked his immune system. Shelties (imagine a miniature Lassie) are known for their beautiful sable-and-white fur. Not Fred, though. My father had to shave him bald to clear up his skin. Fred and I were quite the pair.

In my room, I would grab from my closet the boxes that contained my Barbie dolls, lay each one on the carpet, and spend hours constructing lives for them. Fred lay patiently by my side as sunlight spilled in through my bedroom window. Busily sewing little dresses for them from the sheets I liberated from the linen closet, I created a lovely wardrobe. Crafting furniture out of discarded shoeboxes with festive wrapping paper, I set up a happy home.

In the black artist's workbook that my aunt Pat had given me, I designed elegant ball gowns that I imagined wearing to fabulous galas where I would dance the night away. I got lost in the colors of painting and design, mostly princess gowns with full skirts and lots of tulle. I drew models with long flowing hair and delicate crowns on top of their heads. If I didn't feel like drawing, I wiled away the hours creating a series called *Hello, Fellow.* Making up the life of a successful, attractive, and smart young lady, I set out to create wonderful stories. Upon completion of each chapter, I bound the loose-leaf pages together with pieces of rope I found in one of my mother's junk drawers. With each of these activities, I escaped my reality and entered a fantasy world that was far more appealing.

That happiness only lasted until the next weekday morning at six, when I had to return to school. My mother would sing, "It's time to get up, it's time to get up, it's time to get up in the morning." I rustled around in my bed and covered my face with a pillow. Pretending not to hear, I hoped to delay as long as I could. Because I dreaded going, I was late on purpose. Running with my shoes in my hand out to the bus, I summoned the courage to pull myself together for another day.

In my first year of middle school, the worst of the bullying began. It was another excruciating experience as an awkward preteen, getting through the day. While I had accepted the proverbial dark cloud that hovered over me, when the last class ended, I could finally escape and go home. I moved quickly to the metal fence where the bus waited. Once I got in, relieved, I looked out the window, holding back the feelings of shame that were the result of the day's humiliation. When I arrived at my front door, I raced into my house and fell into the arms of my mother, Mary Jo. As I sobbed uncontrollably, my mom would hold me, caress my hair, and tell me everything would be all right. And I believed her when she said, "I don't know why you're going through this. I am so sorry, my Meggie. I do know that everything has a reason. You're a beautiful, smart girl. You'll be okay. And because you know how it feels, your wisdom will help others someday. I'm so proud of you. I love you so much!"

Mary Jo, my mother, was the most beautiful lady I knew. While she and my father, Michael, had high expectations for their girls to excel, she did share with me her own challenges. She too had a hard time fitting in and finding her place in this world. She had grown up in New York in a family whose patriarch led a very public life as a congressman. She was the oldest daughter of five, a second-generation Italian American born into a family where my great-grandfather had left the poverty of Southern Italy in the late 1880s to travel to the United States to realize his own American dream. An expectation of excellence and an ethos of perfection were passed down for each child to accomplish great things and make the family proud. Politicians, lawyers, judges, doctors, teachers, educators—these were the traditional fields of study to choose from, requiring nothing less than a strong work ethic, each doing their part to serve. She would tell us stories about my grandfather, a man who believed in social justice and who championed the rights of the Italian Americans in New York during a time when Italians were unwelcome immigrants. Because her father ran for political office, she and her siblings were forced into the public arena where presentation was very important. She told me stories of how critical her relatives were of her. *"Mary Jo, you are not smart enough." "Not as beautiful as your sister." "Enunciate your words."* She wanted to escape this too.

My relationship with my mother, especially early on, had its ups and downs. While I wanted so much to be like her, some days it felt too hard to meet her expectations. I hoped she wanted the best for me. But trying to establish my own identity, I rebelled against her, as that was the only way I thought I could save myself. I was so angry that my defenses were constantly up.

Yet, when I needed her most, my mother never let me down. When I was depressed and despondent, she had the perfect words to shift my perspective. She paid attention and motivated me to figure out what interested me. Because I loved learning different languages, she encouraged me to participate in a cultural exchange program where I lived with a wonderful family in Colombia, South America, the summer before my senior year in high school. Because no one knew me there, I got to start over, creating a narrative I chose for myself. That experience changed me. I began to believe her when my mother said the sad times would indeed pass and lead to something wonderful. I was grateful to her for that. Having survived middle school and finding my footing in high school, the night before I left for Boston College, I sat down and wrote to her:

August 14, 1987
Dear Mom,
In my heart, I want you to be pleased with me. I am getting ready to start a new chapter, I need to know you are proud of me. I'm so scared, Mom. I feel I will never be good enough. Please continue to be there for me. I want us to be friends. I want to be able to call you when I need to talk. I really need to know that you love me. I love you, your Meggie

Leaving my safe place to venture out into a world that early on proved to be unkind was still terrifying. I looked for a champion day after day who would protect me from the many verbal lashes, sometimes handling it, other days not. My mother was that champion. While damage to my self-esteem was done, as I grew into adulthood, my mother encouraged me to forgive and let go of the past so I could have a wonderful future.

It took a lot of time to find my way. And it took a lot of time to heal the wounds of my adolescence. But with my mother by my side, I learned how to build a better life founded upon unconditional love of self and for others. As an adult, my mother shared with me wisdom that freed me to move forward. We were good friends, and I depended on that friendship. Not a day went by that I did not pick up the phone to talk to her and get my daily insight, love, and support—until a very sad day in April of 2011. When she took her last breath, I had to figure out something that had been unimaginable previously, how to navigate for the first time facing the world without her. This is the story of how, as grief enveloped me, I had to trust the process through the darkness and allow myself to transform and heal, so that my soul could have a chance to awaken to a new sunrise and fly free. To have taken that chance is true bliss! Read on.

Part One:

Grief—Trust the Process?

"Death consists, indeed, in a repeated process of unrobing, or unsheathing. The immortal part of man shakes off itself, one after the other, its outer casings, and—as . . . the butterfly from its chrysalis—emerges from one after another, passing into a higher state of consciousness."
—ANNIE BESANT, 1847–1933, British women's rights activist

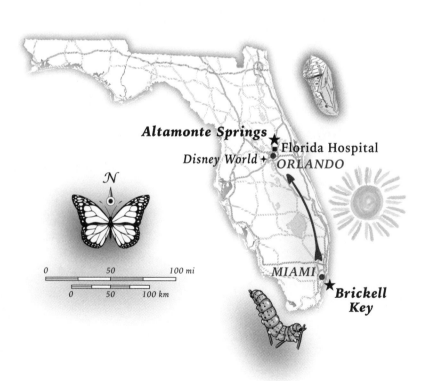

From Miami, Fl. to Orlando, Fl.

CHAPTER 1:

The Journey Begins

"We delight in the beauty of the butterfly, but rarely admit the changes that it has gone through to achieve that beauty."
—MAYA ANGELOU, 1928–2014, American poet

August 2008

On an extremely hot and humid day in August, nearly five months pregnant, I was grateful to be sitting in the cool comfort of the air-conditioned courtroom on the fifth floor of the immigration courthouse in downtown Miami. Intimately familiar with my surroundings, working as a federal immigration prosecutor, the courtroom is where I spent the majority of my days, litigating cases. The bread and butter of my work involved asylum, where a respondent—a fancy term for the noncitizen subject to removal from the United States—had to show that they feared returning to their native land for a reason that would allow them to remain lawfully in the United States.

Day after day, story after story, case after case, I sat quietly listening, objecting loudly at times, furiously taking notes as the facts were set out, only to point out the gaps, the fraud, the lies, the embellishments on cross-examination. And on that date in August, having nine years of experience under my belt, I had listened to thousands of these stories from Haiti, Cuba, Colombia, Venezuela, Eastern Europe, the Middle East, and Central America. Sometimes it felt as if I were in a bad episode of *Groundhog Day*, different applicants reciting the same familiar facts that mirrored the rumors of what would win the day spreading through-out their tightknit, resettled communities. Even though I approached each case with an open mind, the monotony was overwhelming. And on that date in August, it was made worse by the fact that I was pregnant and physically as well as mentally exhausted.

Nine years earlier, when I first got the offer from the Immigration and Naturalization Service (INS), I felt like I had won the job lottery. I was so excited and ready to jump in with both feet tackling an amazing opportunity. While the offer did not come right after law school, I hadn't given up hope. After almost two years of practice with a moderate-sized Miami law firm, primarily handling property foreclosure cases, I knew that crying in the bathroom of my apartment each morning because I dreaded leaving for work was not the future I yearned for. Not liking the subject matter, the billables, the lack of mentorship, or the fairly minimal salary, I kept applying with INS where I had enjoyed my experience as an intern my last year of law school. Eventually, I got an interview and received an offer. I was so happy to move on, having dealt for far too long with a law partner at the civil law firm who was a mean-spirited misogynist. His derogatory, irreverent comments disgusted me. Perhaps an attempt to keep me in my place, he would ask things like:

"Have you passed the Bar yet, Meg?"

"You're not thinking of popping out babies anytime soon too?"

Or worse:

"Come out with our clients tonight and be nice!"

"Bring some pretty friends, it'll be a good time."

Needless to say, I was relieved and excited for a new start. And on the first day of working at INS, I walked into what looked like a conference room to find my workstation. It was in a huge open space with nine big brown oak desks with hutches that lined the four walls, separated by a small gap in between. In the middle, there was enough room for a dance floor, hence its nickname, "the ballroom." There, I met the five other new attorneys who were a part of what was affectionately referred to as the "INS Ballroom Class of 1999." We were all young professionals, excited and ready to learn, and we got along very well together. We worked hard to ensure that justice was done by fairly following the immigration laws by day and played hard on the weekends. I loved working with lots of different people; finally a public servant, it was the legal job of my dreams. I could see myself there for a long time.

After about nine months, we all eventually graduated from that space to make way for the new recruits. Some of my class moved on to other positions within the agency, while others stayed and moved to private offices. However, the camaraderie established in the ballroom was the beginning of lifelong friendships formed from a unique and special moment in time that could not be replicated.

Unfortunately, the magic and novelty of the job eventually wore off. After nine years of a huge caseload, I was burned out from the grind. I guess litigating cases did indeed have a shelf life. As I sat in court in front of one of my favorite judges, I hoped the last hearing of the afternoon would pass quickly. While I was accustomed to long hours on any given day, as my belly was growing bigger, it became more of a challenge to sit still without having to run to the restroom or hold off nausea with a small snack. I was still suffering from hyperemesis gravidarum, a fancy medical term for severe nausea and vomiting. It was my second pregnancy, so I was not new to dealing with extreme discomfort along with a demanding full-time job. I was so grateful that my baby was healthy. Six years earlier, when I was pregnant with my son, I spent a week in the hospital hooked up to an IV to treat severe dehydration and didn't think I would make it through those nine months because I felt so bad. This time, I felt lucky getting away with only a one-night visit to the emergency room to get the hydration I needed to put myself on the right path forward.

As the witness was sworn in on the last case of the day, I had my file ready to go and my legal pad out, drawing a line down the middle of the page to separate the notes on direct and cross-examination. My cell phone was close by on silent. While not all judges allowed food in the courtroom, I had asked permission beforehand because of my condition, and this one made an exception.

The judge, through the interpreter, had the respondent whose case was about to be heard raise his right hand as he swore to tell the truth, the whole truth, and nothing but the truth. This individual was a small-framed young man, whose dark skin and facial features hinted of a

Mayan heritage. He had come over the border at the Rio Grande into Texas without being processed and was subsequently picked up by the US Customs and Border Protection agents. He went through the various channels that brought him to this point, ready to be heard. This man's claim was based upon a common scenario where he had left his home to escape the violent gangs that he emphatically believed had overtaken his small village. He was worried for the lives of his family and feared for his own well-being. While it came out that he himself had not been physically harmed by anyone, he was frightened and could not earn a living in his native land. Clearly, he had come to this country to seek a better future. But, unfortunately, his testimony did not establish a case for an asylum grant. After questioning on direct was complete by opposing counsel, it was my turn. After my short cross-examination and closings by both parties, the judge got up from the bench to deliberate.

When the judge left the courtroom, I looked down at my cell phone and saw that I had missed two calls from my mother. I looked at the time, nearly five o'clock. It was quite unusual that she would call at this late hour; we had already spoken that morning, and she knew I would be in court. After hearing for the last hour about a man who feared for his life and that of his family, I started to feel nervous about the welfare of my parents. I desperately wanted to get up, leave the courtroom, and return the call right away. I grabbed my phone, about to step outside, when the interpreter belted out, *"All rise!"* The judge entered, swooped his black robe behind him, and took his seat at the bench, ready to render his decision. I had missed my chance.

While it only took fifteen minutes to set out his oral decision on the record, I was shifting back and forth in my seat feeling the seconds pass like hours. To get my bearings, I looked around that room I had come to know over the many years. Yes, I was accustomed to the regulation dark blue paint embossed by the seal of the Department of Justice at the front of the room, accenting the two white walls on either side. Yes, I was familiar with the gate that separated the counsel benches from the gallery seating behind me. This was not a strange place, yet, as the judge gave his reasons to deny the application, I was feeling lost and agonizing over the possible reasons my mother might have called.

As was often the case, when things came at me out of the blue, my paranoia took over. Was it my dad? Possibly. He'd had some serious issues with his back recently. Was it my mom? No way. She was the picture of good health. Was it one of my sisters, one of my other relatives? I started to play with my long black hair, nervously grabbing a strand that covered the right side of my face, twisting it around my index finger again and again. My face felt flushed, and my mind continued in overdrive. As I listened to the judge reiterate a summary of the facts, I thought about the respondent's story and the possibility of the horrible things that could affect me. What was going on? I held my breath and tried to brace myself. At that point, I wanted this case to be over so I could go find out why my mom had called and end the catastrophizing.

And at the end of his decision, the judge ordered the respondent removed from the United States, explaining that the decision would be final after thirty days if he did not file a timely appeal. Then the judge turned to me, "Ms. Nocero, do you reserve appeal?"

Again, he said, "Ms. Nocero . . ."

"What?" I looked up. The second time, he got my attention, and I nervously replied, "Oh, my apologies, appeal, reserve, no, Your Honor."

When the judge finished and dismissed all parties, he turned to me.

"Ms. Nocero, are you all right?"

"I'm fine, thank you," I lied.

I wished the respondent and his attorney well, grabbed my laptop and files, placed them in the cart at my side, and scurried out as quickly as I could, given my expectant girth.

When I got on the elevator to return to my office, the phone rang. I quickly answered, yelling "Hold on, hold on!" I knew it was my mother; I got off on the second floor and ran to my office on the left side of the building.

"Are you alone?" her beautiful voice inquired.

"Yes," I replied nervously, hopelessly trying to mask any worry. "I just got out of court. What's up?"

"Meggie," There was a pause. "Dad and I went to my doctor this morning."

Okay, it was medical.

"And we got the results of a biopsy."

A biopsy, what? The facts, the facts, tell me the facts.

"The results were not good."

Here it comes. I stayed quiet and felt the baby, this proof of life, flutter in my belly.

"The lump I found was malignant. I have breast cancer." I gasped. Ah, I could not breathe. I inhaled deeply to feel the air fill my lungs. I exhaled, barely able to hold back tears. Shakily I said, "What?"

Without letting me finish that thought, she hurried on.

"It's in my left breast. I don't want you to worry. We're going to figure out my treatment options, and with God's help, I'll be okay." Then silence.

My mom begged, "Meggie are you there? Are you okay?"

Looking around my office, I saw the words, symbols, and messages of optimism. A "LOVE" plaque hung next to my law diploma, there were beautiful photos of my family at my wedding, and a magnet with a quote on perseverance was stuck to the metal frame on the door. Looking out the window of my corner office, I saw yachts sail by on Biscayne Bay and assumed people must be out there enjoying their day. I sat at my desk, unable to think straight. I couldn't articulate anything. As I felt my baby move inside me, I held on, trying to calm her while my mother was trying to calm me.

Questions, I had so many questions. My lawyerly instincts kicked in. I thought if I got to the bottom of it, a fact-finding expedition, I could control the information that was handed to me. She was talking to me still, but I didn't hear a word. Like a little child facing something she did not understand, my words came out as a plea to the universe, "Oh, Mommy. How? How? How? How did this happen? Are *you* okay?" And in my head, I asked, *Is she going to die?*

"Please don't worry. You need to take care of yourself and the baby. We will get through this. God will take care of me. I love you very much. It's going to be okay."

Always thinking about the other person, why was she always thinking about others? This was about her.

"I'll call you later, okay?" she said.

"Okay, goodbye," I replied and hung up.

I sat staring blankly into space, so much going through my head. Mostly wondering what just happened. I wanted to scream out, *How could my mom have cancer?*

She had spent a weekend with my family in Miami not even a month earlier, helping me, nursing me through the morning sickness after I got out of the hospital. She had been the healthy one, cheering me on. We were celebrating the fact that I was having a little girl, her first granddaughter. We were so excited. I was starting to feel a little less nausea. My life was good. I had a great relationship with my family. I had wonderful friends and colleagues. I had been married to a good man for eight years with a beautiful healthy little boy and was expecting in December. While I was tired of going to court, and my supervisor was blocking opportunities for professional advancement to do something different, I generally enjoyed my job and especially my role as intern coordinator teaching up-and-coming lawyers. I had a lot to look forward to. So why this? Why now?

Then I looked up to the ceiling and noticed water stains in the corner, leftover from what might have been a leak in the window frame from the inordinate rainfall over the past few days. I imagined God was sitting in heaven, ready to unleash a flood with a smirk on His face. I grew incredibly angry. I yelled out, "She has faith in You, more than I ever did, and You do this to her!"

Not able to see clearly, I wiped the free-flowing tears from my face with the sleeve of my black suit. "Well, don't leave her now that we need You the most. Isn't that what's supposed to happen? We pray to You, and You give us a miracle?"

"Please," I begged, "help my mother."

With that, I tried to slow down and get control of my emotions, but my heart was still racing. I got up and organized the papers and files into neat piles on my desk. I whispered under my breath, "Get yourself together, Meg." I reached underneath for my purse and fumbled around for my keys. As I walked out, I paused for a moment and stared at the colorful butterfly paper cutouts that decorated the front of the door to my office, hoping to feel lifted. No such luck. I turned off the light and set off for home, not wanting to talk to anyone. I felt weighed down and slow, but I wanted to run far away as fast as I could. If I didn't say anything, maybe this nightmare would go away. I got in the elevator, went down to the lobby, and left the building without looking up. On the way to my car, I ran into a colleague who knew me well, surely observed my eyeliner smudged at the corner of my eyes, and with concern asked, "Meggie, what's wrong?"

I could hold it in no longer and blurted out, "Fanny, my mom just told me she has breast cancer."

I looked up at her, she held out her arms, and I welcomed her embrace as I broke down. *Oh no*, I thought, *I said it out loud. There's no going back now. This is real.*

CHAPTER 2:

Hello Darkness, My New Friend

"And ever has it been known that love knows not its own depth until the hour of separation."
—**KHALIL GIBRAN**, 1883–1931, Lebanese American poet

February 2011

"Did you call your sister and let her know that we were on our way?" my husband, Frank, asked as we were driving north to Orlando on the Florida Turnpike.

"Not yet," I answered in a daze.

Three years had passed since my mother's initial diagnosis. She had already been through the chemo "plan" that sent her body into remission. However, in July of 2009, we were all devastated as the Computed Tomography (CT) scans at one of her regular follow-up appointments showed new evidence of disease. She thought she had beaten cancer, and I could see this news shook my mother's resolve. However, as scared as she might have been, she told us how strongly she relied on her faith. She would send our family weekly emails and continued to ask for prayers:

UPDATE: Went to South Florida Thursday to see my oncologist on Friday. She is a special woman, and I feel blessed to have her.

She put me back on Herceptin besides the many pills I am taking orally. NO CHANGE SO FAR. She said, "BE PATIENT," something I find so difficult. God has God's hand in this. Thank you for your prayers and love. **If God chooses to take us into deep waters, it is for a reason. The greater the calling, the deeper the water.** *Please pray for patience for me. Much love and prayers for all of you. Mary Jo*

Not knowing what the future held, we all did our best to keep my mother's spirits up by making plans to enjoy as much time together as we could. Among many moments of celebration, my entire family assembled for the Christmas and Easter holidays and summer vacation.

Gathering us all together for her forty-fifth wedding anniversary in the summer of 2010, my mother was overjoyed. We went to her favorite place in the world, their mountain house in Cashiers, North Carolina. My sisters and their families along with my parents' siblings and their families traveled from all over—Florida, Washington, DC, Texas, and New York—to celebrate this major milestone. My mother had spent the majority of her life as a champion for strong and vibrant marriages, and my parents' relationship was a testimony to this. She and my father always told us that love was a decision that they made every day. Through leading Marriage Encounter retreats as well as ministering to others for as long as I can remember, they practiced what they preached. While it had been a tradition for us to get together for a family reunion every summer since my grandmother Betty passed away, this time there was a sense of urgency to show up.

At their anniversary ceremony on July 31, I remembered how beautiful it was to see my mom and dad looking at each other with so much tenderness and love. My father held her hands and told her that she was more beautiful than the day he'd met her at the New York Athletic Club in Pelham, New York, right outside of the Bronx, when she was fifteen. I loved that he shared this story that had eventually led to a fairytale wedding at St. Patrick's Cathedral in downtown Manhattan on that very day forty-five years earlier.

Then, when it was my mom's turn, she shared how much she loved my father and what he and their life together had meant to her for all those years, especially now that she was battling cancer again. After mass, we ended the evening, all twenty-eight of us, dining at a long wooden table in perfect weather on the covered patio of Mica's Restaurant and Pub. Afterward, roasting marshmallows at the firepit overlooking the woods, we sang all the wonderful old Broadway tunes we had grown up with. It was a joyous and memorable evening.

Now, not even six months later, passing the exit to Stuart at mile marker 116, I hoped there was something more that the doctors could do to help my mom. Ever since the miracle drugs had stopped working for her, I knew that my mom was impacted by the haunting tales of others who had lost their lives after the cancer came back. I sensed that while she was trying to be upbeat for all of us, doubt was creeping in.

January 3, 2011
UPDATE ON MY TREATMENT—I WAS TAKEN OUT OF THE CLINICAL TRIAL FOR SUPER HERCEPTIN. MY PLATELETS WERE TOO LOW AND THE TUMORS WERE DOUBLING. AS YOU CAN IMAGINE, I WAS VERY DISAPPOINTED. DR. HAS PUT ME ON THIS NEW TREATMENT THAT HAS HAD GOOD RESULTS IN DESTROYING STUBBORN TUMORS. PLEASE KEEP ON PRAYING. MARY JO

And I wasn't handling any of this well. Not wanting to show my mom I was terrified of losing her, I relied on my best friend, communicating via email and text:

Hey, Lisa—
Can't sleep. I think everything that is going on is really affecting me. I feel like I can't breathe. Pushing people I love away from me. I love my mom a lot. I told her that I can't lose her—she's the only one who really likes me in my family, including Frank. She actually talks to me, listens, and loves me for who I am. Lisa,

it's so hard to see her through all of this—the treatment all over again. Why?? Why is this happening to her? What did she do? I don't think that I could do what she's doing—I am so grateful that she's doing the chemo because she wants to get well. But it's so debilitating, demeaning. Putting her faith in others. I wish I could do more to help her. Thank you for letting me vent.
Love you Lisa, Meg

Then in late January, as we waited to find out if my mom's new medication was working, I emailed my best friend again:

Lisa,
I have been under a lot of stress—mostly anxious and exhausted. I made a request to go part-time—pray that this goes through. It's way too much for me right now! I have been traveling to Orlando on the weekends a lot, so I need it. In fact, we are going to Orlando this weekend—just my sisters with the kids—my dad has been down, so we are taking him to Universal Studios to cheer him up. It's really hard on him—like you said, the family goes through it as well! Thank you again for your prayers.
Love you so much! Meg

And in early February, the stress caught up with me when I had my first full-fledged anxiety attack while conducting legal intern interviews at the local law school. I was really worried about my mom and had gotten very little sleep that week. For the most part, I kept it to myself and did my job as best I could. I thought if I could stay busy, I would be okay.

When we got to the career placement center, my colleague Richard and I were offered coffee before the interviews began. I was so tired that I drank two cups hoping for a pick me up. About an hour had passed when we started on our third interview. I was overly caffeinated, and when I gave the brief background spiel about the position before opening up for questions from the candidate, I started to get very anxious. It didn't help that this particular law student was intense from the get-go and peppered us with one question after another. He was overly passionate, like a first-year law professor demanding that we defend the constitutionality of certain pending Supreme Court cases around immigration law. As I sat fidgeting in the small conference room with Richard by my side, I couldn't handle his energy; I was too sensitive. My head started to spin, and my palms got clammy. As I grabbed onto my chair to get grounded, I felt my heart start to race and my vision became blurry.

I tapped Richard's shoulder while the student was going on and on and whispered, "I don't feel so well. I'm going to step outside."

He nodded. I excused myself in the middle of the interview and left the room.

I approached the receptionist and, as calmly as I could, explained my symptoms and asked, "Can you call 911? I think I'm going to pass out."

After dialing campus emergency services, she proceeded to share her own story of feeling the same way as the result of a stroke. This made me panic even more, and I asked her if I could sit down. She escorted me to a small, narrow work kitchen where I waited for help to arrive.

I wondered, *Why would anyone tell me that? Am I having a stroke?* Terrified, I called my dad, a cardiologist, to tell him what was going on. He stayed on the phone with me to keep me calm.

About ten minutes later, two very muscular, blue-clad paramedics entered the room with their medical gear. I had already been on the verge of tears. Now I felt embarrassed and became even more emotional. As I unzipped the top of my dress so they could place electrodes on my chest to check my heart rate and vitals, I tried to make light of this awkward situation by saying, "Good thing I wore my nice bra today."

The paramedics looked at me, smiled, and continued to do their job. After they recorded all the data from the electrodes, the lead paramedic handed a readout to his partner, patted my hand, and declared, "Your heart looks good. Your vitals are good, but you might want to get a follow-up just to make sure."

I answered back, "Thank God! Can you explain the results to my dad? I have him on the phone on standby."

The paramedic nodded. When he returned my phone to me, he said, "All set!"

I had a quick word with my father: "Dad, I'll call you back when I get home." Then I thanked the paramedic and explained, "I've been under a lot of stress lately and haven't slept much these past few weeks."

"Well," he said, "you could have had a panic attack. Good luck to you, get some rest."

Fortunately, after a follow-up with a stress test and an echocardiogram, the doctor agreed with the paramedic's evaluation. I just needed to manage my stress and take better care of myself. After that appointment, not needing any other excuse to go to the beach, I spent the rest of that beautiful afternoon by the ocean, my happy place. As I sat with my husband, I felt the cool sand on my feet and enjoyed watching the waves roll in. If only time could stand still—I was at peace in that moment.

Life Is a Marathon, Not a Race

While I did my best to calm down and not worry, less than a month later my mother was admitted into the hospital. That morning, I could not shake the feeling of dread that had overtaken me after Aimee called to tell me my mother was very sick. As we drove to Orlando, all I could think of was, *F*ck cancer! Why her?* It seemed so unfair.

In a way, I was relieved that my mom finally went to the emergency room to get help after a week of not eating or drinking. However, I remained incredibly worried about her physical condition and her state of mind. I lived four hours away by car, and while we shared our lives over our daily morning call, I sensed she was protecting me from knowing how badly she was doing. My mom had started a new drug and a brutal round of chemo that past week. After a few days of her new treatment, our conversations had grown shorter and shorter as I sensed her energy level weakening. I knew she remained hopeful that this new drug would be the magic elixir that would eradicate the cancerous cells that had migrated from her breast to her liver, but the harsh side effects of this particular concoction surprised and alarmed her.

As I looked out the window of our SUV, I realized that, while I had taken this drive many times before, this time it was different. I was much more aware of everything. The land around us was very flat and green, with occasional cows or horses in far-off pastures wandering, eating, or just standing there. To occupy myself, I read almost every billboard. Some promised to secure a better financial future if you hired this particular personal injury attorney. Some enticed families to enjoy the time of their lives by offering cheaper tickets to the various area attractions and theme parks. Some advertised for local conservative Christian churches, offering a new lease on life if only one would abandon their sinful ways and believe in Jesus. "I hate fearmongers. My God, some people!" I said out loud after only two hours on the road, and then added, "Are we there yet?"

I looked in the back of the car where both my kids were sleeping soundly, and both my dogs were resting on the floor. My son had just turned eight, and my daughter was two in December. They were too little for all this. To busy myself, I was looking for a sign to reassure me that everything would be all right. Until that point, things had been looking up, and I had not considered that I might lose my mother. Now, after that phone call from my sister early in the morning, her death was the only thing on my mind. I needed a distraction, but the terrain wasn't interesting enough or colorful enough to help me out. At least the day ushered in clear blue skies. I have always loved Florida in February— cool enough to wear a jacket, sunny enough to be outdoors. Perhaps this beautiful day would bring us positive news after all when we arrived at our final destination.

"Is there any way to go faster?" I begged my husband.

"Are you okay? I'm going almost ninety," Frank said, then reached for my hand. I grabbed it and nodded. I was in a fog and could not even recall the events that had taken place that morning. Somehow, we had managed to pack and were now on our way.

After about three hours, I texted Aimee to find out where my mother was located. She sent back the hospital's telephone number and her room number. I called the hospital and asked to speak to her.

"Hello, this is Mary Jo," she said. I was surprised that my mom was the one to pick up the phone.

I said, "Mom, it's me, Meg. How are you?"

I could hear voices in the background; it sounded very busy.

"Is this a good time to talk?"

"Where are you?" my mother asked, sounding rather perturbed.

"We're on the turnpike, about an hour away. I can't wait to see you. How are you doing? What's going on?"

She must have been watching the clock. Still not getting an answer to my question, I heard her laugh and say to someone, "I should have figured it would take her forever to get here."

Then to me, she said, "Your sister told me you were on your way hours ago. We were all placing bets as to what time you'd actually make it."

"Ha, yeah, I'm always late. Very funny!" I didn't mind; I was just happy to talk to her.

As our conversation continued a little longer, I could tell that she was tired, so I said, "Rest and I'll call when we get closer to the hospital."

She replied, "Valerie [her friend] is here keeping me company. The others will be back in a little bit. Just so you know, they put a sign on the door that everyone needs to wear face masks before they enter the room. Apparently, my white blood cell count took a major hit."

"Oh, got it," I said, still in a daze. "I love you, Mom. You're going to be okay."

When I hung up, I felt relieved. It was the longest conversation we'd had in the past week. So much had happened in the last two days. The night before, my husband and I were celebrating our eleventh wedding anniversary. He took me to one of his favorite steakhouses in downtown Miami, The Capital Grill, and did his best to make it a memorable evening. When we arrived at the table, I smiled at the sight of rose petals strewn across the table and a card from the management that wished us well. However, my mind was miles away. The restaurant was mostly dark, with low lighting and strategically placed candles. They seated us at a cozy, romantic booth in the middle of the room, the perfect setting for any couple looking to celebrate a special occasion. While Frank ordered appetizers and my favorite Pinot Grigio to set the mood, my mother's health weighed heavily on my mind, and I couldn't relax. I couldn't shake this unsettling feeling. Although there was nothing I could do for her then, I wasn't in the mood to celebrate and wished that the evening would end quickly so that I could go home and sleep, even though these days I had a very hard time getting any rest.

That evening, I had a vivid and terrifying nightmare. In it, my mother warned me to get a mammogram because she feared for all her daughters. I didn't want to do that. Instead, I decided to drink Clorox to kill off anything bad that was lingering in my system. I felt a burning sensation as it coursed through my body and attacked everything. Then, as I was waiting for the Clorox to finish its course, I had the sensation that God came to me. He looked me in the eyes and said that death is not something to be feared, which made me even more frightened. Then God lovingly advised that I should not let fear control me: "Start enjoying and don't wait until it's too late."

On the way to Orlando, sitting in silence, I thought about this message. But how could I enjoy life when I sensed I was driving away from the peace I had previously known? As I stared out the car window, I felt the magnitude of the moment, filled with sadness and confusion, and I knew a change was coming. I was on my way to take care of my mom. I hoped I could dig deep to find a hidden strength to see me through.

Finally, we arrived at the hospital. My husband stayed in the car with the dogs so that I could go see her. I brought my children with me, hoping they would cheer her up. As we approached the room assigned to her, I noticed a large yellow sign on the door that warned all to wear medical masks to protect her, as her immune system was dangerously low. It made me nauseous to suddenly realize how sick she truly was. Before I entered the room, I put my own fears aside to bring her my most optimistic and positive energy. So dutifully, we pulled the masks out of the box in front of the door and put them on. Then I knocked and entered the room. She was sitting in her hospital gown talking to Valerie, and she lit up when she saw us.

"Meggie—Ava—Michael—you're here!" Each of us hugged her tightly.

After about an hour, Aimee and my father arrived. I grabbed the house keys from my dad so I could bring them to my husband, who had returned to pick up the kids. When I came back to my mother's room, her doctor was explaining to everyone what was going on. He said the most recent chemotherapy had done a number on her immune system and was not working on the tumor in her liver, which was growing and causing the swelling in her abdomen and legs. His first task was to build up her immunity and strengthen her body with antibiotics, hydration, and nutrients. Then, if her levels improved, he would try a new chemo concoction to attack the tumor.

Before then, I never realized how important the liver was to overall well-being. I had grown up as the daughter of a cardiologist, so I always believed that as long as the heart was strong, the body would be fine. I recall that I had once participated in a meditation where I was told to think about the blood coursing through the body as red oxygenated joy. Then I was told to imagine that the joy was pumping through the heart muscle and turning it into a powerful source of love energy that would revitalize the entire body. It never dawned on me to do a meditation for the liver. I don't think I even knew where the liver was located or what the liver actually looked like. However, after seeing how my mother's toxic liver affected her body, I had a greater respect for that organ's role at detoxing the body overall. So now there was a plan, and we knew what we had to do; we had to help her rebuild her immune system and then focus on breaking down the tumor in her liver so that it could do its job. Luckily, my father said, my mother's heart was still strong.

CHAPTER 3:

Ground Zero—
Entering the Cocoon

"Life is pleasant. Death is peaceful. It's the transition that's troublesome."
—ISAAC ASIMOV, 1890–1992, American writer and professor of biochemistry

When day turned to night, everyone left for the evening. It was my turn to take the first shift and stay with my mother. The hospital room felt tiny. A twin bed was pushed up against the wall, and a brown recliner in the corner almost touched the top of it. A small table sat under a window where you could see the ambulances and traffic below. On the other side of the room, a small sink was surrounded by medical equipment and sanitized hospital supplies. Although we decorated with photos of all the grandchildren, placed a statue of the Virgin Mary, and created a shrine for healing, it unmistakably felt like we were in a hospital.

When the lights went out, it almost seemed like we were in an actual cocoon. It was dark, tight, and difficult to move around. And the smell—I will never forget the smell. It was a pungent aroma, sweet and antiseptic. One moment, I was a happy-go-lucky caterpillar, plodding my way through life. Going to work. Taking care of my family. Struggling with challenges, not wanting to change. The next moment, I was ready to fight to keep my mother alive so my world could stay the same, so I could stay a caterpillar. I did *not* want to go into the cocoon, but I unwittingly followed my mother in.

While my mother rested and tried to sleep, attached to an IV that delivered her antibiotics, sedative, and fluids, I sat in the recliner covered by a very thin hospital blanket. I would not let myself fall asleep. She was experiencing a lot of abdominal pain, and I had to call the night nurse several times to increase her medication so she could rest and allow her body to recover. I was happy to be there. This was my chance to repay her in a small way for all the love and support she had given me over my forty-one years of life.

The oncology floor was a very sad place. Each room held families surrounding their loved ones, who were worn down, sick, and in pain. The energy was depleting. I am so sensitive that I was overwhelmed by emotion and holding back tears. I wanted my mother to get well enough to leave. I did not want her to catch the hopelessness that loomed around every corner.

My father, my sisters, and I stepped up as my mother's designated spokespeople—the warriors who protected her from being just a name on a whiteboard on the oncology floor of a major hospital. I thought my mother would be empowered, knowing that we had her back, but after spending the first night with her, I could sense that her resolve had weakened, and I didn't know why. Just two weeks earlier, she had been optimistic that this last treatment would work, but now she was acting as if she were ready to quit. As I looked down at my mom, not only did I see her in pain, but I felt her fear for the first time. She was incredibly anxious and withdrawn. Here was a woman who normally stood strong in the face of any challenge, now acting as if her days were numbered.

The next morning, when Aimee took over, I returned to my parents' house to shower and change. I hoped that would help me shake the feeling that something was very wrong with my mother's mental state. Arriving at the house, I opened the front door and walked toward the bedrooms. It felt so empty without her there. I went to my childhood room, sat down on the brown pullout couch and massaged my neck, hoping to alleviate the tension in my muscles. I rubbed my forehead back and forth, overwhelmed by the feeling that my mom was giving up. Exhausted, I fell to my knees and cried out in sheer desperation, hoping God would not ignore my plea:

"I don't understand, what happened here, what changed? Why do I feel her slipping away?"

I felt totally out of control. I started to beat my hands on the ground, hoping to get rid of some of the pent-up anger that I'd stuffed away since arriving at the hospital. When my fists hurt too much, I stopped, held my hands out, and closed my eyes. At first I saw mostly blackness, but as I visualized moving my hands back and forth over my mother's body, an indigo dot appeared and grew larger. I attempted to provide long-distance Reiki, a Japanese technique using a spiritually guided life force energy for healing that I had studied that past year. I knew indigo was the color associated with your intuition and third eye. After about ten minutes, I felt foolish. I let out a desperate wail and allowed the tears to come for the first time in days.

"Who am I kidding? What am I doing? What can I do? Mommy, how can I help you?"

No one was at the house except for my dogs. It was safe; my mother and father would not see how weak and scared I really was. When I finally stopped crying, I curled up on the carpet in a fetal position with my dogs, Leo and Giorgio, by my side and fell asleep.

Later that afternoon, after getting cleaned up, I returned to the hospital and prepared to stay with Mom until the evening when it would be Aimee's turn. My mom looked much better. The nursing staff had removed the warning outside her door. The blood work showed that her immune system was improving. She was more energetic, and her appetite was slowly returning. We kept a journal that set out the day of the week and the time of the day when the nurses came to check on her vitals, as we wanted to make sure there were no mistakes. It had been two long days already.

On the third night, I returned to sleep at the hospital again. A nurse brought my mom dinner, and she sat up to eat it, still noticeably in pain from pressure under her right breastbone.

"Are you okay?" I asked. "I'm glad to see that you're eating. Hospital food sucks, right?" She nodded.

"Maybe I can smuggle in something good for you. Just let me know what you want, okay?"

"This is fine, I just wish they could do something about the pain here," she said, pointing to a spot above her belly.

"I'll let the nurse know."

When I returned, I told her, "The nurse is coming, Mom. By the way, I spoke to the kids a little while ago. They are praying for you. Frank took them back to Miami yesterday so they could go to school today. Michael is doing well—you know he got Peacemaker again?"

At my son's elementary school, the teachers acknowledged each month students who demonstrated leadership qualities with the coveted school's Peacemaker award. This was Michael's third recognition.

"Yes," she smiled.

"Oh, and Ava—you heard her, she sings all the time. She is so confident too. Not at all like I was, huh? So many people have told me to put her into an acting class. Channel that energy now before she turns on me."

My mom looked at me, smiled, but still did not say much. Uncomfortable with the silence, I continued, "An actor just like you, right? I'd love to show her the photos of you as Roxanne in *Cyrano De Bergerac*. Maybe I'll look when I go back to the house."

She still did not engage in conversation.

I looked at her with growing concern. "I know you don't feel well, but I sense something else. Are you okay, Mom?" She seemed so distant and scared. "Mommy, what's going on? It feels like you're giving up."

She sat up a little taller and leaned against the heated pillow that was in place to relieve the pain in her chest. When she looked down, I saw large teardrops gently fall down the right side of her face. I moved closer, handed her a Kleenex, and she wiped the tears away. Then she told me what had happened when she was first admitted to the hospital.

I sat quietly and listened as she spoke. "On the first night, I was so dehydrated and very confused. Your dad and sister went home after I was finally admitted after many hours there. I got a temporary bed and was brought to a holding area to wait for a room on the oncology floor to open up. I was alone when I started to receive the IV fluids and antibiotics. On the other side of the curtain, I could hear a conversation with a woman talking about her last will and testament. I was so confused, I started to get scared thinking that the woman was talking about me. I was frightened and alone. No one was around to ask what was going on. Then a trusted priest came to see me. He sat beside me and appeared to be giving me last rites, telling me that it was all right to let go and go to Jesus. I thought I was dying."

She drank some water to clear her throat and continued, "They finally brought me to this room very early in the morning. When my doctor arrived, I asked him what was going on and he told me I did not look good." At this point, my mother could no longer control her tears. "I don't want to die. I'm not ready."

"Why didn't you tell us sooner?" I grabbed her hand. "Please, Mom, you aren't going to die. We'll get you the help you need. You're going to get strong. We need to get you out of the hospital and home where you can continue to heal."

I finally understood why she had been despondent, and I was furious. I told my dad and sisters what had happened. Each of us pledged to get Mom out of that hospital, that cocoon, and get her home. Against this backdrop, we met our first angels: Placido, Shannon, and Dr. "Angel."

CHAPTER 4:

Angels All around Us

"Her angel's face,
As the great eye of heaven shined bright,
And made a sunshine in the shady place."
—EDMUND SPENSER, *1553–1599, English poet*

The hospital was such a loud place. It seemed to me that patients would need quiet to heal, but noise came from all directions, and each machine had its own particular language. There were the *bings, rings,* and *bleeps* coming from the machines that monitored my mom's heart, her medicine, and her breathing. There were emergency calls coming over the loudspeaker in a numeric code that only the medical staff understood. The humming from the air conditioner and other various systems was constant. *Humm . . . humm.* It bothered me at first, but after a while I got used to it. My least favorite was the inflating noise, that *whooshhhhh,* that came when her blood pressure cup inflated and the sucking noise, *su-su-su-suh,* that followed after a reading was taken. No, that's not true—my least favorite was the *beep* that went off when the bag of nutrients and antibiotics that was attached to her IV was done. A sudden loud *beep, beep, beep* that made me stand upright to look for a nurse to assist. All these noises, these horrible noises, were a reminder to me that she was sick. I spent most of the evening watching her sleep; I wrote in my journal to clear my head before I nodded off:

2/22/11 1:41 a.m. *I'm trying to make sense of it all—I have faith she will heal, longing for the ignorance of childhood—loving her in every moment—how strong she is! How lucky I am that she's my mother!*

"Good morning, Mommy, how are you today?" I asked the next morning, hoping for a response that indicated she was doing much better. She clutched the area under her right breast and squirmed to get comfortable.

"Hi, Meggie—we're still here, huh?" Then she remembered. "What happened to your race? Weren't you supposed to go to a Minnie Mouse race at Disney World?"

I laughed, as I'd totally forgotten that I'd signed up for the Disney Princess Half Marathon Weekend. It was aspirational anyway, as I was not really a fan of walking or running long distances.

I replied, "You're trying to get rid of me already? Yeah—13.1 miles of Disney happiness sounds like what I need to do after three days of no sleep. I'll do it next year when you can join us."

She smiled, sat up, and tried to get comfortable. Then she looked over at me and asked, "What are you doing?"

Looking up from my laptop, I declared confidently, "I'm writing a book."

"Really!"

"Yes, really. I want to share with the world how I grew from my early challenges to a more positive perspective on life."

She smiled and said, "So all those years I spent hours and hours teaching you to write will pay off?"

I laughed. "Unbelievable, right? I tortured you—procrastinated until the last minute as a kid, and now it looks like all those late nights will pay off after all."

And I couldn't have asked for a better teacher. My mother was well-educated with a BA from the College of New Rochelle, an MA in Social Studies from Hunter College, and later in life, an MA in Religious Education from Loyola University.

She continued, "You know how proud I am of your new attitude on life. It's not only wonderful for you and your family, but it will lift the rest of us when we're down. Just remember that this new attitude is a gift from God. Continue to stay close to the Lord to sustain yourself when the going gets tough. Jesus will give you the grace you need."

I smiled and nodded, "I'll do my best, but first the focus is on you. We need to get you out of here." While my parents raised my sisters and me as Catholics, I never drank the religious Kool-Aid when it came to catechism or church doctrine. Questioning everything, I disagreed with a lot of the Catholic church's dogma, especially the limited role of women, their stance on marriage, and other divisive and archaic positions. And with the latest sex abuse scandals involving Catholic priests, I further questioned the divine authority of a church institution that could let these crimes continue to happen. Growing up, while I believed in God and was inspired by the teachings of Jesus based in unconditional love, I truly felt uncomfortable with a church that used fear of damnation and guilt to maintain and control its community.

This feeling of not belonging changed after I attended Boston College and was introduced to the Jesuits' teachings in support of tolerance, education, and free thinkers, coupled with the message that we find God in all things. Subsequently, my mom and I used to have lively discussions about spirituality and the church. She even gave me sound feedback after I wrote my senior paper on "The Ordination of Women in the Catholic Church" for my canon law class in law school. I learned so much from her; it was my mom's desire to be a seeker in this life, and it was her faith, not her religion, that empowered me. She believed so incredibly in the love of Jesus and had faith in the healing power of prayer. If she still attended Catholic mass, found peace there, and believed that Jesus's grace was what she needed to get well, this was not the time to challenge her. I had no problem going to mass with her, as I still aligned with the words of the Jesuit priest Anthony de Mello: "I have wandered freely in mystical traditions that are not religious and have been profoundly influenced by them. It is my church, however, that I keep returning, for she is my spiritual home." In reality, my mother was the founder of my community of faith; she was where I found my church and spiritual home.

Placido

We were suddenly interrupted when a man entered the room. I looked up, ready to write the name of this new character in our hospital journal. It was about seven thirty in the morning, and my eyes were very tired. I heard his voice before I saw his handsome, young face and wasn't sure if he was a doctor or a nurse.

"Good morning, everyone, how are you doing this morning?" he asked with a bright sunny smile. He introduced himself as Placido.

"I'll be the nurse caring for you this morning, Mary Jo. By the way, your vitals look so much better," he happily advised. "Let's see if we can do even better today so that you're on your way home."

My mom smiled, and I immediately liked him. "So you got the presidential suite," he joked as he moved around. "This is the smallest room. They really rolled out the red carpet."

It was such tight quarters that I had to retreat into the bathroom to get out of the way when more than one visitor was present. "I guess they don't want me to get too comfortable here," my mom said wryly. Now he smiled again.

As kindly as possible, I advised him that at least one member of our family would be there with my mother at all times and that we would like him to explain what was going on with her medical care and the state of her health as things progressed. He took this in stride with a smile that acknowledged that we wanted the best for her.

When he came in to relieve the night nurse, his enthusiastic personality brought a renewed sense of energy to that little cocoon of a room. What was once a dark place immediately lit up with his presence. And I could see the resulting effect on my mother's face. She, who had been anxious and nervous for the last two days, relaxed for the first time. And fortunately, he told us that he was assigned to our room for the next couple of days as well, so we all breathed a little easier.

In mid-morning, Aimee showed up. It appeared that she had gotten some much-needed rest, as she was happily chatting away with Placido too. He was that kind of person, warm and amiable. He administered the medicine that helped lessen my mother's pain, and at the same time he addressed her spirit as he shared his friendship. He advised that he would be getting us a copy of the report that would show how my mother was improving. He also let us know well in advance who was scheduled to come to the room and what procedures would take place that day. He explained that my mother was scheduled for a venous Doppler exam to determine why she was experiencing so much discomfort under her right breast, and that she also would be getting a diuretic to try to reduce the overall swelling in her body.

After spending some time learning about his family and his love for all things Italian, especially Italian food, my mother confided that she made an amazing red sauce. When we got her on her feet and out of the hospital, he had a standing invitation to join us for a traditional Italian Sunday night spaghetti and meatball dinner.

My father had arrived later that afternoon after work and introduced himself as a cardiologist who worked in the hospital. Without missing a beat, Placido respectfully brought him up to date on my mom and chatted with him about the hospital as well. Grateful for the distraction, we were happy to see him whenever he came to check on my mom and were grateful for the synchronicity that had him caring for all of us.

During the day, Placido helped us understand what the numbers stood for as her vitals were taken. I took down the times that her drugs were administered and the times that blood work was done: 8:30 p.m., 1:30 a.m., 4:00 a.m., and 5:40 a.m. I took down her temperature, her blood pressure, her oxygen levels. I wrote down when she went to the bathroom, when she asked for assistance because of the pain, and even when she sneezed and developed a bloody nose.

I took down the dosage of her medicines. She got five hundred mg of Vicodin for the pain. She got Pepcid for acid reflux. She was given a multivitamin to fortify her body. She was given potassium. She was given topical Benadryl to help with the itching because they thought she had cellulitis, an infection of the skin that affects individuals with weak immune systems. She was taking the antibiotic Zosyn to reduce the chance of being affected by drug-resistant bacteria while in the hospital. Her potassium came in at 3.5, the low end of normal. Her white blood cell count improved from 1.7 to 2.8. They determined that she was a high-end neutropenic and not as prone to infection as when she arrived three days earlier. Her platelets were low at fifty-five thousand, a residual effect of the chemotherapy. But she did appear to be improving. A dietician arrived to see my mom, as well as a doctor who specialized in infectious diseases and the primary care physician on call. It was nonstop action.

Before they took her for the venous Doppler exam, her oncologist returned with a resident. After she told me what happened the first day in the hospital, I imagined confronting him and accusing him of taking away her hope and killing her spirit. But when he came into that room, I saw my mom's desperate eyes, still looking to him for some good news, something to hold on to. So I put my own anger aside to listen to what he had to say.

At first, he presented my mother's case to his student without even addressing her. Interrupting them, I spoke up. I looked at the resident and asked his name.

When he answered, I said, "I'd like to formally introduce you to Mary Jo, my mother, the patient."

She was not just a case. Her doctor looked at me and then at my mother, decided to sit next to her, and referred to her as "dear."

"I reviewed the results of this morning's tests. It looks like this is the sickest you have been since the initial diagnosis."

Trying to tame my sarcasm, I thought, *Really? We know. Way to point out the obvious.*

He continued, "We are going to address the swelling and discomfort first. Give you some relief. Then we'll address the tumors in your liver. Your vitals are improving, which is great news. Keep it up. Do you have any questions?"

I wanted to ask, *How about giving her something she can hope for?* She replied, "No."

After he left the room, I sighed loudly. I had managed to be cordial to him, but when he was no longer there, I broke down in tears from the need to release the anger, fear, desperation, and sadness. This was a whole new world for me, a whole new language. Feeling lost, I looked down at my hand at a simple silver ring my friend Teda had given me and read the inscription aloud: "This too shall pass." Things had to get better.

At the end of Placido's first shift with us, we asked who the next night nurse would be. He said that a nurse named Shannon would be taking care of us and reassured us that she was a wonderful, dedicated nurse whom we would love as well. With that, he completed his shift for the day and said his goodbyes until the next time we would meet. We waited with eager anticipation for the moment when our next angel would arrive and pick up where Placido had left off.

Shannon

Aimee and I were with my mom the night Shannon walked into our lives. Having been told that she was wonderful, we were looking forward to meeting her when she arrived.

Shannon was beautiful, and her smile radiated pure love. She was tall with porcelain skin and beautiful long blond hair. She wore dark-rimmed glasses and carried herself with an air of self-confidence and experience. She gave off a positive energetic vibe as well. That night in the hospital, it was her aura of self-confidence and ease that assured us that God had not abandoned my mom. The only thing she was missing was a pair of wings. She clearly knew what she was doing. And from the moment she walked into the room, we all, and especially my mom, felt instantly comfortable with her. From the way she addressed us, it was clear that her energy was filled with compassion and love.

Shannon was an integral part of the hospital experience. Once again, we were blessed with a nurse who cared for my mother's spirit as well as her body. We were excited when we heard that she would be on for most of the nights we were there. We knew that my mom would be well taken care of. And, with the help of these very capable and loving nurses, my family made a deep connection with two perfect strangers because our paths had crossed at a time where we all needed divine assistance.

Dr. "Angel"

After almost a week in the hospital, taking turns sleeping on the reclining chair, watching my mother to make sure that she was comfortable, and praying she would take a turn for the better, things started to look up. Dr. Angel, the infectious disease specialist, appeared for the next procedure, and I could have sworn that an aura of white light surrounded him. While he did have a full head of white hair that one could mistake for a halo, there was also an incredible healing energy that attached itself to his calm and soothing presence.

My mother was still having a hard time breathing. The venous Doppler test earlier in the week showed a tremendous amount of fluid accumulating under her right breast above her lung that was making it difficult for her. This doctor would be responsible for draining the fluid to relieve the pressure that was causing her so much discomfort. While this procedure could have been extremely risky, this doctor had such a calming effect on all of us when he walked into the room that we trusted that all would be okay. While I was hoping not to have to be present for the procedure itself, when the time came to take my mom to the surgical room, she held my hand, squeezing it so tightly that there was no way I could leave her side.

We rolled her down the hall on the gurney, into the elevator, and down two floors. The attendant carefully helped transfer my mother, who was noticeably in pain, onto a surgical table. My dad took her hand and lovingly guided her the rest of the way. My mother sat there, hoping to get this over with. Then Dr. Angel walked in. When he was ready, the nurse painted iodine on my mother's back to ensure the location was free from germs. They were monitoring the area with an ultrasound machine to determine exactly where the needle should enter her back. My mother had to bend forward as Dr. Angel masterfully inserted the tube into the area right below her breastbone and above her rib cage. The whole time my father and I each held one of my mom's hands. I looked away and noticed that the room was painted with a lively jungle theme. I smiled at the monkeys, giraffes, lions, and butterflies on the bright yellow walls behind the examining table, perhaps an attempt to diminish a small child's fear. I felt like those images were there especially for me.

I closed my eyes and repeated over and over a prayer that all would be well, secretly hoping that I would not pass out after seeing the needle. I hated needles. Dr. Angel carefully and safely removed approximately a liter of fluid without any complications. Almost immediately, my mom felt much better. After we returned to her room and got her settled, Dr. Angel informed us that there were no signs of cancer in the fluid, and my mother breathed a sigh of relief. Then, after nearly five days in the cocoon, we moved into a bigger room that would better accommodate our large family. Mary was driving up, and my mom's three sisters were planning to fly in that week to help us out. My mom's brother and my dad's sister would arrive later that week. Everyone was prepared to help my mom in this fight for her life.

After the procedure, it was clear that my mom was on the mend. She started once again to talk about her work as a Family Life minister and even told us to contact the parish center to reschedule the appointments she had canceled for the following week. While her blood levels were noticeably improving, and my mother was feeling better, her doctor now wanted to go after the tumor and advised her to continue with the same chemotherapy treatment that had put her in the hospital in the first place. I wanted to interrupt, *I thought you were going to try something new? No! That poison almost killed her.* In fact, the chemo was so dangerous that the nurse had to wear protective covering to place it into her IV. But it appeared that my parents were left with no other options and decided to use the only thing that was presented to them.

After they administered the first round of chemo, we were able to get my mother released from the hospital that week. It was almost the end of February. We were relieved that she would be able to continue the healing process at home. None of us wanted to repeat those two long weeks again.

I returned home with her and wrote this poem for her entitled "Illness is a Call for Love":

Illness is a call for love,
Today I make way for love.
Illness is a call for peace,
Today I surrender all thoughts that hurt.
Illness is a call for joy,
Today I release every judgment that I ever made.
Illness is a call for forgiveness,
Today I give up my old wounds.
Illness is a call to be present,

Today I let go of the past and the future.
Illness is a call for wisdom,
Today I will listen to my higher self.
Illness is a call for wholeness,
Today I will rest in the grace of God.
Illness is a call for grace,
Today I will receive a healing gift.

I wanted my mom to hear me clearly: "We are here for you, Mom— we love you—get well—you don't need this illness anymore."

CHAPTER 5:

Would the Angels Follow Us Home?

"When I die, I shall soar with angels, and when I die to the angels, what I shall become you cannot imagine."
—RUMI, 1207–1273, thirteenth-century Persian poet

When my mother was finally given the green light to return home, many people offered to help. But we had no idea what we would need to take care of her as her strength returned. My mother had been extremely independent until that point. Now she had difficulty walking and caring for herself because her legs had swollen so much that her balance was off. In the hospital, a physical therapist came to my mom's room to show her how to use a walker. This lady spoke to my mom as if she were a small, ignorant child, incapable of functioning on her own. This woman did not know my mom. I laughed quietly to myself and thought that if the therapist did not leave, even as weak as she was, my mother was going to hit her with the walker.

Knowing she would need assistance, we researched companies in the area that provided home health care so we could plan the next step. We wanted to believe that whoever came to our home would be preordained, that somehow our next angel would walk through the door, halo and all. Based upon a referral, we called our first candidate to meet with us and my mom. We should have known immediately that she was not the person for the job when she handed us the program for the funeral of her last patient. We had just liberated my mom from the cold and dismal hospital stay, and here this lady was in our face, so proud of the fact that she had arranged the details of her former employer's passing. We should have asked her to leave on the spot, but not wanting to turn away a potential employee, we continued the interview in spite of ourselves.

We brought her into my mom's bedroom, aware of how much illness robs one of their privacy. My mom was polite even though she was exhausted. Happy to finally be back in her own bed in her own room, she trusted us to do the right thing. After my father and sisters returned to the kitchen, this woman took me aside and shared that her brother had died of lung cancer. While I offered my condolences, I did not want to talk about death. Between planning a funeral, and now this, the interview wasn't going very well.

"Yeah, he died last year, but the ganja really helped him."

"Marijuana?" I asked.

"Yes, the green ganja!" she answered. "I can score you some for a price; it'll take the edge off for your mom."

"Are you saying you're a dealer and can score drugs for my mom?"

Neither one of my parents was about to smoke a joint, even if marijuana provided huge medical benefits. No one even smoked cigarettes in our house. When I once asked my mother if she'd ever partied and used drugs in the sixties, she looked at me like I had three heads. I could not imagine this lady taking my father aside to inform him that she could deliver a year's supply of the finest grass to their doorstep.

"No, I don't deal. I just know where I can get some," she said.

"Oh, my God!" I laughed, not sure what else to do.

I suggested, "Well, I would not mention drugs or ganja. It's not something my parents would welcome in their home."

It's ironic that this lady picked me to talk to about drugs, as I was the one who worked with law enforcement. Then, walking back to join the others, she turned to me and said, "Looks like your butt is as big as mine."

I paused after I processed what she just said, thinking, *What the hell? Who says that in an interview?*

I was done being polite; it was time for her to go. Without even joining the others, I escorted her to the front door. Opening it, I said, "Thank you very much for your time. We'll let you know."

Returning to the kitchen, my sister asked where she had gone.

"Yeah, right, there was no way in hell we were going to hire her. She started talking about funerals, told me she could get drugs for Mommy, and then insulted my ass. I think she crossed the line more than once. Not for us." We laughed.

After several other unproductive interviews, we met with a Haitian American nurse's aide named Dina. When we introduced her to my mother, she reassured us that she would be serving my mom as she healed. Even in her weakened state, my mother understood and accepted her help. That was the first time that I'd seen my mom smile since she came home from the hospital. Dina told us she had received her certification to work in home health care right after her arrival from Haiti. She added that family was paramount, that she had three boys, and that her faith was very important to her. She was a great fit.

In the weeks that followed, Dina cared for my mom beyond anything we could have imagined. She would lift my mom from the bed and help her with whatever she needed. I'll never forget her beautiful laugh, gentle and uplifting. Dina was a vital part of our team. She protected my mom's dignity by helping her to bathe and care for herself so the cancer couldn't rob her of that too. When she started working for us, I would always smile when Dina came in the morning. *Beautiful* was the word that came to mind. In a world where many people focus on the ills of society and what is wrong, Dina was an expression of what is right. My mom was in good hands. Now that I felt my parents had the help they needed, I could return to Miami the second week in March. I was so excited to see my kids; I missed them so much. It was time to catch up on home and work after being away for so long.

CHAPTER 6:

Hope, Where Have You Gone?

"All that I am, or hope to be, I owe to my angel mother."
—ABRAHAM LINCOLN, 1809–1865, sixteenth president
of the United States

March 2011

I had been back in Miami for about two weeks, but I worried daily about my mom. My dad's seventieth birthday was coming up, so I decided to return to Orlando to celebrate and see what was going on. Thank God I did, because that would be the last time that I would have a real conversation with her.

When I got to the house, my mother greeted me at the door with a huge hug. My kids ran past both of us, carrying their luggage into my old room. After four hours in the car, it was late, and they were tired. Traditionally, when I came up from Miami, my mother and I would sit in the kitchen, where all the good stuff in an Italian home happens, and talk for hours. Topics varied from theology to philosophy to our hopes and dreams. When I arrived that March night, I was happily surprised that she was able to join me in the kitchen again.

"It's so good to see you. I told you I would make it up here this weekend. How are you feeling?" I asked.

Leaning over and rubbing her forehead, she said, "I'm not sure. After the second treatment, I felt horrible. They told me my liver was really compromised. But after a few days, I started to feel so much better."

"And now?" I asked.

She said, "Meg, I'm exhausted, really drained. It's awful. My brain is in a fog."

She was obviously weak. Even the simple act of writing was hard for her. When I saw her signature on my father's birthday card, her usually meticulous handwriting was jagged and illegible. I was looking for anything, a sign that would give me some hope that she could overcome this. Unable to offer medical help, I adopted the role of motivator. To offer my mom a glimpse of hope, I told her I had contacted a healer to work with her spirit on another plane.

"The healer said she saw you in a dream state. She said this disease was giving you a chance to receive love from others after giving so much of yourself. She said your spirit felt very strong. It's time for you to receive."

After I'd shared the healer's words with my mother, she started to cry.

"Why are you crying? Did I say something wrong?" I grabbed her hand.

She shook her head and spoke through her tears. "How do I get past all this? The cancer came back, and my doctor is telling me that this disease is chronic and will eventually kill me. How do I believe that I'll beat this when the person in charge of my healing doesn't believe it?"

She continued, "I wanted to show him before . . . to prove him wrong. But maybe he is right?"

I begged her, "Mom, you're the only one in charge of your healing. You can't give your power away. You can't give your hope away when it's all you have. Faith is what allows for miracles. You taught me that. If you don't trust the doctor in charge of your care to do his best to treat you, then find another doctor. You need to believe that you will get better."

My mother looked exhausted and scared. I bent down to hug her and help her up. "Okay, let's go to bed. It's late. I love you, Mom. We all do, and we will do everything we can to help you." I hugged her with all my might.

Mary came up with her family the next day to help our mom. At the end of the weekend, I decided to stay longer. I called my office to let them know that I would be taking sick leave again, and I sent my kids home with my sister. We were in this fight to hold hope and encourage my mom, despite evidence to the contrary. Even in the face of what others saw as a losing battle, we all started to look for other solutions, other doctors who could help with my mom's treatment.

We called a massage therapist to come and help release some of the stress on her back and body. We would massage her legs ourselves to try to relieve the swelling. Mary brought compression tubes to see if they would help, even a little. I continued to have energy healings done for her. We sought second opinions from doctors at MD Anderson in Orlando and Sylvester Cancer Center in Miami, and we discussed other cancer experts. My aunt Betty suggested that we look into possible trials near where she lived in New York City that could address her type of cancer. We explored nutritional changes that would strengthen her body's immune system. My aunts and uncle would arrive in shifts to do whatever they could for her.

When we felt that we had nowhere else to go because traditional methods were not working, Aunt Pat and I sought the help of a Chinese acupuncturist to see if Eastern medicine could offer her healing. We would do whatever we could to help relieve my mom's considerable pain. We had to; we couldn't give up. As long as she was still breathing and willing, we were going to fight for her when she could no longer do it for herself.

Dr. "Namaste"

Namaste means "I bow to the divine in you" in Sanskrit. It is used for both greeting and leave-taking. I say it to show respect and gratitude. As the next doctor we encountered brought us the hope we were desperate for, I symbolically bowed slightly, hands pressed together, welcoming him and giving him the nickname Dr. Namaste. The circumstances that surrounded our initial meeting with Dr. Namaste were surreal. Knowing the benefits of acupuncture treatments, my aunt Pat had researched those doctors who practiced in Orlando and had experience treating breast cancer patients. We found one who had an excellent reputation and called to find out if he could help. When we spoke to him, he offered to evaluate my mom in his office. In her weakened state, there was no way that she would be able to travel or that my father would permit it. I had learned from reading that acupuncture can be extremely effective in releasing and distributing the energy in the body, thereby helping the body to heal itself. We were searching for alternatives to the chemo that was poisoning my mom. This sounded like a good option.

My mom was open to meeting him. She was open to anything that offered her relief. When we spoke to Dr. Namaste, we explained that it would be too difficult for my mother to travel to his office and asked if he made house calls. Although he normally did not, he was moved by her situation and agreed to come to our home. We had researched his background and felt guided to trust our instincts. He had over thirty years of clinical training and expertise in Traditional Chinese Medicine and acupuncture, specializing in women's issues.

The morning he was to arrive, the weather was horrific. Lightning and thunder filled the sky, and it poured like a monsoon. This storm continued throughout the day. Despite the weather, Dr. Namaste confirmed that he was on his way. Visibility, especially for a driver who wasn't familiar with the directions, was terrible. We were expecting him around two o'clock and told my mother the same. When he did not arrive, we grew concerned that he was lost or had canceled. We called him and left messages. By three, we still had not heard from him, so we waited. I even went out to the end of our street in the pouring rain to look for the hero who was to arrive in a white car to save the day.

I stayed outside for over thirty minutes, refusing to come in. I stood in the street, soaking wet under an umbrella, as the rain came at me sideways. My aunt Pat called out to me from the front door over the thunder and lightning, "Do you see him yet?"

I looked up, and there he was coming down the main road.

"Yes, yes!" I yelled back. I saw his car turning up our street and jumped up and down to get his attention. I ran toward him, waving and yelling, "We're over here!"

Finally, he saw me. I guided him up the road to our front path. My aunt stood at the door with two towels. I brought another umbrella over to his car, opened it, and offered it to him. He got out of his car and we both ran to get out of the terrible weather. After he dried off and I returned from the back of the house in dry clothes, my aunt Pat and I sat down with him at the kitchen table. Dr. Namaste's appearance in person matched the vision I had in mind of what a Chinese doctor would look like: a refined and well-dressed, middle-aged Asian man who spoke with an accent.

"So," he sighed, "I'm finally here. What a day!"

He reached into his briefcase and pulled out the papers we had faxed him earlier. "Thank you for the initial information. What's the status of Mary Jo's medical condition today and what treatment has she received so far?"

I pulled out our journal that documented everything and handed it to him. He talked about his background and his extensive work with the treatment of breast cancer. After looking over our journal, he proceeded to examine my mother.

"So, Mary Jo, good afternoon. I'm Dr. Namaste. I'm here to see if there is anything I can do to help you." She smiled.

"I'm going to check your pulse and look at your tongue. Let's see."

"Very good, Mary Jo. I'm going to talk with Pat now and perhaps some herbs will assist you."

When we told my mother that he was there to help her, she was incredibly grateful. She was so relieved to see a new face and was so happy about the possibility that someone would offer her another option that I believed I saw the glimmer of hope return. After he examined her, we returned to the kitchen.

Dr. Namaste explained his observations and what they meant in Chinese medicine. He told us that her condition was serious. Her tongue showed serious dehydration, and the swelling in her legs was cause for great concern. He said that her difficulty with digesting and excreting toxins from her body posed a serious problem for her as well. He offered us some herbs that could help her, but he advised that her disease was well advanced. Then he told me that the herbs would be ready for pick up the next day at his office. He wished us both well and left. By that time, the rain had finally stopped.

She did try to take the herbs in applesauce but to no avail. When it came time for my aunt Pat to leave several days later to return to work in New York, I watched my mom cry and hug her tight. When I ran out of leave from work and had to return to Miami as well, I said to her, "I don't want to leave you."

She looked at me and said, "I love you too!"

CHAPTER 7:

Time to Go Home

> *"We are eternal beings. We lived as intelligent spirits before this mortal life. We are now living part of eternity. Our mortal birth was not the beginning; death which faces all of us, is not the end."*
> **—EZRA TAFT BENSON**, 1899–1994, American religious leader

April 2011

On the evening of April 7, 2011, for the first time in weeks, I sat with three close friends from work enjoying Indian fare and music. I drank a few glasses of wine as I relaxed on a beautiful spring night in downtown Miami. Behind the restaurant, you could see the lights of the city. Miami still amazed me, and the skyline was more beautiful than it had been nearly twenty years ago when I first moved there. The cityscape of Miami since 1992, like so much else, had changed. Of Miami's eighty tallest buildings, only eight of them existed then. Even though Miami was a mature city when I arrived there, it had grown even more. While its geographic boundaries were the same, it grew on the inside. Much like each one of us, by our twenties, although we've reached our mature adult body externally, we never want to stop growing inside.

On my first trip to Miami to search for an apartment to rent, my mother was with me. I remember it as if it were yesterday. I had just turned twenty-two and been accepted for a master's degree in Inter-American Affairs and International Security and Conflict at the University of Miami's Graduate School of International Studies. We had such a wonderful time exploring the city of Miami together. I had brought my dog, Alfredo Luigi, nicknamed Alfie, which limited my choices to pet-friendly rentals. Because of Alfie, I found Brickell Key, a place that became my home, where I'd matured, married, and raised a family of my own. Those are good memories.

Enjoying dinner and reminiscing, I felt so much love and gratitude for these friends. We had been through a lot together over the years, and it felt so good to be with people with whom I could be myself, no worries, even for just a couple of hours. Toward the end of the night, I saw a black crow appear beside our table. I read once that the black crow is considered to be a totem animal that is an omen of death. I tried to ignore the symbolism. When it would not leave after what seemed like an eternity, I waved my hand in its direction and yelled, "Shoo!"

When it finally flew away, my cell phone rang. It was Aimee calling to tell me that they were admitting my mother to the hospital again. *Thanks a lot, stupid crow!* My sister was extremely upset, understandably agitated, and worried beyond belief. As I attempted to calm her down, I felt devastated.

Aimee said, "They are going to try to schedule a procedure tomorrow to relieve the swelling in her legs."

I said, "So this is a good thing for Mom. Hopefully, she will see improvements soon afterward. It will be all right. I'll come back tomorrow morning."

Aimee replied, "Good, I hope so. I'll let you know."

After we hung up, I was so agitated and despondent. Doubt invaded again. I had just returned to Miami from weeks of nursing my mother back to health in Orlando. I had done my best and left feeling that she was making progress and had turned a corner. However, the last few days, my mother would not take my calls. I felt tremendous guilt for having returned to something of a routine existence while Aimee and my dad were left to manage as best as they could. I felt I had abandoned my mother. Had I stayed there, perhaps she would have continued to make progress. Unfortunately, I'm not God; I couldn't control what happened to my mother, no matter how hard I tried. I now knew that nothing was under control.

From the expression on my face, my friends knew it was not good news. I told them what was going on and then asked for the check; after paying it, we hugged and said our goodbyes. I would leave for Orlando the next day. This time, my husband and children came with me, but we made the decision that my kids would not go into the hospital room. Aimee said that my mom was writhing in pain and struggling to get comfortable. She was very confused about where she was, who she was, and what was going on. No, my kids would not see her like this. They would remember her the way she was before cancer and chemo took a toll on her body. That evening I could not sleep. I felt that my mother's cocoon was getting tighter and darker.

When we arrived in Orlando, my kids stayed in the children's lobby on the ground floor of the hospital. The Disney movie *Up* was playing in the background, an animated feature which I had seen many years earlier about an older gentleman who had lost his wife, the love of his life. *Up* was a story about how he was assisted by a young Boy Scout who wanted to get a service badge. I suspect they play it because the children there often have elderly family members who are dying, and the movie was about not forgetting your loved ones who have passed, because they were still with you. A sad journey at times, but it has a happy ending. If this was a sign, it was very clear and precise . . . one that foreshadowed an ending I would never have chosen.

CHAPTER 8:

My Mother Became a Beautiful Butterfly

"Perhaps the butterfly is proof that you can go through a great deal of darkness yet become something . . . beautiful."
—**BEAU TAPLIN**, American writer

E ver the optimist, I thought this hospital visit in April would be like the first time that past February when, after a full week, she got her strength back to the point where she sat up and demanded to go home. When my family arrived in Orlando late at night, my mother smiled; she was happy to see me. Clearly uncomfortable from swelling in her legs, she still seemed hopeful that the doctors could help her.

Months earlier, my mother had bought a beautiful doll that played the Swedish pop group ABBA's song "I Have a Dream" when you pressed a button. She loved it, and it brought her a lot of joy. On the second day at the hospital, hoping that music would help, my aunt Pat and I sat by her bed, singing her the words of the song.

She smiled at us with such appreciation and love. However, later in the day, her pain got worse, and the nurse gave her stronger medicine to make her comfortable. After a day of taking a high dosage of Dilaudid for her pain, she slipped away, and we never communicated again. Sitting by my mother's hospital bed was agonizing, and I prayed she would get relief soon. Although she was in what appeared to be a drug-induced coma, she never fully closed her beautiful eyes, what Shakespeare called "the window to your soul." Holding her hand so she felt my presence, I repeated, "Mommy, it's going to be all right."

For the next three days, she lay on her back connected to the IVs, showing movement only when she bent forward to gasp for air. When this happened, I would grab her and pull her up hoping she would not choke. I had no idea what else to do. My sisters, father, husband, aunts, uncle, brothers-in-law, and I spent three days going back and forth to the hospital and taking turns sleeping on the cold hard floor. We prayed she would wake up so we could all go home together.

On the evening of April 11, 2011, after a full day by her side, my dad and I went home to get some sleep. It had been a rough few days, and we were feeling the deleterious effects of insomnia. Mary, who had to return to her medical practice, had driven back to South Florida with my husband Frank and our kids the day before. Aimee stayed with the private night nurse we hired to make sure my mother's needs were taken care of. That same day, I had communicated with the healer who had helped me before. I explained what was going on and asked her to assist with another long-distance healing for my mom. In light of the circumstances, she graciously agreed to do a healing that night. I still had a lot of faith that everything would be all right, that somehow my mother would experience the miracle of a second chance. I believed that her spirit would not choose to let go of her physical body yet. I wanted my mother to stay with us.

The next morning, I received a text from the healer indicating that something happened; she was not allowed to share the information with me at this time but would do so when she had permission from her guides. I thought this was good news, that something good had happened. I was actually excited. So when we received a phone call at six in the morning from the night nurse telling us that we needed to come quickly back to the hospital, I was hopeful. I still did not believe that she was dying. I really believed that there would be a miracle.

When my father and I arrived at the hospital, Aimee was already by her side. There was a heaviness in the air. It felt like I was walking into a dense fog. During the daytime, through the window, you could see people below walking on the path that encircled a manmade lake. Now it was dark outside, the window was black, and only a small light in the room shone on my mother who was laboring to breathe. The night nurse was sitting in the reclining chair located by the window. When we came in, she spoke to my father and left. He then went to my mother's right side with Aimee, and I sat on a chair on her left side leaning against the bed holding her hand, no longer praying, but begging for our miracle. My eyes were closed as I started negotiating with God. I promised I would change, do better, be a better daughter, not ask for anything, if only we received a miracle.

In that moment, my pleas were interrupted by a vision. As I sat in the chair next to her bed, laying my head over her body, eyes closed, I saw an unusual white lighthouse surrounded by the bluest sky. In a flash, a burst of such blinding white light surrounded the lighthouse that I would have wanted to cover my eyes if they were open. I felt her voice say, *Let me go!*

I was confused. What was going on? I'd never had a vision like that before. That was only for spiritual or holy people, enlightened ones. Not me. But I was sure my mom had relayed to me a message the only way she could. She was finished here on Earth, and it was time to say goodbye. I opened my eyes, looked at my dad and Aimee, and started to cry as unimaginable words escaped my lips, "Mommy's going." Not even seconds thereafter, she stopped breathing and was at peace. Just like that, our fight was over. It was done, finished. All those months of her suffering and pain culminated in this moment in time: April 12, 2011, 8:10 a.m. The end of her journey here.

"No, no, no, it can't be true," I whispered, sitting beside my mom's hospital bed, as she lay there lifeless. "Why is this happening?" I was not wanting to look at my father for fear of seeing his heart broken after losing his soulmate. Not wanting to look at Aimee for fear of seeing myself in her eyes. Not wanting to move from that spot by my mom's side, knowing that if I did, her physical body would be taken away forever. While I had been raised to understand that this is the ultimate homecoming, the soul returns to heaven leaving earthly pain and suffering behind, I could not be happy for her. I could not be joyous for her. I could only think of myself. And I was devastated.

Then there was lots of movement. Most of it was a blur. I am certain that my mother's sisters and brother, who came to visit for weeks at a time to help my mother, were there at some point to say their goodbyes, but I don't remember many details. Still standing at her side, I do recall that my dad asked us to reflect on what we would remember the most of my mom. My sister and I commented that the worst things we could hear at this time were "I'm sorry for your loss" and "She's in a better place." When her oncologist came to pay his respects after he found out she died, he said just that: "I'm sorry for your loss" and "She's in a better place." I looked over at my sister, smiling through tears, and rolled my eyes.

Seeing her lying there was surreal. I wanted to crawl out of my skin and leave this dimension as well, to travel with her wherever she had gone. Instead, I hid in the corner by the food cart that was stored near the door of the hospital room and sobbed uncontrollably.

When a volunteer brought rosaries into her room, I stood up and accepted a blue one that was offered. I wrapped my mother's hands with it. Like Lazarus in the Bible, I hoped that she would rise again. But all I felt was coldness where there was once warmth. She had gone. I took a photo of her beautiful hands so I would never forget what they looked like.

Then the business of sharing this awful news began. I called my husband to tell him my mother had died. When I begged him to bring our kids back to Orlando so I could hold them in my arms when I gave them this awful news, he did not think it was a good idea. He explained that they were exhausted and had just gotten back to Miami. Under other circumstances, I would have understood. But I needed them then. Unfortunately, "Honey, I'll be right there for you," was not the response I received.

I was so disappointed. I'd never felt so alone. As my mother lay lifeless in the hospital room, it was difficult to process what was going on around me. I begged my husband to come back. Then, when my father suggested that I go home and be with them, I missed my mother even more. I wanted to ask her what to do next. Here I was, so absorbed in my own pain that I could not see that this profound moment in time had weakened my strongest allies. Not at all like the serene image of calm and collected individuals paying their last respects, I was yelling at everyone, but mostly at the injustice of this incredible loss. As a member of an Italian family, I'd learned to feel passionately and love passionately. I guess I felt a little louder than most. I was feeling the pain of an unimaginable loss, and they were too.

As tempers cooled and emotions settled a bit, we all bid farewell to my beautiful mother, saying our last goodbyes. My father hugged me and told me he loved me, something I desperately needed to hear. Aimee told me she did not want me to leave. She too did not know how she was going to face the next days. And how was I just supposed to go back to normal, to work, as if nothing had happened? I was experiencing incomprehensible sadness and pain and was going to need my family now more than anything.

When we finally left the hospital and returned home, I got an email from the healer I had spoken to the night before. She wrote:

> *After Jesus had come through me and we laid her body back down, I felt us move up to the top of her head and give her a halo. It was all really beautiful. Also, I'm not sure if I conveyed that as I was going through this with her, I just knew that she was aware of what was happening. I could really feel It. I thought you would like to know.*

After reading this, I felt in a small way that I had been given a gift, a glimpse into the great mystery of the afterlife—what Wayne Dyer describes as "going from the now here to the nowhere again." It was her time to move on to the next realm. I emailed the healer back:

> *Thank you so much. I am so glad you sent this to me. My mother passed away at 8:10 this morning. We are heartbroken.*

Then I emailed my best friend:

> *My mom died, Lisa. I don't know what to do now. How am I going to get through this? Where is God in all of this?*

My husband did drive the four hours back to Orlando and showed up that same night. I was grateful that he did. When I saw my eight-year-old son, Michael, he asked, "Why are you crying, Mommy?"

I held his hand and replied, "I have to tell you something very sad."

He asked, "Is Grammie still at the hospital? Is she going to come home soon?"

"Michael, Grammie passed away and went to heaven." As he processed what I said, he started to cry and hugged me tightly.

Then Michael sat in my lap. I said, "She's going to be our angel now in heaven. She's going to watch over and protect us." Leo, my dog, sat right beside both of us and poked at our hands until we scratched his head.

Michael then said, "I love you so much."

Holding each other through this challenging time made processing it easier to deal with.

The next two weeks were a blur. I stayed in Orlando to help plan the funeral arrangements with my sisters. *Tangled*, the last movie my mother had seen in the theater about the adventures of Rapunzel, became a favorite for my daughter, Ava, as she played it over and over. And I had vivid dreams over the next few days where my mother came to me, assuring me that it would all be all right. In one dream, I didn't remember exactly what was going on, but I did hear the song "A Horse with No Name" sung by the folk-rock band America playing in the background.

Maybe the symbolization of the message was simple and beautiful: my mother suffered like the heat of the desert, she met with death as the river dried up, and then her spirit let go as the water symbolized a renewal of life. For, it was true, she was now free.

This was a very mystical time. I felt her presence in the wind, huge gusts that shook leaves on the trees. I felt her watching over all of us, not leaving us quite yet. And my father even shared with me that she came to sit next to him on the edge of their bed, reassuring him and loving him still. And then there was Zachariah, the Sheltie that my mother and father had adopted toward the end of her illness. He was a quirky dog, afraid of so much, but not my father. He loved him, never leaving my dad's side. He would bark as if he knew that my mother's spiritual presence was still in the house. He offered companionship during this very difficult time, somehow knowing this was his job, to take care of my dad for my mom.

When the day of the funeral arrived, well over three hundred people showed up to remember her and to pay their respects. As she had many priests as friends, twelve of them honored her on the dais as we bid her farewell. Perhaps to make sure we knew she was watching over what we were about to say, just before my sisters and I presented the eulogy, a surge of power caused a blackout in the entire church that certainly got our attention.

"What the heck was that?" Aimee said.

Having heard it said that spiritual beings communicate through electricity, I laughed and said, "Mommy is here, and she is paying attention—we better make her happy and not screw this up."

After Aimee and I spoke, Mary finished with an acknowledgment of the kind of force my mother was: "We know that you are going to shake things up in heaven and set things straight on the church's positions concerning women."

Then each of the grandchildren had a chance to elegantly state how much she meant to them as well. And for the communion processional, our lifelong friend Misha sang what had become my mom's theme song, ABBA's "I Have a Dream." It was a true celebration of life.

The day after the funeral, we honored her in a private service, gathering as a family to pay our last respects and release her butterflies. My mother's metamorphosis was complete. But this loss was already too much for me to bear. It was time for me to leave and return home to Miami. It was time for me to face life without my mother. While she had emerged from her own cocoon, I was still in mine. It was getting tighter and darker as I braced myself for what was to come. I had no idea how I was going to live without her. I could not shake the feeling that I had failed her. Because I could not convince her to stay with us, I felt that I had failed myself as well. I was perplexed by the vision of the lighthouse I'd seen before she died; it stayed with me. When I looked up the symbolism, I read that a lighthouse offers help in navigating the way through rough waters and represents strength, guidance, and hope. Feeling exhausted and emotionally spent, I lacked the energy to process this. I had no idea how to navigate grief. I wanted her guidance. I needed her to tell me what to do; I wished with every bone in my body for the chance to ask her in person. Sadly, I knew that was no longer a possibility.

CHAPTER 9:

To Dream an Impossible "Oprah" Dream

"The whole point of being alive is to evolve into the complete person who you were intended to be."
—**OPRAH WINFREY**, American media executive, actress, talk show host, and one of my mentors

I have always had a difficult time dealing with change. If a certain lifestyle worked for me, when circumstances changed, I would fight them. In 2006, three years after the birth of my son, Michael, I was sure that if I organized myself and delegated better, all would be well. But it was not working. I would attempt to make my old routine fit into my new life. Instead of allowing the new to be what it was, I refused to surrender the past. I felt like I was losing my mind. I was working full-time, taking care of a toddler, renovating and redecorating our small apartment while we lived in it, and still trying to get back into shape. I was exhausted, increasingly depressed and my relationships, especially with my husband, suffered. I felt stuck. I felt more and more resentful as I looked in the mirror and saw the shell of the person I once had been.

During this time, I asked the universe for help. A colleague from work suggested that I change my perspective, another friend introduced me to the law of attraction, and then I came upon the inspiring acceptance speech given by Oprah Winfrey for the Elie Wiesel Foundation. Listening intently to her speech, I received many God-winks, a term coined by SQuire Rushnell to define personal experiences that are seen as signs of divine intervention. I asked myself the questions that Oprah posed so eloquently: "Dear God, how do I fulfill my potential here on earth? Dear God, how can I be used in service to that which is greater than myself? Dear God, am I on the right path?"

Until then, I had never thought about living intentionally. I was moving through life, numb. Good things happened some days, and other days I just hoped to survive. Now I forced myself to really pay attention to the song in my soul. Oprah went on to say that we are all blessed with privilege, and when we leave this Earth, we will be asked, how did you serve, who were you able to save, what did you do for the powerless, broken, and suffering? The *Aha!* came when she said we were all free agents for the Divine, managers for the spiritual forces within us. We have the power to transform our lives and the lives of people we know. Late at night when I heard this, I felt that God was talking directly to me.

I was convinced that service would save me as long as I taught and inspired exactly where I was. Only there would I have the power to transform. Wow! This was huge. While I had always been a fan of Oprah, now I saw her as magical too. From that point on, I looked to Oprah, alongside my mother, for insight and inspiration. I became a voracious reader of all things aligned with the power of intention and the spiritual inquiry into my purpose, calling, and consciousness. Oprah became a part of my Mastermind Group, a concept described by the author Napoleon Hill in *Think and Grow Rich*. I was in search, both in a real and imaginary sense, for mentors, great thinkers, and history's greatest achievers who could help me envision my own purpose.

How did this help me as I faced my new normal now that my mom had died? Well, in reality, it did not. With my mother's death, I felt like the leader of my Mastermind Group had abandoned me. I reverted to a victim role and chose not to remember anything that could help me. My mother fell ill around the same time that Oprah announced she was going off the air after twenty-five years. I know it sounds self-focused, but I felt that Oprah had abandoned me as well. So ultimately, I felt that

I'd lost my mom, my mentor, and the chance of realizing both seemingly impossible dreams.

Let me explain. One of my mother's favorite songs was "The Impossible Dream" from *Man of La Mancha,* the musical inspired by *Don Quixote,* the seventeenth-century work of one of the world's preeminent novelists, Spanish writer Miguel de Cervantes. The words of this song encouraged those who listened to never give up as they reached for the unreachable star. So with this focus, I set out to find a way to keep my mom's hope for healing alive. By dreaming big and realizing something considered to be impossible, my "plan" was to show my mother a miraculous experience could happen. Fueled by this impossible dream of meeting Oprah, I made a new vision board. On it, I put photos of my mother protected by angels and right next to that, I put a photo of me and a photo of Oprah waving at her audience. On a mission, I set out to get tickets to one of Oprah's final shows in Chicago.

I told everyone my plan, and they helped as well. I felt that if I grabbed onto my impossible "Oprah dream" and it came true, then my mother would believe that all things were possible for her as well. Silly and simple, I know, but I didn't want to let go.

Impatient and unwilling just to wait, I called my best friend, Lisa, who was always up for an adventure, and asked her if she wanted to go to Chicago in October of 2010 to see if we could get last-minute tickets. Knowing how much this meant to me, she said yes. Then Aimee joined the fun, though truth be told, more importantly she came to see her beloved Notre Dame play football.

When we arrived at the W Hotel on a Thursday night, we asked the concierge if he could help us. He looked at us with incredulity, as this was the hottest ticket in town. On Friday morning, we took a taxi to Harpo Studios in hopes that divine intervention would allow us into one of the two shows. As we approached the studio, we saw the audiences lined up for the two tapings. Bursting with excitement, everyone was waiting for their big chance to meet Oprah. I was jealous. It was like Fort Knox—security all over. We took pictures outside the studio and then crossed the street to the Oprah Store and chatted with the staff and other guests about our half-brained optimistic scheme. We hoped they would give us three tickets for the last show of the day. It did not happen.

Two dreams died within a matter of two months: My mother passed away in April of 2011, and Oprah went off the air in May. I felt defeated on both fronts. I remember sitting on my couch watching Oprah say goodbye to her audience on that last episode and experiencing my mother's final moments all over again.

I slipped into a depression when the grieving process began. The evidence showed that prayers were not answered, and dreams do not come true after all. I started to question everything I had learned thus far and had no earthly idea how this whole experience could ever be a part of my evolution to become the person I was meant to be.

Part Two:

Transformation—
Metamorphosis through
the Darkness

"There is a sacredness in tears. They are not the mark of weakness, but of power. They speak more eloquently than ten thousand tongues. They are the messengers of overwhelming grief, of deep contrition, and of unspeakable love."
—WASHINGTON IRVING, 1783–1859, American short story writer

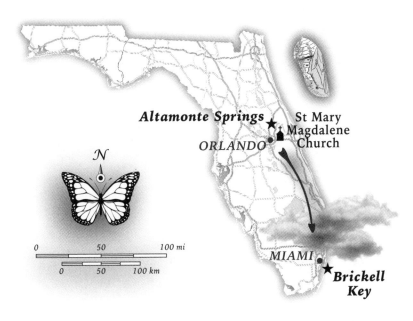

From Orlando, FL back to Miami, FL

CHAPTER 10:

Follow the Butterflies

"If there never was any change, there would be no such things as butterflies!"
—**WENDY MASS**, American young adult novelist

And there I was, a little girl again, looking to my mother to give me guidance, to protect me, and to tell me she was proud of me. But unlike my childhood, when I needed her to hold me and tell me everything would be okay, she was no longer physically there. Where did she go?

The morning after my mother passed away, we looked for her butterfly. As our Italian tradition goes, when a family member dies, that person returns as a butterfly—a sign that a metamorphosis has occurred from the physical to the spiritual dimension.

When my mother's grandmother Mary passed away, my mother took me with her to New York where my Italian American family held a wake and a funeral, then afterward celebrated Grandma Mary's life. Lots of people came together to remember what a wonderful woman she was. They told stories of how her parents had come to America from Italy and settled in Texas where Mary was born. Then she emigrated back to Italy where she lived until she returned to the States as a young woman to marry Charles. They raised two children, Betty and Rose. I was proud to be related to her and also feeling very sad, but my mother explained that after her death, Grandma Mary wasn't really gone, that she would come back as a butterfly. Just then, a yellow butterfly flew past us. My mother pointed it out and said, "Hello, Grandma."

About five years after that, when I was ten years old, my mother's parents came to Orlando to celebrate Easter with us. Grandpa Fred was about six feet tall, had broad shoulders, walked with a cane, and was larger than life. His *big* physical presence was matched by his *big* personality. When he walked into a room, everyone knew a formidable man was present. I always looked up to him but was a little scared of him too.

Before he traveled to see us, Grandpa Fred and Grandma Betty spent a week at Hutchinson Island where he suffered a fall. By the time he got to our house, something was brewing inside him. A few days later, when Grandpa Fred woke up in the morning, he could not breathe well. Chaos ensued. They called an ambulance. I went upstairs to see him. And there he was, this giant of a man sitting on the side of the bed in his undershirt and a pair of pajama pants. When I peeked in, he looked my way and smiled.

"Hi, Grandpa, can I come in?"

He nodded. I ran in and hugged him. "You're going to be okay. We're praying for you." Then I ran out to find my sisters. We sat on the grass across the street from our house with Aimee's best friend praying in a circle. From there, we saw the ambulance come and watched the medics take him away. We held hands and asked God to take care of Grandpa Fred. Then we stayed outside until we saw our mother arrive home. That's when my dad opened the front door and yelled for us to come in.

We sat at the kitchen table where my parents told us the terrible news; Grandpa Fred had gone to heaven. Through our tears, we saw it there perched outside of the window of the kitchen—a formidable and majestic brown butterfly fluttering its wings against the screen. "Hello, Grandpa!"

Now, thirty-one years later, the morning after my mother died, we looked for her. On my daughter Ava's shirt, Mary pointed to a big beautiful purple butterfly and said, "Hello, Mommy!"

Laughing, Ava danced around as if she were flying free.

And on April 21, 2011, the day we interred her ashes, I found this story that Native Americans told called the "Butterfly Indian Legend":

*If anyone desires a wish to come true, they must first capture a
butterfly and whisper that wish to it. Since a butterfly can make
no sound, the butterfly cannot reveal the wish to anyone but
the Great Spirit who sees and hears all. In gratitude for giving
the beautiful butterfly its freedom, the Great Spirit will always
grant the wish. So, according to legend, by making a wish and
giving the butterfly its freedom, the wish will be taken to the
heavens to be granted.*

After I finished reading it out loud, we released seventeen monarch
butterflies as we wished my mother safe travels. I whispered to her butterfly
spirit, "Please take care of us."

CHAPTER 11:

Purpose for This Pain?

"Grief can be the garden of compassion. If you keep your heart open through everything, your pain can become your greatest ally in your life's search for love and wisdom."
—**RUMI**, 1207–1273, thirteenth-century Persian poet

On Sunday, April 24, everyone had gone home. It was time for me to leave as well. As I packed my stuff, I sat in my room and realized that I'd no longer share any more "night befores" with my mom. On the night before an important event, I would always sit with her in my room or at the kitchen table or anywhere, really, excitedly talking about it with either great anticipation or lots of trepidation.

For instance, the night before I traveled to Colombia, South America, for a three-month cultural exchange, my mom helped me pack, talked about my exchange family, and expressed excitement that I would learn Spanish. The night before I left for Boston College, we both eagerly discussed the classes I would take, the friends I would make, and the new chapter I was about to begin. And the night before my wedding, I rested my head on my mother's shoulder as she brushed my hair and calmed my nerves. We talked about the beautiful moments we'd shared planning everything—from the glorious day I said "Yes" to finding the perfect wedding dress to booking the Portofino Bay Hotel for our big Italian affair. We excitedly anticipated a wonderful day.

The night before my son, Michael, arrived, Mom was with me at the hospital when doctors discovered that his umbilical cord was wrapped around his neck causing him distress. After labor was induced, we spent the next thirteen hours watching favorite old movies. We rejoiced when he arrived—healthy. The night before my daughter, Ava, was born, Mom calmed me down over the phone when the doctors told me they had to perform an emergency C-section. After a difficult surgery, with salsa music playing in the background, Ava arrived singing at the top of her lungs.

I'm lucky to have experienced so many night befores with my mom—so sad there won't be more.

Sitting in my childhood room, the night before I returned home from my mom's funeral, I let a lifetime of memories with her flash before my eyes. Once I left the house, I did not believe I would survive this dreadful feeling that cut so deeply into my soul and pained a heart that longed for her gentle motherly embrace. Leonardo, my Shetland sheepdog, looked up from where he sat by my feet as I cried. Giorgio, my other Sheltie, as if on cue, moved closer to me. What would I do without them?

It was getting late, and I had a long car ride ahead of me, so I willed myself to get up, grabbed my suitcase, and put leashes on both dogs. About to close the door to my childhood room, I lingered for a bit looking at it. I wanted to consciously hold on to my memories of a time that was no longer.

Just then my dad called to me from the other side of the house. "Meg, it's time to go. It's getting late!" Glancing to the right, I could see the lamp by "her" side of the bed with the five butterflies clipped to its shade. I remembered how my mom used to walk me to the door when I left to return to Miami. Not this time. I walked away alone.

After placing my luggage in the trunk of my SUV, I turned around and grabbed my dad to hug him tight. I hoped he, my only living parent, would help me navigate now. I kissed Aimee goodbye on the cheek, telling them both I would call when I got to Miami. Then I opened the door to my car, got in, and started the ignition. Lowering the window, I looked back. During my mom's illness, all of us stood together fighting for her. Now that she had passed, I felt helpless. I did not know how

I could even begin to face this loss, forget about consoling my dad or sisters. Yet, my dad promised that he would be there for us. And, if my dad could move forward after fifty years together, I could too. Under my breath, I declared, "Here goes nothing!" Then I waved and drove away.

CHAPTER 12:

Navigating through
the Darkness

"*Deep into that darkness peering, long as I stood there, wondering, fearing, doubting, dreaming dreams no mortal ever dared to dream before.*"
—EDGAR ALLAN POE, 1809–1849, American writer

Nightmares, Closets, and Dragonflies

For the next few months, I had nightmares almost every night about looking for my mom. On the night before I returned to work, sleep transported me outside the back door of her house.

> *I rang the doorbell to see if anyone was home. There was no answer, so I went to turn the doorknob, and to my surprise, the door was open. "Hello, is anyone here?" I yelled. I heard voices, and it sounded like a party was going on. Walking in, I thought, Why wasn't I invited to the celebration? "Hello, is anyone here?" I yelled again. No one replied. As I walked through the kitchen, the floor felt cold and damp. I looked down and wondered where my shoes were. Passing the dark dining room and our living room, I came to the door before the hallway that led to the*

bedrooms. I opened the door, more curious than afraid as to who was there. I went directly to my room where the noise was coming from. The door was wide open, and as I peeked in, I gasped. All my belongings were strewn everywhere. Books that lined the walls had been tossed around the room. The wooden platform bed to my right was flipped, its mattress ripped apart. Picture frames that contained photos of me throughout the years lay torn on the carpet, shards of glass from the frames surrounding them. A heap of old clothes was piled up in the middle, my old prom dresses on top ripped to shreds. And five snow globe keepsakes from my favorite places—New York, Italy, France, Miami and Colombia—lay broken on a water-soaked rug.

"We've been robbed, someone help!" I ran to see if my mother was in her room next door. There, things looked far worse. All her furniture had been moved to a corner blocking the sliding glass door that led out to the backyard. The portrait of the Madonna and Child was torn in two. The furniture was too heavy for me to move back. Desperate, I fell to my knees and begged, "Mommy, where are you?"

I returned to my room and placed the garbage that used to be my most treasured memories in a bag. Grabbing my white prom dress off the pile to wipe the tears from my face, I froze, sensing someone was there. I felt a hand on my shoulder that had to be my mother. I turned around, and a bright light blinded me. Readjusting my eyes, I saw a beautiful diamond ring lying against one of the photos of my high school graduation. It was cracked. Where did she go? I placed the ring in my pocket, called the police, and went back to cleaning the room until they arrived.

Strangely enough, two good friends from my office appeared; one was all knowing, the other formidable and strong. Confused, I asked, "How did you know? Why are you here?" Without answering, both investigated the scene, gathered evidence, and called for backup, saying, "Meg, we will take care of everything." Grabbing my hand, they led me to a little red Mini Cooper that was parked in front of the house. In that cramped little car, the three of us drove in circles for what seemed like hours looking for my mom. When we finally got to the police station on the river, a man dressed in a black suit called out, "They killed her, don't waste your time looking here, her body is gone." No, no, no! I opened the car door and jumped out. I ran toward an old school telephone booth on the corner of the street, got in, and closed the sliding door. Like in the film The Matrix, when I picked up the payphone, I was transported back into consciousness and woke up to an alarm that would not stop.

I opened my eyes and said, "I'm back." When I realized the alarm was coming from my clock, I turned it off and started to cry again. Here, in this reality, my mom really *was* gone.

I looked over at the clock, which said six thirty, and groaned, "Noooooooooo!" It was time to get out of bed, get dressed, and return to work, like nothing had happened, like my life was not forever changed. I shuffled to my closet, rubbed my eyes intently, and murmured, "God help me!"

I sighed loudly and shook my head. I wanted to crawl into a ball in the corner and go back to sleep. I sat back down on my beige beanbag to plot out how I was going to call in, tell them I didn't feel well, and stay safely there inside my cocoon. Taking a deep breath as I pondered an out, I lay back on the beanbag for a couple more moments and looked around.

My closet was the walk-in kind and rather spacious. I could stay there forever if I wanted to. We had renovated our apartment right after I gave birth to my son about eight years earlier. When our two-bedroom condo became too small for the three of us, we purchased the one-bedroom next door and tore down the wall in between. Our master bedroom used to be the living room of the one-bedroom condo, and my closet used to be its kitchen. We contracted with a closet company that came and added the perfect number of shelves and drawers to suit our needs. The mahogany-colored wood blended perfectly with the deep burgundy red we chose for the walls. We picked a decorative Pottery Barn oriental rug to cover the laminate wood floor. And when I closed the curtain that acted as a door, my closet became the perfect hideaway from the world. I felt good here; it was a safe place for me. I flirted with the idea of staying there and falling back to sleep.

Not wanting to get fired, my responsibility to provide an income and health insurance for my family trumped my desire to hide away. So I willed myself off the floor, found a black stretchy dress with a matching suit coat, got a pair of black pantyhose and heels from my shoe rack, and left the closet. As I caught a glimpse of myself in the bathroom mirror, I felt ashamed. I hadn't worked out for months, and it showed. I quickly jumped in and out of the shower, hurriedly dried my long black hair, and mechanically put on my makeup, hoping that the concealer would do its job to hide the dark circles under my eyes. I wore black on the outside, and I felt black inside too. I grabbed my purse, reaching for my keys. Exasperated that they weren't there, I yelled, "Does anyone know where my keys are? I'm going to be late!" Tears started to form in my eyes, but I held back. *Oh, no you don't—not now, not this early in the day.*

I returned to the closet to see if they were there. Happily, I resolved that if I could not find them, I had an excuse to stay home. There, on my bureau next to my jewelry, I saw the big Romero Britto butterfly keychain and sighed. Turning to leave again, I nearly fell over a box on the floor.

"Ugh!" I screamed. Then, furious, I kicked over the box as I struggled to keep my balance. When I reached down to throw the box, I noticed that on the top was a red sticker label with the words, FRAGILE— HANDLE WITH CARE. Horrified, I dropped my purse and keys, grabbed the box, and opened it carefully, making sure nothing was broken inside. Once I set aside the bubble wrap and dug through the packing peanuts, I pulled out a small dragonfly lamp with its instruction manual. I inspected it carefully, and it looked intact. Curious as to why my friend Gracie had sent me a dragonfly lamp, I read in the manual that, according to Native American legends, the dragonfly is a symbol of resurrection, transformation, and spiritual renewal after hardship. Of course, I smiled. I unwrapped the lamp and placed it on the table near a photo of my mom proudly holding my daughter the day that she was born. As I plugged the lamp into the wall and turned it on, I said a silent prayer:

Mom, please watch over me. I don't know how I'm going to survive without you.

I turned off the light in my closet and left the dragonfly lamp on. I thought, *I'll be back later; she's here.* I grabbed my purse off the floor and left my apartment to join the living and my dreadful new normal.

No Part-Time for the Weary

As time progressed, I felt worse, and my grief didn't subside. My emotional wounds were not healing; they continued to ooze with a profound sadness each day as the sun rose and set. Restful sleep was a thing of the past. Grief evolved into a depression I could not shake as I longed for my mother's embrace. I needed her to tell me that everything would be okay. Numb, I wanted to be numb. Facing hopelessness, how could I live without her unconditional love? Everyone around me went back to normal. It felt like those same people willed me to do the same. Why couldn't I? Darkness followed me wherever I went. Even though I showed up each day armed with my smile, I was literally dying inside.

At work, in the courtroom, my anxiety worsened as I listened to stories over and over again of people fleeing persecution. My right brain, the creative side, dwelled on the various renditions as told by the respondents in court of how relatives died at the hands of a terrorist group or how they feared harm as well. Could this happen to me? After twelve years of dealing with cases that involved immigrants at their worst, I began to think everyone was similar. There were cases that had merit, but I was growing tired of lies. My negative thoughts were only interrupted for a moment when the immigration judge or opposing counsel addressed me. While my attention was fully on each case, the facts were routinely the same so I could focus on other things. Going through the motions, standing up, sitting down, taking notes, and asking questions on cross. Returning cases to the file room, processing the paperwork, dealing with phone calls. Check in in the morning. Check out in the evening.

As the hot and oppressive Miami summer approached, I braced for horrendous humidity and the possibility of hurricanes. I used to enjoy this time of year, looking forward to going to the beach and playing in the sun. Now I only prayed for this despair to end. Something needed to give. My husband had just opened his own law practice. Knowing we still needed the income, I could not quit, but I could ask to work fewer hours.

Before my mother passed away, in December of 2010, she encouraged me to request part-time because I was exhausted even then. Begrudgingly, I submitted the request, even though I knew it would be frowned upon in my office under the current family-unfriendly leadership. Now it was June of 2011, nearly six months later, and I had heard nothing. I sent an email to my supervisor as to its status, and he replied, "Because your mother passed away, we did not think you were still interested."

Horrified, I emailed back, "I didn't withdraw my request. I was told it had been elevated to headquarters. Of course, I'm still interested."

"Okay." Again, I had to wait.

About a week later, coming back from court, I saw the voicemail light blinking red on my phone. The head of my office wanted to see me that afternoon as soon as possible. It was already late in the day, time to go home. Presuming the call concerned my part-time request, my curiosity prevailed. Generally, we all avoided his office whenever we could. One did not want to experience his wrath if he was in a bad mood. So many stories circulated how he would raise his voice when he lost his temper or belittle my colleagues when they did not meet his expectations. I never got the feeling that he actually liked being around people unless it was at a tailgate or happy hour. While he may have offered kind words at one time or another, I never thought I was a favorite. I tried to get to know him. Even a shared love of learning, history, travel, and dogs did not bridge the gap.

We found ourselves at odds more often than not. I always conducted myself with integrity and was horrified the time he accused me without any evidence of forging a supervisor's signature on an application for a program. Or when he presumed that I had an ulterior motive because I got to know people on a deeper level in the office. I wasn't an ass-kisser or braggart. I genuinely like people and hoped that my work ethic and job performance would speak for themselves. Unfortunately, that wasn't the way things worked there. Now I wasn't looking for recognition; I just needed a reprieve from a really stressful period. My body tensed up thinking about having to face him. I placed the files for follow-up on my desk and mustered the courage to go up one flight of stairs.

I knocked on his door, and asked, "Is this a good time?"

"Come in and close the door."

The last time I was there, I had threatened to file an EEO complaint against him for failing to recognize my contributions as the lead intern coordinator for our office. While the male counterpart on my team received an award, he reasoned that taking a short period of time off for maternity leave after the birth of my daughter disqualified me, even though I did high-caliber work the rest of the year. We all sensed how he felt about women who chose to be mothers. In fact, he made it clear when he called me at home while I was on maternity leave to advise that I didn't get a promotion, that he thought time off with a newborn was a vacation. At that last meeting, I was supported by another colleague. Having done the research, we knew the law was on our side. This time, I approached his corner office alone and knew that the law had nothing to do with the outcome; his decision to grant or deny me part-time work was discretionary.

There he was, sitting behind his desk, leaning back with his hands behind his head, waiting for me to take a seat. His body language communicated that he was in a position of power. I sat up as straight as I could, waiting for him to begin. It was clear that he was excited about the fact that he would be retiring soon. That was the first thing he said. He spoke about his plans happily. Usually, I would show more interest, but I was too tired to care. I wanted to know the verdict with regard to my request.

He started, "Headquarters gave me the green light to do whatever I deemed fit."

I was hopeful.

"You know I approved it and elevated it in the first place," he continued.

He placed his hands on the desk and moved his chair forward, looking me in the eye, and as matter of fact as he could, dealt the final blow.

"While headquarters let me do whatever I wanted, I'll be retiring this month. The office is short-staffed. I did not want to make that decision, knowing that one person working less than a full-time schedule would be a hardship here. So instead of deciding myself, I let the managers who would be responsible when I'm gone vote. Of the six individuals, only one person agreed that you could have part-time, you should be happy about that. The rest of them voted no. I'm sorry that I have to deliver the bad news, but your part-time request is denied."

Having held my breath up until this point, I exhaled as I took in what he just said. The others denied it? Who? Why? He could have said yes. What kind of place is this? I bent slightly forward and shook my head. This man could have said yes. I was only asking to work slightly less and get paid slightly less. No special favors. I needed the time to heal. How could an individual be so cruel? What was wrong with him—did he have such little regard for me? Being blocked from advancement on my professional path was one thing. But being blocked from the chance to get back on my feet for a breather was another. He said he could have approved it here—yet I got a no?

Sure, he was the one who gave me the chance to spearhead and elevate the office intern program when I started in 2000. Eleven years later, you would think I had failed at it, but my track record proved that I delivered year after year, creating one of the best programs in the country. I did seek his approval, knowing full well that he was the one person who could open doors to move up in that office. In addition to doing a good job litigating, writing (I was named as the prevailing party in a published seminal decision at appellate level), and addressing clients' needs, I organized social committee events and led training sessions for my coworkers. On my own dime, I got certificates from the best time management training programs and brought the information back to help my colleagues with work/life balance. He asked for innovation, and I stepped up to the plate.

Yet he still denied me any opportunities to advance my career, from refusing to fund me after I was accepted as a fellow with the Council for Excellence in Government when he had the budget; to not picking me as a senior attorney on three occasions; to overlooking me as a supervisor for Miami; to bristling after he couldn't stop me from participating with the ICE Mentoring Program. Fine, he was leaving, he didn't have to write a letter of recommendation on my behalf to anyone. However, I needed a break and he ultimately said "No!" I wanted to tell him off and quit then and there. He had done a lot of crappy things, but now, I thought, *How cruel, how terribly cruel*! I was a warm body that they needed to go to court and do the grunt work they didn't want to do. Nobody cared about the condition of that body, it just had to show up. From what he said, other members in management clearly did not care about me, even though they gave lip service otherwise.

Because of his place in the chain of command, I held my tongue. I stood up, smoothed out my skirt and calmly said, "Thank you for your time. I have nothing else to say to you."

I quickly left his office, and under my breath declared, "Asshole!" I went from angry to despondent in a matter of seconds. For so long, all I wanted to do was impress him. I worked so hard to do my best, and got nothing, not even this. Hatred. That is what I wanted to feel. Apathy. I only wished I did not care. Utter disappointment. That is where the pendulum settled. Still, I so desperately wanted to be liked, so desperately wanted to be a part of something, a longing that has stayed with me since I was a child. But killing them with kindness had done nothing for my career. Speaking up when others were wronged got me passed over. Integrity, do the right thing, play the game and it will pay off? Wrong. Properly navigating the chain of command got me nowhere. Favoritism played its part. Where was the just outcome in all of this? I revisited what I used to tell myself: *Be a team player, Meg. Be a good employee, Meg. Move along quickly and accept this, Meg, don't ruffle any feathers. Don't stir things up or you will bring negative attention upon yourself, Meggie.*

Back in my office, I swore that I'd had enough. I didn't deserve this. I worked hard, brought results. I needed a *f*cking break*. And all I saw in front of me was his smug little face, telling me, "No." That was the last time. Screw all of them. I secretly wished that they all felt even a fraction of the pain and exhaustion that I was going through. I prayed that the karmic gods would one day wreak havoc. I had to get the hell out of there before I did or said something I would really regret. I grabbed my purse to leave, turned off the light in my office, and slammed the door. That is when I spotted one of the managers who voted me down. I couldn't hold back. Frustrated and at my wits' end, I declared through tears of betrayal:

"How could you vote against me? How could you? I have had the most challenging three months of my life. I have given my everything to this place. I gave my everything to my mom. I never ask for special treatment from this office. *Never.* You think I wanted this? I needed this. I'm *done.* I can't believe you people."

He stood there wordlessly as I walked away and headed to the elevator. Then, not wanting to wait for it, I ran down the stairs and left the building.

When I got to my car, it felt like a hundred degrees inside. It was June, and the temperature gauge read ninety-five degrees. I turned on the car to get the A/C started and got in. It was so hot that I felt the leather stick to the backs of my legs. I pulled out of the parking lot and headed toward my house. At the stop light, I pulled my long black hair into a ponytail and noticed the people in the car on the right chatting animatedly, laughing while they waited for the light to turn green. I hated them for experiencing joy. I hated everyone. I wondered if they ever felt the kind of sadness that I was feeling. I wondered what was going to happen to me now. I wanted to crawl out of my own skin and yell out, "My mother is gone. How can anyone laugh and enjoy life? How could my boss say no to part-time?"

As I approached the Brickell Key Bridge that led to my neighborhood, I saw all the lean bodies swiftly running past me and thought, *There must be something wrong with me.* And as I customarily would do when things did not go my way, I examined my own flaws to find evidence that I was unworthy of good things. I started to berate myself. I examined my own body, disgusted at how I lacked the discipline to keep it together. If I were beautiful and fit, I would be able to handle whatever the world threw at me. If I were the picture of perfection, I would get the breaks. No matter what I do, I will always be that little girl who was harassed and bullied daily because she was less than. I will never be worthy. I thought, then, how disappointed my mother must have been with me. I couldn't even help her survive. I couldn't even help myself now. I felt like my head was about to explode. I wanted to get home, change my clothes, and curl up into a ball in my closet with my dragonfly lamp on and cry some more. And when I arrived home, that is exactly what I did.

On the last day of work for the head of the office, the top lawyers from Washington, DC, were in town to oversee the transition and announce their new pick to lead our office. After work, they hosted a happy hour, and I went with my office colleagues. At the bar, I saw the head of the office coming my way. I tried to dodge him, but I was standing in the middle of a crowded and narrow space and couldn't move. It was too late, he was right in front of me.

"Meg—this is it," he said.

"Yep, good luck." I replied quickly.

"You too," he said. "I hope you get exactly what you want in life."

As confidently as I could, I replied, "Thank you, I most definitely will."

As the words left my mouth, I had to believe them. I actually walked away thinking that he must be laughing at me for thinking I could rise in the ranks there. He had certainly made sure to stand in the way of any professional opportunity that came my way. I had no faith that the other managers would be any different. And I had no idea what I would do next. I knew that if I stayed in this job, my career would stall out. I wanted to continue learning, but I felt trapped with no possibility of advancement. Truth be told, my nerves were shot.

Tinnitus—Anyone Know a Cure?

In August, around the four-month anniversary of my mother's passing, I woke in the middle of the night to a loud whistling sound. I got up to go to the kitchen to see where the noise was coming from. I never thought for a moment that the whistling tea kettle sound was coming from my own head. Finding no evidence of faulty electronics or burners left on, I cleaned out my ears and shook my head, but the sound was getting louder and louder. As I paid more attention to its origin, the left side of my brain seemed to scream out like there was a three-alarm fire, so loud and high-pitched that I turned on the television in the living room in hopes of drowning it out, but to no avail. I spent the rest of the dark hours wandering around my condo, unable to sleep because of the ringing. It followed me. It was maddening.

Like a dutiful hypochondriac, I spent those waking hours searching the internet with vigor looking for the reason behind this newly acquired symptom that left me exhausted beyond measure. I found everything from the serious possibility of cancerous tumors to the less devastating overexposure to loud noise, but not wanting to get medical help, I hoped it would get better on its own. After three weeks of worrying, I finally made an appointment with an ear, nose, and throat (ENT) doctor for an evaluation because it was driving me crazy. I couldn't concentrate at work. I couldn't function without sleep. I would retreat to my closet once again, wanting to die. After seeing my mother go through tests and treatment for the past two years that left her worse off than when she started, I was terrified of doctors, even though they took an oath to do no harm. In the buildup to my appointment, I nervously anticipated a horrible diagnosis that would line up with my own fear of a terrible, drawn out death. The eventual tinnitus diagnosis took away any remaining chance for peace.

After being checked out by an ENT doctor, an ear specialist, and a cardiologist to find out if there was a clear physical problem that could be addressed, I was sent for a physical exam, hearing tests, an exam to see if the arteries to my ears were blocked, and finally magnetic resonance imaging (MRI).

Once I changed into a gown for my MRI, I took the headset offered and got up on the platform, waiting for the operator to move the table into the long tube. As I lay still for what seemed like forever, the music playing in the headset could not overcome the really loud noises of the MRI—which exacerbated the loud ringing in my head. It was almost intolerable. I thought, *This must be how people go insane.* Hoping that my high threshold for pain would save me from the embarrassment of running out of there, I held my breath and like a good girl stayed quiet for the duration of the procedure. All the while, I wanted to scream, "How did I get here? Somebody help me!"

When all the tests came back normal, the doctors offered to prescribe antidepressants or anti-anxiety pills, but they could not guarantee that either would help me. Once again, as a dutiful hypochondriac, I read the warnings and side effects that seemed to guarantee more pitfalls than salvation. Before I left his office, the ENT doctor turned to me and said, "As of yet, there is no known medical cure that will stop the ringing. Tinnitus is something that you might have to just live with for the rest of your life."

During the ride home from his office, I bawled. Over the past months, that seemed to be all I had done—cried hysterically. The more I tried to keep it together, the faster I fell apart. Perhaps all the joy and laughter had been buried alongside my mother's ashes. So here I was with a loud, persistent ringing in my head, so loud at times that I couldn't hear conversations right in front of me. I was stressed out in what seemed to be a dead-end job that I could no longer stand. Unable to sleep more than three hours a night, I was barely functioning yet still had to take care of kids and go to court during the day. The only medical option offered, antidepressants, made me even more nervous. And finally, the one person who could always calm me down was no longer alive to assist. I was trapped in a living nightmare. Suicidal ideations danced around in my head as the only certain way for relief. But how could I do that to my kids? And my partner, the man who vowed to be by my side in good times *and* bad, didn't understand and grew increasingly frustrated as I got worse.

I did not want to live like this anymore—I didn't want to live anymore. Panic set in. Even a much-needed trip to the Bahamas for five days offered little solace. Desperate and strung out, I locked myself in the bathroom and called my dad from the hotel. He listened to me as I tried to catch my breath. "Daddy, what is wrong with me?"

And when I paused, he yelled over the phone, "Dammit! C'mon, Meg, snap out of it! This is not the young woman your mother raised. Get it together."

Just as when he had raised his voice to get my attention when I was hysterical as a kid, it worked, and I stopped crying.

He continued, "Meggie, I am sorry. But I know you are stronger than this. You have to calm down and figure out what you can do. I can't help you while you're there."

I unlocked the bathroom door and sank into the corner between the doorway and the wall of the hotel, feeling the full weight of the world on my shoulders, "Okay, Daddy, okay. I'll do my best."

When I hung up, I dropped my head in my hands, completely distraught, and whispered, "Mommy, please help me! Where are you?"

My two-year-old daughter, Ava, approached me and said, "Grammie says she's okay, she wants you to move on." Then she sang, "Don't Give up! Don'tcha give up! Never Give up! Never Give up!"

Wiping the tears from my eyes, I held my little girl and knew that this was not how I wanted her to see me.

"Get it together, Meg! You are stronger than this," I whispered, repeating the words of my father.

I promised myself that when I returned home, I would be the strong woman my mother raised. I just needed help to figure out how. I reached out to my family in an email:

I have been having an exceptionally difficult time these last few months dealing with the loss of Mommy. I thought I could numb myself to these overwhelming feelings. I underestimated how not having her physically here would affect me. I do believe she's at peace now—I do believe that she lives on in all of us. I do understand that what I am feeling is grief, and I am going to see someone to help me with that because I am having a hard time functioning and sleeping—so I ask you all to please keep me in your prayers and that I too have FAITH that I can move on out of this sorrow.

CHAPTER 13:

Let the Healing Begin

"Ask, and it shall be given you; seek, and ye shall find; knock, and it shall be opened unto you."
—**MATTHEW 7:7**, The Bible, King James Version

Needles & Moxa

Those days, I didn't have faith in many people to help me. Yet I knew I had to ask a trusted few as I could no longer go it alone. At my mother's funeral, one of my good friends in Miami promised to check on me each morning to make sure I was all right. When she called me on a Wednesday before I went to court, I finally admitted to her that I wasn't doing well at all. Closing my office door to protect my privacy, I told her that I couldn't take the ringing anymore, I didn't want to live like this; I didn't want to live. Then I started to cry.

"Meg, I'm really worried about you," she said.

"Me too, "I replied.

"There is a doctor in my networking group who might be able to help you. I think she does acupressure or acupuncture. I'm not sure which one. If you want, I can call her and find out if she can see you today."

"Okay, all right." I needed to do something. "Thank you so much. What do I have to lose?"

Before hanging up, she said, "I'll call you right back. Gimme a sec."

I replied, so grateful, "Thank you, I appreciate this so much."

When she called me back, she told me that everything was set. I had an appointment for that afternoon, and she was on her way to pick me up from work and take me there. I remembered how Dr. Namaste brought hope to my mother during her last days. While I hated needles, perhaps this woman could help me, as I was desperate for hope. When we arrived, Dr. Eva welcomed me immediately with an embrace and sat me down to determine what she could do to help. She looked nothing like Dr. Namaste; she was a young blonde woman from the Czech Republic.

I said, "It has been so long since I had a full night's sleep."

She looked at my bloodshot eyes, the window to my troubled soul, and replied, "I can see that."

After explaining that my mother recently passed, I continued, "I feel like I'm being punished for not being able to save my mother." Then I lowered my head, fully feeling the shame of those words.

Through tears, for over thirty minutes, I detailed the beginning of the ringing in my ears. I told her about the anxiety that had overwhelmed me since April. I explained how lost I had felt. And I told her about my job and the stress there as well. She checked my tongue and pulse and then let me choose the treatment room. I liked the one painted bright orange; it felt happy. After I changed into a patient's gown, she explained how Chinese medicine using acupuncture points could help to reduce the tinnitus and decrease my anxiety. She showed me her herbal "moxa" stick and slowly placed it at various points along my back, explaining how it could invigorate the flow of energy. Trusting her, I closed my eyes as she placed the acupuncture needles in strategic locations all over my head, my ears, and the rest of my body. She covered me with a blanket and placed heat lamps over my stomach and legs. She turned off the light and turned up the music, asking if I was okay, then wished me sweet dreams. As I lay there afraid to move, I listened intently to the music hoping it would drown out the noise in my head. The song "Only Time" by Irish singer and musician Enya, played in the background. That song made me smile. Time, I needed time to mourn the loss of my mother. And I consciously inhaled and fully exhaled, in and out, over and over again. *Breathe, Meg!*

After what felt like over an hour, Dr. Eva came back in, peeled back the thin blanket, and took out all the needles, one by one. I got dressed, feeling a bit more rested and thinking for the first time in a while that maybe this was a step in the right direction. There was hope for me yet. While the ringing was still there, I felt calmer. Grateful, I hugged Dr. Eva. This was the first piece in the puzzle as I began to assemble my team of healers. I committed to my self-care; I was going to go twice a week for the foreseeable future.

Beginning to Write My Way Out

That same August, after sharing with a therapist friend that I was having a hard time navigating the grieving process, she offered to meet with me. After listening for over an hour as I tried to come to terms with how I felt and the way my life force was depleted, she suggested that I dedicate some time each day to talk to my mom and reconnect. Acknowledging my exhaustion from caring for a dying loved one, she validated my need to take a leave of absence from my job to recuperate. She thought it would be a good idea as long as I had a plan. So I set out to make it happen and created one.

First, after researching what I needed to obtain a leave of absence under the Family Medical Leave Act, I sent a formal request through my supervisor, supporting it with evidence in the form of a medical evaluation of post-traumatic stress disorder as the underlying cause for the tinnitus diagnosis, along with my doctor's letter and weeks I proposed to take off. By this time, the previous head of the office had retired, and the one who replaced him assured me that he would do whatever he could to get it approved. Second, as synchronicity would have it, that same month, I made lunch plans with another friend who was finishing up her certification to become a life coach. So I asked her if she could coach me for the six weeks I wanted to take leave. Because she needed the hours, she agreed to take me on as a pro bono client. Third, I set some savings aside so that I would not have to worry about the additional financial stress on my family.

True to his word, my new head of the office advised that my leave of absence was approved beginning on September 11, 2011. With the help of my life coach friend, I was determined to make the most out of the time that I had. Each week I set out goals to catapult myself forward and at the same time honor my mother's memory. Following my therapist friend's suggestion, *I turned to writing as a healing tool. I started simply; I would wake in the morning and read from a book that resonated with me. When a quote or a passage spoke to me, I grabbed my journal and channeled at least three pages of longhand about what I felt my mother would want to communicate.*

Then I started to detox and take care of my mind by caring for my body. Eating better and exercising more, I tried yoga, spinning, Zumba, and swimming. I took contemplative walks where I really paid attention to my surroundings. I even organized a group to walk in the Susan G. Komen Race for the Cure in memory of my mom and another friend who passed away from breast cancer. And, with the support of my father and husband, my family set up the Mary Jo Nocero Leadership Award for Outstanding Achievement in Tennis, honoring an outstanding female tennis player at my former high school. Ensuring that my mother's legacy would not be forgotten, I became a human "doing" hoping for ways to keep her in my life. At the same time, I was looking for ways to heal myself and alleviate the ringing in my ears and the pain in my heart. This was proving to be a more difficult task.

Not Every Group Is Supportive

At my mother's funeral, I was told that hospice offered support groups for individuals dealing with grief; others recommended that I look to my church to see if there were any programs offered there. Neither existed near my home. Because I was dealing with tinnitus, on the advice of a colleague, I called the local hospital to see if I could participate in a behavior modification program. As I was not addicted to any controlled substance, I did not qualify, but they did refer me to a grief group that met once a week in the evenings. So I decided to try it out. After all, what did I have to lose?

When I pulled up to the entrance of a three-story facility with ambulances coming and going, I froze. My heart started to race and pound wildly. As I hadn't been in a hospital since the day my mom died, I started to panic. Maybe I should not go. I wanted a support group, not to be admitted. I took a few deep breaths, parked my car, and against my better judgment went in. The automatic doors opened wide, and the freezing temperature and sweet antiseptic smell brought me back to her final days. Before I could escape, the person who was running the group saw me and beckoned me to come in and take a seat in the circle. I dutifully complied.

There were six others there, all women except the facilitator. After welcoming all of us, he invited each one to share whatever we wanted concerning our loss. One woman lost her husband at thirty-eighty and was left with two small kids to raise; another's sister was murdered by a former lover. One older woman shared how alone she felt now that most of her friends and close family had died; another's husband passed away from a heart attack after years of alcohol abuse. I felt the palpable pain in that room. I was surrounded by so much sadness it was almost killing me to be there. I just wanted to sit quietly until I could leave. Then I could return to my closet and hide. When it was my turn, all eyes were on me. It was time to share.

I began, "My mom died in April as a result of breast cancer." As if the word *cancer* were her cue, the older lady to my left cut me off before I could continue.

She said, "Well, my husband recently died after a long battle with lung cancer. His kids tried to evict me from my home as they only want his money. And if it were not for my little white dog, I would have walked into the ocean months ago. I don't want to live anymore!"

And, with that statement, she took the liberty to go around the circle repeating each person's reason for being there until she stopped at the woman who'd lost her husband because of alcohol abuse and announced, "I get why everyone else is here. From murder to loss, but why you? You knew he was an alcoholic. You should have seen it coming. Why are you grieving him? Why are you here?"

I turned and looked in horror at the facilitator, who sat there saying nothing. The lady on my left looked like she was ready to unleash again, while her target uncomfortably repositioned herself while holding back tears. This wasn't a safe place at all.

Before she could go on, I touched her hand, and said, "Grief is grief. Don't judge her."

She looked at me as if she were about to say something, stopped, and looked down as if she were ashamed. I felt so bad confronting her in front of the others. I wanted to say that I was sorry and that I understood how she felt—angry, despondent, lost. Then I felt a stabbing pain in the pit of my stomach. I clenched my jaw tightly and my ears started ringing even louder.

I touched her hand again and whispered, "It's okay. I get it."

The meeting couldn't end fast enough. In the silence of my car, my tinnitus was ringing out of control. I turned on the radio as loud as I could stand, but it just aggravated the situation as I felt a tension headache coming on. I began to berate myself for putting myself in such a bad situation. I should have left when I saw the meeting was in the hospital. I would certainly not be going back. But I couldn't help wondering if I would ever feel comfortable in my skin again. This meeting had set me back. Would I ever get the help I needed to move forward?

Still in So Much Pain

I returned to work and my regular routine in late October. Three months passed slowly and agonizingly. I still felt out of sorts. In the midst of my grieving process and wearing "gray-colored" glasses, I couldn't even appreciate a January sunrise over Biscayne Bay. The oranges and reds and yellows that burst from the sky as the sun greeted the day were once something that I would look forward to. However, it had been five days in a row now that I had gotten less than a total of three hours of sleep, and it had taken its toll. And then on one lucky night, I passed out exhausted at midnight and woke at three cursing the darkness. I would walk around the house, looking to clean or organize what I could. My head was aching, and I couldn't think straight. My ears were ringing beyond belief. My eyes were bloodshot and itchy. I could barely see the television that I turned on to drown out the noise in my head, half-watching the sort of old movies that aired only during the wee hours of the morning. I sat up on the couch, kicked off the red throw that I used as a makeshift comforter, and looked at the kitchen clock in disgust. *I can't believe it's six thirty again.*

The acupuncture treatments had helped a lot, but with the added stress, the insomnia took over. For the last week, my husband had been in Orlando at a conference, and I was left to hold down the fort alone. It was time to help my son get ready for school, to dress my daughter, and to get myself ready for work. On no more than six hours of sleep in the last six days, I had no idea how the hell I was going to function.

As I let this thought ruminate, I started to cry—wail actually. I ran to my bedroom so I would not worry my kids, although at this point I don't think much would have scared them anyway. I had been crying uncontrollably for months.

As I grabbed for the phone, I thought twice before calling my husband. I knew he wanted to believe that things were back to normal after my six-week leave of absence from work. But back at my office since late October, all the positive groundwork vanished when the stress of balancing work, life, and grief overwhelmed me again. Now in January, I saw myself sliding backwards.

I felt my heart race and started to hyperventilate. "I can't go on like this, I can't," I wailed.

I held the phone in my hand and dialed New York City. On the other end, my aunt Pat picked up the phone. I fell to the ground begging her, "Please help me! Please help me!"

"Meggie? Is that you?"

"Patty, I can't breathe, I feel like I'm going to die."

"Take a deep breath—you have to take a deep breath. It's going to be okay. Just breathe."

Michael, my eleven-year-old, came into my closet to see where I had gone. "Mommy, are you okay?"

I couldn't even look at him.

"Mommy I love you, are you okay?" Ava trailed along behind him. It was dark except for the little dragonfly light in the far-right corner of my closet. I was sitting on the floor soaking wet and wrapped in my towel with the phone held tightly to my ear.

I wiped my eyes, looked at them, and smiled. "I love you both so much. I'm okay—don't worry," I lied.

"I have to go, Mommy. I took the dogs out," Michael said.

I looked at the clock and it was 7:05; his carpool driver would be downstairs any minute. I thought, *I'm a terrible mom, I can't even protect my kids from this craziness I am experiencing. I never wanted this for them.*

"I love you, Mikey. Have fun at school." And with that I kissed him on the cheek. Ava, my three-year-old, started to sing one of the Disney tunes that she loved so much and returned to her bedroom to watch Mickey Mouse Clubhouse on the Disney Channel.

Patty said, "Are you still there?"

"Yes, I'm okay," I said hopefully. "I'm going to get dressed to go to work. I promise I'll call you later."

Over my objection, my husband had gone to Orlando so he could get his continuing education credits. I'd begged him not to go. I told him that I wasn't ready to handle everything on my own. But he had insisted.

I thought, *How can he be so selfish when I desperately need his help?*

I don't think he wanted to be bothered by me; maybe he didn't even care. He left on Monday; now it was Friday, and the conference was over. He would be gone for two more days, as he had scheduled a trip to Tampa at the tail end. I was doing my best alone but felt like I was falling apart. Dutifully, I got up, grabbed clothes from the closet, got dressed, and left the house after our nanny arrived at eight thirty to take care of Ava; at least she was in good hands.

As I started up my car, I realized I was scheduled to be the duty attorney that day and would be responsible for answering all the questions that were fielded in our office. Sitting at the light, about to turn into the parking lot, I cried out loud, "Oh, my God, this is a joke! I can barely keep my eyes open. Are you kidding me? Are you really kidding me? Are you there, God?" I banged on the steering wheel. "How could my husband not have compassion for me? How could he be so heartless?"

Then my tears returned once again. I thought to call my husband. I needed to call my husband. I dialed my husband's number.

He answered, "Hello?"

I begged, "It's me. I need you to come home."

"Meg, what's wrong with you? You know I can't do that."

"I'm jumping out of my skin. Please come home. I'm so exhausted; I can't handle another day like this without any sleep."

"I have one more day of lectures, and then I promised my parents that I would see them this weekend."

"Please, please."

"C'mon Meg, I have to go. I'll call you later." And he hung up.

Weeping, I looked at the phone and prayed out loud, "Help me! Help me, Help me! If you don't want me to give up, then You have to help me. I can't go on like this." The ringing in my head got worse, and now the headache from crying made it very difficult to see.

I arrived at the public parking lot near my office. I had made it through traffic over busy Brickell Avenue and crossed the bridge that linked the financial sector to downtown Miami, all without realizing it. I parked, looked into the rearview mirror, and applied a new layer of lipstick, hoping that would somehow transform my face and hide my exhaustion. I got out of the car and walked about ten minutes across the street, praying I would not run into anyone I knew as I made my way into the office.

Not even thirty minutes into my day, the panic returned. The phone was ringing over and over, and my heart was racing. Only ten more hours and I could go home. In the meantime, I couldn't let anyone know what was going on. I was so ashamed, I thought maybe I would be fired or sent away if they found out what a mess I was. I called my aunt Pat again, and she pleaded, "Go home, Meg. Call your supervisor and go home."

Desperate and lacking the energy to argue with her, I called my boss, told him I was not feeling well, and turned off my computer to leave.

As I grabbed my purse to go, I remembered one of my best friends, Teda, advising me long ago, "Don't go to the hardware store for bread." My husband couldn't handle me right now, so I called Teda, told her what was going on, and asked, "Will you help me?"

She said, "Come over."

I did.

After I got there, we decided to go to the emergency room to rule out anything really serious.

Sitting in the hospital waiting room with Teda, I stared off into the distance, grateful that I was not alone. I was desperate for help. The earlier events of the morning had really scared me. Thinking the worst diagnoses—stroke, heart attack, or possibly cancer—I held back tears.

To level out the panic I felt, I repeated my go-to mantra: "I am healthy, happy, beautiful. I am strong, smart, and all is well."

I liked to think I was a recovering hypochondriac and could keep my anxiety under control, but the effort to do so that day took a level of effort that not even Wonder Woman could handle. Since my mother passed away, I felt I had been holding my breath and doing my best to stay ahead of any bad news on the horizon. Well it was time for release, because I needed to face the music as the built-up anxiety over the past nine months finally caught up with me. That day, I'd lost my ability to numb out and just do my job.

When the nurse finally called me back, she checked my vitals and asked me some questions. Then a doctor arrived after she received the results from the various tests. She said, "You are okay. It appears you had a panic attack. From what you said, you have been under a lot of stress that's resulting in insomnia. We are going to give you something to help you and ask that you follow up with your primary physician. Take care of yourself." I sighed, grateful, confused, and exhausted. Easier said than done.

In the treatment room, they gave me anti-anxiety medication to calm me down. As it began to take effect, I finally felt my body rest. It was getting late in the day, and I was so grateful that Teda stayed with me the whole time and made sure my kids were taken care of as well. She said she would take me home too. Then, at around five o'clock, my husband appeared.

"Teda called me, I canceled everything and drove back."

"I didn't think you would come." I was surprised. He had been adamant about staying.

He said, "Look I came back, I'm here. I talked to the doctor. They're releasing you now. Let's just go home."

Dazed from the Xanax, ashamed of myself, and without the energy to argue, I grabbed my things, and we did just that.

Journaling a Divine Shift

I was at a crossroads. While I had been going to traditional talk therapy for some time, clearly it was not working for me. I spent hour-long sessions each week ruminating about everything that caused me so much pain.

In my mind, I kept subjecting myself to evidence that there was so much wrong with me. Now I began to fear that my husband might leave me.

After the emergency room episode, my husband said that he'd had enough. He begged me to go on medication, as nine months had passed since my mother's death, and he had not seen any improvement. Facing the possibility of being alone at an emotionally vulnerable time, I called a psychiatrist to see if I could get an appointment to satisfy my husband's insistence that I speed up my recovery with mind-numbing meds. Nothing was available for a few weeks. I chose not to schedule anything and hung up relieved. I had done what I'd promised, but my soul rebelled. *I don't want to take drugs. There has to be something better for me!*

Knowing I could no longer handle full-time work, I submitted a request with supporting documentation to work a flexible schedule at eighty percent. Much to my relief, my request was granted without question. Then I reached out to my friend who had started a holistic healing practice out in California.

"Bella, I'm not good." I endearingly called all my closest female friends Bella.

She replied, "Listen, call this therapist. She does things differently. She has a better approach. I know that she will help you. I think you really will like her."

Trusting her recommendation, I made an appointment with the psychotherapist who introduced me to eye movement desensitization and reprocessing (EMDR), neuro-emotional technique (NET), and Psych-K to free myself from subconscious, limiting beliefs as a part of her treatment. In our first session together, she spent the first part listening to my story, but the second part, she had me moving through it. She was the first one who explained to me that emotions need to move. If they get stuck, that is when anxiety sets in. She said, "The Latin root of emotion is *e*, out of, and *motere*, to move—emotions, both good and bad, need to move out of us."

Then she had me wrap my arms around my shoulders, calling it a butterfly pose. I closed my eyes and visualized my happy place at the beach, feeling the wind in my face and the sand covering my feet as I moved my butterfly wings from side to side. She introduced Psych-K as a self-empowering process to impact the neural pathways on a cellular level and had me repeat this mantra: "Magical work for magical pay, magical service every magical day." These weekly sessions had me safely going within to get in touch with what was going on so I could move out of a past that frightened me into a present of possibility.

I continued getting deep tissue massage and a technique called Rolfing to relieve the tension in my facial muscles and my body. One time, when I desperately called my massage therapist to come to my aid because the ringing was off the charts, I was so immensely grateful that she rescheduled everything to accommodate me. She not only helped to minimize the pressure in my jaw, but also the emotional love and support were vital. Then I worked with a healer who practiced cranio-sacral massage, body talk, and meditation. She even acted as a medium so I could connect with my mother. And I got an appointment with one of the best orthodontists in Miami to figure out how realigning my bite with Invisalign could minimize the inflammation in my temporomandibular joint. With each of these actions, my goal was to reduce the ringing and reset my nervous system. And my situation did slowly improve. It took a lot of work, but I was getting better.

I finally found a support group as well. I received an email from the healer who had worked with my mom's spirit on another plane during her final weeks. She invited me to join her Divine Mentoring Group. She told me that her intention for the program was to help the participants clear stuff out so each person could move forward to "live the life they wanted." Enthusiastically, I joined the Divine Five telephonically, saying yes in hopes that I could continue the momentum for more positive shifts.

Instead of ruminating over what was wrong with me, through weekly sessions, I had a chance to look at my gifts. After goal sharing, the healer explained that she would hold an intention of clarity for my purpose. After I shared that I had a hard time with change, she pointed out, "One thing that is tough to see, especially when we are in the thick of transition, is that we are exactly where we need to be. So we need to learn how to be more patient with ourselves. Because we are older souls, we have this burning calling inside of us that tells us that we should be doing something that we haven't been doing and get to it already—always a sense of urgency. The more time you take for yourself, the clearer you will be able to see."

Then she pointedly asked me, "What will it take for you to truly feel worthy? What do you think is the real lesson in all of this for you? All this stuff is happening all at once. Let's start with your mom's death—what lessons do you have with this? Your work? Your family? Why is there part of you that wants to stay stuck in the emotional state that you're in right now? What's the purpose of it?"

I replied, "While I say to myself that I don't care what people think, in reality I do. Although I've been repeating to myself over and over again that I'm enough, without the approval from my mother that I depended on for so long, I'm stuck. There have been so many lessons in all of this for me. I saw my mom succumb to a horrible illness and have not felt any peace since. I miss my mom's guidance and love."

I continued, "I hate the question, why do I want to stay stuck in this emotional state? I don't want to be stuck in anything. I really want peace and freedom to become aligned and not have to prove myself. I think that is the only way I can heal. I don't have a guide that I can look to—but I want to get there, to that place of peace."

And a common theme appeared. Each therapist suggested the same thing: "You have to learn to be your own guide, Meg. It's time."

Nearing the end of the mentoring program, I discovered the works of Joseph Campbell, the author of *The Hero with a Thousand Faces*, who introduced the myth of the hero's journey. His quote, "Follow your bliss and the universe will open doors where there used to be walls," became the adage that guided my way. As I worked through so much, I got more clarity around what I wanted. I began to believe that I was meant for more than what I was experiencing. I began to realize that the label "government lawyer" was too limiting. For the first time in twelve years, I allowed myself to think outside the box and declare, "My calling is too loud to stay (at my job)."

Continuing to journal and spend mornings in contemplation, I thought about the difference between living a life doing things that were expected of me and one where I did things I wanted to do. Until then, I never thought about moving on to do something outside of where I was, even though I hit a wall each time I tried to advance from within. While my mother was alive, I guess I was okay to remain where I was as long as we explored the curiosities of life together. But when she died, I was no longer satisfied with the way my life was unfolding. My own father beckoned for me to wake up, get it together, and face my issues so I could move forward and hopefully have no regrets. This was a beginning to "follow my bliss" in hopes that the universe would open doors. And as Goethe wrote, "Whatever you can do or dream you can, begin it. Boldness has genius, power, and magic in it." It was time for me to be bold and no longer resist my own call toward a greater purpose. I just had to figure out what I was passionate about to determine what was waiting for me.

CHAPTER 14:

Your Life Purpose Is Calling— Are You Paying Attention?

"You're only given one little spark of madness. You mustn't lose it."

—ROBIN WILLIAMS, 1951-2014, American actor and comedian

Soul Talk and Synchronicity

From 2007 to 2011, my soul sisters and I gathered each week for what we called a "Soul Talk," a circle of friends nurtured by compelling topics, enlightening conversation, and a tea ritual. There, we held a safe place to support each other through challenges while educating ourselves on different topics. We were diverse women with varying backgrounds and worldviews brought together by a desire to share different perspectives that could help each of us live a more satisfying life.

Every week, one person would host, choose the subject matter, and prepare the materials for discussion. From the creative to the sublime, we investigated authors as varied as Albert Camus, Carl Jung, Don Miguel Ruiz, and Dr. Seuss. We participated in exercises that had us rock stacking, the act of balancing stones to practice patience, and created chakra bracelets for spiritual cleansing. Always ending with a meditation, we gathered each week with an open mind and left far better off than we came. Yet, as with all good things after a great run, our time together came to an end. Due to significant changes (moving away, divorce, and dealing with loss, to name a few), our core group went our separate ways. As I learned when we studied Jung and his concept of synchronicity, the universe provides meaningful connections for each of us exactly when we need them most. The question remains, are we paying attention?

Reflecting back on the events that impacted me, the way that my parents met was seemingly serendipitous. My mother, fifteen, and my father, seventeen, were both on a summer break enjoying themselves poolside at the New York Athletic Club on Travers Island in Pelham. My mother, dressed in a white one-piece, caught his attention as she took her place high above on the diving board ready to jump in. As the story goes, my father, normally very shy, stood mesmerized at the side of the pool garnering all his courage to speak to her before she swam over and climbed out. When she did, he boldly engaged in lively conversation which led my mother to walk him over to introduce him to my future grandmother, Betty. My mother began by saying that my father was in town on a semester break from the College of Holy Cross in Worcester, Massachusetts. Then Betty immediately asked if he knew a young man by the name of Michael Nocero, who attended Holy Cross as well. Before he could answer, Betty started singing the praises of this young Italian American pre-med student who had such a bright future that it was imperative that they meet. When Betty paused, my mother turned to her new friend with a smile, and my father proudly exclaimed, "*I* am Michael Nocero." With Betty's blessings, that was the beginning of a love affair that lasted over fifty years. After six years of dating, they married in a glorious celebration in New York City. Synchronicity.

Even in my own life, the power of intention crossed paths with divine intervention, opening up amazing connections. While in law school, bored with studying for exams, my friends and I grabbed the law school's book of our classmates' photos. We decided that we were each going to cut out a photo of an individual who we thought would make a good match for the other two. After perusing, they cut out a photo of a young Italian American kid in our class, stapled his photo on my straw, and placed it in the potted plant next to the door. Fast forward, we graduated and were studying for the Florida Bar Exam in the University of Miami's law library when the guy who was on my straw showed up daily and sat down right next to me. On breaks, he and I would go outside and spend the time getting to know each other. Over time, seeing how much we both had in common, we became more attracted to each other. In February of 2000, I married the Italian guy on my straw in front of three hundred and celebrated at Portofino Bay Hotel, a resort designed to look like the Italian port city. Synchronicity.

From my own experience, even before I knew what synchronicity was, I believed in it. The "Soul Talk" crash course encouraged me to pay attention to what would come. And with the formation of so many soul sister bonds, I knew these incredible women would forever be a part of my life as the next chapter unfolded. I just needed to have faith and dwell on the possibility. In one moment of self-doubt, questioning my path, one of my soul sisters sent me a song by Natalie Merchant called "Wonder" followed by an encouraging, "You'll make your way, Meg!" This was my hero's journey coming together, soundtrack and all.

Paulo and The Pilgrimage

As a part of my morning ritual, I started voraciously reading every uplifting spiritual and leadership tome that resonated with me. I was on a deep inner journey of self-discovery that I hoped would deliver me further out of the darkness. I wanted to get as much inspiration as I could, for I was ready for a big change and was tired of playing it safe. That is when I crossed proverbial paths with one of my mentors, the mystical master himself, Brazilian author Paulo Coelho.

Prior to the worst days of my mother's illness, I volunteered for a women's retreat through my church. Having already participated six different times, I knew the time commitment that was required as a member of the team would be hard for me because I was traveling back and forth to Orlando. Because the leader was a close friend, I asked if I could still participate even though I could not be at the retreat house the entire weekend. She knew what I was going through and let me serve the way I could. I needed to be surrounded by good energy to counterbalance the sadness in my life. They agreed to put me in one of the back rooms on Saturday with the leader of one of the committees. Open and vulnerable with her story as I was with mine, as soon as we greeted each other, our conversation started and did not end.

"Do you believe there is an invisible energy among all of us?" she asked.

"Of course I do. You can call it what you would like—God, the universal energy, or otherwise. I believe that once we wake up and recognize this loving force, we are all better off."

"Well, have you ever read books by Paulo Coelho?"

"No, not yet, is he good?"

"You have to—he's amazing. He talks all about the mystical in his books," she said.

"Then I definitely will."

She had an inquisitive edge and a desire for knowledge that matched mine. Like me, she didn't know how special she was. Having made choices that led down a certain path, we both were figuring out where to go next in order to offer our gifts to the world. Here, organizing love notes, we talked about the power of possibility and dreams. I found another magical connection. We bonded. And after the weekend was over, knowing I had gone to Orlando to be with my mom, she provided a lifeline, checking in and keeping me in her prayers.

After my mother passed away, she gifted me my first book by Coelho, *By the River Piedra I Sat Down and Wept*. Here, he specifically addresses love and spirituality, setting out the theme, "But we must never forget that spiritual experience is above all a practical experience of love." I was having a very difficult time reconciling my disappointment that the clergy she worked with failed to show up for my mother at the end. Still seeking spiritual sustenance, I wondered if there really was a God of Love. I was nursing the wounds that my mother's death left behind. This physical separation had me questioning everything. When I started reading Coelho's book, I saw a lot of myself in the protagonist Pilar. She was a strong, independent woman raised in a Catholic Church that was supposed to be a moral authority. Like her, I too was examining what I understood to be truths and looking to find spiritual happiness outside of my religion. I loved his writing style and his approach to such important questions. The minute I finished this book, I wanted more.

The Alchemist was next. Inspired by the protagonist Santiago's magical search for his personal legend, the reason that he was alive, I enthusiastically tore through its pages, wanting to start my own journey to discover my calling. Instructed to listen to my heart, pay attention to signs, and follow my dreams, this book invited me to move in the direction of possibility rather than disappointment. Coelho said, "And when you want something, all the universe conspires in helping you achieve it."

In my search for help navigating the spiritual path, I next turned to *The Pilgrimage*. Page by page, I was fixated on Coelho's walk in Northern Spain on El Camino de Santiago de Compostela and didn't truly understand why. I would never describe myself as a hiker or a lover of nature and the outdoors. I was a beach girl; sitting by the ocean enjoying the breeze was more my speed. I thought it was crazy to imagine actually walking over mountains through the wilderness to find myself. First of all, I would never find the time. Second, I had no desire to go. Backpacking and sleeping under the stars or in hostels wasn't my idea of a vacation. But reading about all the spiritual signs Coelho encountered on his pilgrimage, his journey to the sacred place where St. James was buried with Petrus as his guide, I too wanted to go on that kind of journey.

If I did go on the pilgrimage, I was curious as to what lessons I would learn along the way. As the story in this book unfolded, I felt like I was peeking into a crystal ball looking at a possible future event that was waiting for me. I even googled the history behind El Camino and saw for the first time a picture of the lighthouse at the end of the journey at Finisterre; it was the same lighthouse I'd seen in the vision I received sitting with my mother right before she died. Now the mysticism of his tale intrigued me even more, and the seeds of a potential adventure were planted in my psyche.

Happening upon Coelho's work was a good omen for me. As I better navigated through grief, I felt the same as Coelho did at the beginning of his travels: *"This immensity made me very anxious; it created a terrible fear that I would not be able to succeed—that I was too small for this task."* But at the end, knowing he did succeed, maybe I would too.

Around the same time I found Coelho's work, I had my first mammogram ever. Reading in his books about omens and signs, I was paying attention to everything. Sometimes this is good, but when the hypochondriac part of your personality takes over, it could be very bad. I thought how clichéd for the next chapter of my story to unfold—girl loses mom to a disease that sends her into a spiraling mess, only to find herself facing the same thing. The last thing I wanted to do was go to a diagnostic center and place my boobs into a vice that held them still so that the technician could look inside. I'd had enough of breast cancer awareness. I was plenty aware.

There I was, standing half naked, one arm outside the robe at a time, feeling violated as they searched for any issues lurking below. I felt ashamed of my body, as my breasts were uncomfortably exposed. It made me think of my mom. She must have felt such fear when she located the malignant lump on the left side. It must have been torture for her to be examined and then have to wait for an answer as to her fate. This mammogram was an awful experience, from beginning to end, and I prayed it would be over soon. Following up with an ultrasound, pressing hard against my skin, probing to see if anything lurked within, I attempted to crack jokes, making small talk as I watched the screen, not knowing what I was seeing. After the exam, I retreated to the dressing room to put my clothes back on. My chest was pounding from the pain of the vice and the fear of the unknown.

When the results showed a suspicious cluster of cells and the doctor set up a biopsy to see what was going on, I freaked out. This was an awful place to be ten months after my mom passed away. My nerves were already shot. Add this to the mix, and I thought I was going to pass out. My mind went crazy, and all I could do was take deep breaths to engage my logical brain, reciting the multiplication tables to hold a panic attack at bay.

My husband drove me when I returned two days later. In a cold sterile room, I lay face down so that the nurse could place my offending breast in a cutout hole on the table. The scans of my chest were hanging on the wall to the right so that the surgeon could guide herself accordingly. She pointed out the area that she would be inspecting further. After numbing it, she took a big needle and punctured my skin. It took about thirty minutes, but it felt like an eternity as I could not calm myself down. My heart raced the entire time. I felt that I had to explain why I was such a mess and on the verge of tears.

"My mom died of breast cancer last year in April. I thought I had enough to deal with without this."

Mary, the nurse, reached out and held my hand.

"I don't want to be here," I said.

"You're going to be all right, darling," she gently replied, and I started to cry.

When all was done, I got dressed again. I was careful not to irritate the skin that boasted a fresh new stitch and bandage. It was Thursday. The doctor had said she would try to get the results to us before the next day, so I only had one day to go home and ruminate. The ringing in my head was out of control. A symphony of shrieking and intermittent high-pitched sounds invaded once again. The only thing I could do was to take deep breaths and remind myself of the words that were engraved on my silver ring, "This too shall pass."

The next morning, looking for Jesus' grace my mother had said to rely on, I decided to go to the children's mass at my son's school. It usually was an uplifting service filled with wonderful music. There, I ran into some of my friends from the church retreats. One of my favorites was a teacher at the school who was also a Eucharistic minister who emitted the most incredible positive energy. I needed some of that. So when it was time for communion, I stood in line to receive the host from her. As I walked to the front of the church, I prayed silently, *Let the tests come back negative. I need a better story for this next part of my life!* Person by person, I stepped closer to the altar. The violin singing out the melody of "Here I Am, Lord" played from the rafters.

As I stood before my friend to receive the Eucharist, she smiled and held up the host. It looked like a small, circular piece of cardboard before me. In her raspy tone, she said, "The body of Christ."

As the words left her mouth, when she placed the host in my hands, I felt a magical rush of energy flood over me. Then a strange tingling sensation ran throughout my entire body. I got goose bumps all over.

I answered back, "Amen."

I walked back to the pew, not really understanding what had happened. I felt peaceful. This was another strange happening. After seeing a lighthouse and hearing my mother's ethereal voice before she died, experiencing dreams where specific messages were accurately relayed, and now feeling an incredible electricity course through me, I hoped I wasn't going crazy. As I knelt down, I wanted to hold onto this feeling for as long as I could. Crossing my arms over the back of the bench in front of me, I stayed there until mass was over.

Sitting in my room later on, it was nearing five o'clock, and I still hadn't gotten the results of the exam. Then the phone rang.

"Is this Meg Nocero?"

"Yes, who is this speaking?" I sat down on the couch to brace myself.

"This is Mary from the Diagnostic Center. I wanted to call you to let you know that your test came back fine. All clear. Good news before we left for the weekend. Now you can enjoy it!"

"Thank you so much," I said with relief. I felt like I had won the lottery. "Good news indeed."

I didn't have breast cancer. The unfolding of events over the last couple of days felt like evidence of what Coelho meant when he wrote, "The secret of life, though, is to fall seven times and get up eight times." I was so relieved. My prayers had been answered.

Knowing that she was praying for me, I wrote to my new friend to share the wonderful news and thanked her for turning me on to Coelho and his books. She replied:

> Always remember ASK, BELIEVE, and RECEIVE! It's not too early and sometimes even seems impossible to do, but it truly does work. I know that of the three, we both seem to struggle with the last one, receiving. Remember we are not alone. Thank you for being there for me! You are more than you'll ever be able to realize. I love you very much.

Ask, believe, and receive. All right, universe, bring it on.

Just as Coelho wrote in *The Alchemist*, I too was figuring out that there was something bigger than I could see going on. Lessons to be learned, people to meet, as Coelho declared, "We are travelers on a cosmic journey. . . . We have stopped for a moment to encounter each other, to meet, to love, to share." Grateful for the encounters with so many magical souls, now I was ready to run toward something really wonderful. There was a connective process that had me releasing my fears, moving forward into my fabulousness. With a newfound mystical understanding, I was grateful for my mother's presence on a different plane. No longer moving forward on this journey in isolation, I invited others to walk with me. It was all a metamorphosis with a glimpse of the butterfly becoming; I had to trust it. It was going to be as cool as what my best friend Lisa and I used to repeat, "Jandy de La O, here we go!"

The Artist's Way

And with that, in June of 2013, I started the next phase of my journey with a twelve-week course based upon Julia Cameron's book entitled, *The Artist's Way: A Spiritual Path to Higher Creativity*. This was my opportunity to expand my creative soul and see where it could take me. Asked to sign a personal contract for accountability, I committed to writing what Cameron called Morning Pages, three pages each day in longhand of whatever came to mind. Then I batted around ideas for Artist's Dates, the one time each week that I set out alone to discover something creative and new. Week after week, my group gathered to check in and share our experiences. I took art classes and went to the movies alone. I even attended voice lessons with my four-year-old daughter.

Showing up at the Coconut Grove Conservatory on a Saturday morning for Ava's first voice lesson, we were introduced to a lovely young woman who was finishing up her masters in vocal performance at the University of Miami School of Music. She said hello to Ava and walked us toward the back of the studio to a soundproofed room set up with three chairs and a black upright piano. Ava decided to sit in the corner, play games on her iPad, and refuse to participate. Instead of begging her or calling it quits, I saw this as an opportunity to further my creative recovery process.

I asked, "I know you are supposed to teach kids here, but I already paid, and clearly Ava is not interested. Would you teach me?"

"I don't see a reason why not. Let's do this."

After going through a few vocal warmups, I chose a few songs from the sheet music that she had with her. Our first song from the musical

Chicago, "When You are Good to Mama," felt appropriate and within my vocal range. Ava grew more and more interested and joined in.

"Mommy," she laughed playfully, "if I were a coach on *The Voice*, I would not turn around for you."

"Not nice," I replied, "This is for fun. Not a competition. Besides, I'm not so sure I would turn around for you. Let's see what you got."

After six months of voice lessons, Ava and I flourished and gained more confidence. We discovered that Ava had a natural ear for music and a beautiful singing voice. At our first recital together, the ages of the participants ranged from four to twelve. Apart from the parents, I was the only adult in the bunch. As I stood on stage and saw the audience, I was nervous and actually very excited too. I love to sing, and music makes me feel alive. Ava sang a solo from *Tangled* called "Healing Incantation." We followed up by performing "Goodnight, My Someone" from *The Music Man* as a duet. And I finished proudly singing "Memories" from the musical *Cats*, clearly sensing the synchronicity as I pondered the profound lyrics remembering happiness of a time gone by, welling up as I chose to embrace a new day as it begins. Reviving a creativity that had lain dormant for quite some time, I saw in real time the possibility of a more colorful future. Yet, still grappling with expectations and the fear of disappointing myself and others, I set out to investigate what other career options resonated with me. This inquiry took me to the back room of an Italian Pizzeria in South Beach, all ready to start my first-ever memoir writing course.

Memoir Class 101

As I looked around me, I noticed that the room was painted almost entirely white. I welcomed the opportunity to be there, even though white was the color most movie set designers used for mental institutions. Snickering a bit, I dismissed the notion that I was crazy. After I found my seat at the end of the table, I was happy to see the bright orange wall at the back of the room facing me.

Eleven chairs surrounded the table. As food was ordered and delivered to us throughout the night, the room gained more charm like one of my Italian American family gatherings. Delights like eggplant Parmesan with mozzarella cheese melted on top, decadent tiramisu with layers of cream, cappuccino as a pick-me-up, beer, refreshing Perrier, Greek salad, and seasoned broccoli adorned the table for our enjoyment. It was a makeshift classroom in a restaurant, after all.

The aromas brought back memories of Friday nights of my childhood. My family would go to the local Italian pizza place where garlic clearly was used as a main ingredient. It also brought back memories of my junior year abroad in Rome, where I would often go to the local trattoria to enjoy the company of good friends and good food.

Out of all the students in the room, I gravitated toward a most colorful and insightful fellow student. With a short, bleached-blond, spiky haircut, a fancy cane, and wit to match, you could tell she was an artist. I wasn't surprised to learn she was curator of an art gallery; her writing skills and comments were as bold and confident as her career and appearance.

"Nice to meet you," I said.

"Nice to meet you too. Nice bright yellow jacket."

"Thank you. I love your blond hair."

"So you're a writer?" she asked.

"That's the goal. Excited to be here, you too?"

"Yes I am. I'm excited too."

During the next three hours we spent together that night, she shared her compelling story that left me in awe of what she had overcome. We chatted briefly about the ideas we had for books, inspired by each other and enjoying the creative collaboration. I was excited to return there. Plotting out the first part of my plan for a new career, I was an artist on my way to creative recovery. My purpose was calling, and I was most definitely paying attention. And I wanted to share what I was learning with whomever would listen. I felt a spark of creativity—perhaps it was a bit of wonderful madness—and I wasn't about to lose it.

CHAPTER 15:

Meeting My Magical Mentors

"Invest in the human soul. Who knows, it might be a diamond in the rough."
—MARY MCLEOD BETHUNE, 1875–1955, American educator

Through the years, I have met many inspiring and beautiful people in person and through social media. When I started my blog and continued email blasts in November of 2012, I set aside most of my insecurities and shared my daily insights with these beautiful ones. And it is truly my belief that people come into your life at the perfect time. One such person was Amy Butler, a well-known ambassador of beauty and quilt patterns. In 2012, she contacted me to ask if I would collaborate in an upcoming digital magazine that she was about to launch. In an email, she said:

Dear Meg,
Hello! I trust my note finds you well. I am reaching out to you about your beautiful writing on J.K. Rowling's quote. It truly touched my heart. I am in the process of producing a new online magazine. I am an artist and designer, and this is a completely new venture for me. I'm hoping you might be interested in allowing me to publish your writing. I would design it into a beautiful image. I think so many people would be inspired by your heartfelt words. I know this is an "out of the blue" request,

but I couldn't pass up the opportunity to reach out to you. In any
case, thank you for writing so soulfully, it means a lot!
All my best,
Amy

I wrote back:

Amy,
How exciting! You are very talented! I am very happy you were
touched by my writing. I absolutely love your mission statement
for your magazine —I think it would be a great match. I love
your idea! Yes!
God bless,
Meg

I was going to be published in this artist's journal about living life
authentically. A dream come true. Being part of one person's beautiful
vision lent encouragement to bolster my own. I kept moving forward.

As I did not go silently into that good night—thank you very much,
Dylan Thomas—I began to find my voice. Holding on to my dream, I
didn't give up. By writing my way out, I felt like I was rising from the
ashes of depression and anxiety like a phoenix ready and willing to speak
my truth. I had a vision—a wonderful one. I was becoming a storyteller.
It made perfect sense in that I had spent my entire career listening to
other people tell me their stories in court. It was my turn. At first, I
thought I had to keep this vision to myself, to protect it and tuck it away
for that day when I could give it my whole attention. But it wanted to
dance around in the universe and grow *now*, so I let it see the light of
day and went looking for a team of magical mentors to help bring my
dream of being a published author to reality. And I thought that women
collaborating with other women was always a good idea.

Having started this whole writing process in June of 2013, I needed
an editor. At my book club called Reading Between the Wines, the
founder invited her author friend, Wendy Shanker, to talk about her
book, *Are you My Guru? How Medicine, Meditation & Madonna Saved*

My Life. Really enjoying the evening and her story, afterward I contacted her asking for any advice or wisdom she could share. She kindly took the time to respond. She suggested that I join an online community for women writers called She Writes and sent me the contact information of someone who could help me.

The recommended professional, Devan Sipher, was a writer of a column in the *New York Times* and was also a published author of fiction. I hired him to review and edit the outline and first three chapter of what was then called *Sunrise of My Soul's Bliss.* Initially, my idea for the book was part memoir and part insights of the day. After looking at my work product, he asked me if I had considered separating them into two books. Then he encouraged me to look at other authors' works, like Joan Didion's *The Year of Magical Thinking,* to get some insight into the genre of memoir.

After his suggestion that I explore other expert storytellers and already enamored with the mystical Paulo Coelho as the male guru for my future book, I decided to pick author Liz Gilbert, who was equally spiritual, as his female counterpart. So when I found out that Gilbert was coming to town to present her new book called *The Signature of All Things,* I excitedly made plans to go see my female guru in person. Doing the background research beforehand, I learned that Liz got her inspiration to write her bestseller *Eat Pray Love* after her own creative rediscovery with Cameron's *The Artist's Way.* After sharing this with my Artist's Way crew in October of 2013, we all set out on a final group Artists' Date to meet Liz. I wrote to Liz on Facebook:

> *Liz:*
> *I am so excited—just picked up your new book and got the vouchers to hear you speak in Miami on Wednesday!!! I was inspired by* Eat Pray Love—*read* Committed *and was so happy to see that you were also inspired by Julia Cameron's* Artist's Way. *I am just finishing up the last week of the twelve-week commitment and would love to hear more how* The Artist's Way *impacted your life (I think that I read somewhere that you actually planned out your* Eat Pray Love *adventure when you did the* Artist's Way*). I am in the process of writing my memoir in addition to other*

*creative projects that have gratefully been recovered. When I was
starting to write my book, I was told to find an author that I liked
and use their style as a tool and a guide. Your writing is my female
guide and Paulo Coelho is my male guide!!! Looking forward to
seeing you and would feel incredible lucky and grateful to meet
you. Keep inspiring all of us and thank you!*
Meg Nocero, Miami, FL.

Since we wanted to get front row seats, I picked up Teda an hour before so
we could get to the auditorium early. Arriving at the downtown campus of
Miami–Dade Community College, we presented our tickets and walked
in. Happily, it was a small venue. We chatted with the other guests who
excitedly waited for her to show up. About thirty minutes later, the rest of
our party arrived and joined us in the front row. Turning down the lights,
Liz appeared in a sunshiny yellow A-line dress to read to us from her new
book. It was so cool to be in the same room with her, have the opportunity to listen to her, and perhaps talk to her as well. When she opened the
forum up for questions or comments from the audience, I raised my hand.

I said, "I really love how you write. You have such passion. Is it true
that you were a student of *The Artist's Way* and that is how you conceived
of your idea to go on your *Eat Pray Love* journey?"

She smiled and nodded. "Yes, that was a wonderful experience. The
first time I did the program, I had decided by the end of it that I wanted
to travel to Italy and learn Italian, go to an Ashram in India, and return
to Indonesia to study with the old medicine man I'd once met there. We
all know what *that* decision led to. . . . Without *The Artist's Way*, there
would have been no *Eat Pray Love*."

I continued, "I'm here tonight with my Artist's Way group. Couldn't
think of a better way to finish off the twelve weeks. Hopefully, we can
get a photo with you at the end of the night."

Liz said, "You got it."

When the lecture was over, the moderator invited us to line up so
Liz could sign our copies of her book. We took a photo of the four of

us together as evidence of my ladies of *The Artist's Way* on the ultimate Artist Date with Elizabeth Gilbert. We all had a wonderful evening in what Liz described as "liquidy and sexy" Miami.

I left on cloud nine, with the added inspiration to keep moving forward as well. Wanting more, I signed up on her website to continue getting posts from her. In April of 2014, one such email announced that she would be returning to Miami, this time with my favorites Rob Bell, Iyanla Vanzant, Deepak Chopra, and . . . drum roll please . . . Oprah! When the tickets went on sale, I immediately purchased two. Having failed in my quest to meet Oprah in Chicago in 2010 and aborted a trip to LA in 2012 for her "O" experience because my anxiety was off the charts and I was afraid to travel, I was not going to miss her when she was coming to my own backyard. I posted on Facebook:

> *OMG! I got awesome seats to go see Oprah at the American Airlines Arena in October! Living the dream! I'm going to see Oprah in person in Miami!!!!!!! I'm gonna pass out!*

Six months out, I signed up to attend a Hay House Writing from Your Soul workshop in Ft. Lauderdale led by the "father of motivation," Dr. Wayne Dyer. Having read many of his books about manifesting into reality, I looked forward to the opportunity to see him in person.

In May of 2014, I set out to the Broward Convention Center ready to learn as much as I could. At this point in time, having experienced many solo artist's dates, I didn't mind going alone. Because Dr. Dyer suggested that an author should create the cover of the book before even starting to write, I created a cover of *The Sunrise of My Soul's Bliss* and had it in hand. I took my place in the audience and listened as Dr. Dyer motivated everyone to wake up to their purpose. On a break, as a line formed, I marched up to the front and waited for my turn to shake his hand and ask him to write something motivational on the back of the card of my cover. Enthusiastically, he did.

Bubbling over with excitement, I said, "Dr. Dyer, this is such an honor."

He smiled at me. His energy was so peaceful. I continued, "Here are Give Love Rocks from a project that I have with my kids. Happy Birthday. And look, like a good student, I made a cover, so now I have to finish the book—can you sign this?"

He took the cover, signed his name on the summary side and commented, "Nice, *The Sunrise of My Soul's Bliss*, I like that a lot—nice cover too! Keep going. You're on to something!"

Inspired by Dr. Dyer, I felt positive momentum building. I began to format my book proposal with the help of my cousin and readied it for submission in November to Hay House. Nothing was going to stop me now. I worked day and night on my book and told anyone who would listen how excited I was about Oprah's Life You Want Weekend that was coming in October.

As the Oprah event drew near, my optimism grew, and my attitude changed even toward the monotony of my job, as I looked for opportunities to share my enthusiasm and excitement during my workday. And, returning home in the evening, I felt like something magical was about to happen as I thought back over the whole unfolding of the past months. It played out like a game of six degrees of separation of Oprah, where I started to see the six or fewer social connections away:

First, it was the encounter with Liz Gilbert, signing up for her email, and noticing that she was going to different cities starting in the fall with Oprah.

Second, I traveled to New York City with my daughter, Ava, to attend a National Organization of Italian American Women Awards Gala where my aunt Betty was honoring Lisa Oz, accompanied by her husband Dr. Mehmet Oz, a regular guest on *The Oprah Show*. I met them both.

Third, on our way home to Miami, Oprah's finance expert guest Suze Orman boarded the plane and sat right behind us. I posted on Facebook:

Well taking our flight home and Suze Orman gets on the flight! No kidding—ha-ha—6 degrees of the big "O"!

Fourth, in September of 2014, after Oprah started the tour, I would follow her Facebook page as she went from city to city. I wanted so much to meet her that I posted a brief version of my story and in bold letters at the top of the post wrote: READ THIS! Well, a woman named Linda who had gotten on stage with Oprah in Atlanta responded and asked me to message her. Curious, I did, and she left her number with a message to call.

She wrote, "Meg, I never do this, but was moved by what you wrote and had to contact you." I called her. She told me Oprah had chosen her to come up on the stage after she came down into the audience to pick out a few individuals who moved her. Why was this wonderful lady calling me if not to give me more hope that my dream would come true? Then Oprah Winfrey's staff called me two separate times to confirm details about the weekend. I was so excited; I texted my best friend:

Lisa—I just got a call from Oprah's people again confirming my seat. I just know that we are going to meet her—I can feel it!!!!!

And fifth, my friend and I entered a contest on Oprah's webpage for tickets to her Miami event. That same evening, on October 22, 2014, we learned that each of us had won two additional premium tickets. We were able to invite four people to join us. All six of us together on the first day of the event, October 24, 2014, I posted:

Today, I get to see Oprah on stage for the first time in person! I am so excited—something wonderful is definitely about to happen and I am so ready for it!!! Bring it on—can't wait to share with all of you who are going and those who are not—I will be posting!!!! Checking this one off my vision board!!

Between taking my first Twitter selfie with my new magical friend Chris to being reminded that whatever has happened to me has happened for me, I was energized. When my friends and I went out for cocktails later that evening at the Mandarin Oriental Bar on Brickell Key, we were gushing about how amazing the entire evening had been and ready for the next adventure.

And sixth, on October 25, 2014, I realized one of my biggest dreams. It was the second day of Oprah's Life You Want Weekend at the American

Airlines Arena in Miami, Florida. Before I left my house, just for luck, I grabbed a copy of best-selling author Pam Grout's *E-Cubed*, a book of nine experiments to get yourself in alignment with what she calls the "field of potential" or "FP." Opening up the book to Experiment 9 entitled "The Yabba-dabba-doo Corollary," I followed the instructions and asked the universe to show me a "transcendent moment" within the next seventy-two hours. Specifically, I asked the universe to meet Oprah in person.

When we arrived at the arena, my energy was high. After seeing Oprah on stage the night before, I was looking forward to seeing her again with the rest of the speakers. As we found our seats on the arena floor, many were dancing to the DJ's high energy music and buzzing around with enthusiasm.

Two days before the Miami event, I had the following dream: *I was sitting in the audience at the Oscars chatting with Steven Spielberg and his wife, Kate Capshaw. After a short time, I looked up and saw Oprah in the crowd coming my way. When she was about two feet away, she stopped, looked at me, then turned and walked off. I remembered wanting to scream, "Come back! Why are you walking away?"* I woke up in a panic, having to convince myself that it was not a premonition but only a dream. So without ruminating further, I let it go. Besides, for the entire month before, I had been visualizing that I would actually meet Oprah on stage in front of the entire crowd. Just as when I'd met Bob Barker in 1991 on the *Price is Right*, in my visual, Oprah would call to me and invite me to join her by saying "Come on down!" Without hesitation, I would obediently climb up on stage next to her. I would be as lucky as the day that I spun one dollar on the *Price is Right* wheel. True story.

At the Miami event, sitting next to my friend, dressed in a "not to be missed" canary yellow jacket and wearing a tiara, I was spotted by my friend Mari, who had somehow made her way down to the floor from the nosebleed section to find me. And serendipitously, there was an open seat right next to me. Surrounded by my friends and with the high energy in the room, I was ready for something magical to happen. Suddenly the music stopped, and Deepak Chopra took center stage with Oprah, encouraging all of us to join in meditation. At the end of the meditation, as calm music continued to play, Oprah asked all of us to journal on what we wished for our loved ones. Then, as my Facebook friend Linda described, Oprah descended into the audience to pick people to share their answers on stage. Because I was sitting right in her path, Oprah was heading for me. I was so excited I was jumping out of my skin. I was actually bouncing up and down in my seat.

My friend Mari was unusually at ease. She looked at me, put her hand on mine, and whispered, "Calm down. It's going to happen."

Then Oprah approached and stood right in front of me, looked me in the eye, and smiled. I was giddy and overjoyed. Then she glanced at Mari sitting to my right, read her journal entry, smiled, said, "I like you," grabbed Mari's hand, and returned to the stage.

I whispered to myself, "Oh, my God, that's it. That was my Oprah moment? What just happened?"

As she walked away, I dropped my head, devastated. How could my chance be over? Then I remembered my dream with Steven Spielberg and thought, *It was a premonition after all. Oprah just walked away from me! And I had such a good feeling about today.*

Trying to make sense of what just unfolded, the message Oprah shared the night before came to me again, about how she got her part in the movie *The Color Purple*: Oprah said she desperately wanted to play the character Sofia and had auditioned. A few weeks passed by when she didn't hear from Spielberg, and she was worried that her "dream role" was slipping away. She said she thought it was because she was in such bad shape. So she went to a health spa to do what she could. She said while she was running, feeling her thighs rubbing together, she stopped and felt her life whisper to her that this was ridiculous; she needed to trust and let it go. When she did, Spielberg called her that same evening and she got the role.

Oh my God! Steven Spielberg was in my dream, she just walked away from me—she said let it go—she let it go—he called her—Mari said it's going to happen. I have to trust.

So, like Oprah, I was convinced that if I allowed the universe to handle it and let it go, I would get my chance too. I happily cheered for Mari as she stood on the stage next to Oprah.

Not even minutes after I did, I heard Mari on stage say, "I love you, Oprah, but I can't be up here without my friend Meg."

I thought, *What did she just say?*

Oprah asked, "Who got the tickets?"

Mari answered, "My friend Meg."

Oprah said, "Well then, where is Meg?" Mari pointed and Oprah laughed, "Aren't you glad I'm bringing her up here?"

Then, like Bob Barker, Oprah invited me to come on down. I stood up and waved like I'd won the lottery. Then I headed straight for the stage. I climbed up the stairs from the left, hugged Mari, and thanked her profusely, taking my place next to her and waving to the audience.

"Oh, my God!" I said.

Oprah said, "Meg, put your crown on your head and wear it. That's so great."

After Mari shared what she dreamed for her loved ones, Oprah asked me what I had written. I said, "I know, but I get so nervous. I'm shaking. All my friends here know how much I love you."

Oprah replied, "I believe it. That's okay. What did you write, Meg?"

I opened up the journal I had and nervously declared, "This is not even my book." The audience laughed and clapped. Oprah said, "Let's help Meg out."

Then, I waved to the audience, "Hi, Miami!!"

After I finally got my journal, I shared with the audience what I jotted down.

Oprah said, "This is wonderful. This is what I want to say to everyone who wrote and dreamed big for your family, your beloveds."

Then she looked at me and said, "C'mon up here, Meg, this is the moment—you don't want to miss it."

She locked arms with Mari and me and said, "You can't offer someone else that which you don't already have and wish for yourself. It's that first principle." Oprah had explained earlier that the first principle that rules her life is the principle of intention, knowing what you want.

She went on, "Even that woman who wants her son to drive a Bentley, I think that you may want that a little more than he does." Everyone laughed, and Oprah continued, "Everything you have written down for your beloveds is what you also hold in your heart for yourself."

"Amen! Alleluia," I said.

Oprah then said, "Meg, you see that for yourself? That is true for everybody. This is the first real glimpse of the life that you want, because for so many people it's easy to do it for someone else. It's about opening up the heart space."

At that moment, I looked directly into Oprah's eyes, the windows of her soul. This icon, who was so much for so many, had amazing eyelashes and skin, but her eyes looked so very tired. She had been on this tour for some time, giving everything of herself each weekend in a new city. I saw her humanity outside of the celebrity. And I was so grateful that she had come to Miami to offer her brand of inspiration. How incredible that I had that moment to stand next to her. I was grateful for the chance to meet her, someone I had admired from afar for so long. Yet, standing next to her, I realized how human she was. This gift of sharing space with her, when its magnitude finally dawned on me, made me start to cry.

"Meg, you're going to hate this picture, stop crying." The audience laughed.

I said, "I'm going to hate it, I am going into the ugly cry."

"Meg, you're going into the ugly cry. You're not going to like it. This photo is going to live a long time; see he's taking our photo—say hi!"

Mari, Oprah, and I smiled and waved at the photographer.

Then she said, "By the end of the day, I want you to open up your heart space and be able to dream for yourself." I dreamed this. I intended for this to happen. And I knew that my mother opened up the way to show me that nothing is impossible. I looked up to the heavens and nodded, "Thank you, Mommy!"

Then Oprah said, "Thank you both for doing this exercise. Thank you, Meg!"

As she walked Mari and me off the stage, I said to her, "Thank you so much, Oprah—you have no idea what this whole experience has meant to me."

Returning to my seat, I was floating on a cloud. I was sure my feet were not touching the ground. How amazing that one person can make you feel so elevated, that so much was possible. I, of course, continued to jump up and down with everyone in my row when I got back there. My friend was so excited. I hugged her so hard. It made it even more special that she was there. We all had this incredible moment with Oprah:

Meg: I was on stage with Oprah Winfrey!!
Aimee: OMG! U did it!!!
Meg: I am on cloud nine! I got on stage with Mari and had my moment with Oprah, dreams come true!!
Giseli: OMG!!! I knew it!! I was praying for this moment!!
Nick: Yahoo!!!! Woohoo!!! Omg I've got goose bumps for ya!!! Way to go Meg!!!
Maite—My Dear Friend! I have tears of joy for you!!! I am so proud of you Meggie!!!
Eva: NOOOOOO WAYYYYYY! Remember, all the airport bookshelves will have it. Congratulations!!!!!!!!!!!!!!
Janet: ~AWESOME~~AMAZING~~BRILLIANT~
Michele D: Rock on!! I love it. You so earned this through blood, sweat, and tears and an outpouring of constant Goodwill like I've never seen from another human being. I am super proud of you. I wish I had seen it! Super congratulations.

Oprah's photographer came up to me, introduced himself, and gave me his card.

"Congratulations!" he said. "After the weekend, send me an email, and I'll mail the photos for you and your friend."

I shook his hand, "I'm so grateful. Thank you. I will."

So happy, I beamed. Then I looked at his card and saw that his name was George Burns, the same name of an actor who played God in the movies *Oh, God!* and its sequels in the seventies. Pay attention, God is in everything! In that arena, that afternoon, I experienced the "Oprah effect." I had watched her show every afternoon as she inspired others through telling stories, but actually standing next to her in her light was better than I could imagine. And leaving the stage, wrapped up in her energy! When others in the crowd realized that Mari and I had been on stage with her, they wanted to take photos with us too. While I didn't know what impact this would have on my life, I was ready to live intentionally. I promised that I would finish what I started and keep going, even though the path ahead remained very uncertain. Not even twenty-four hours after I tapped the field of potential to give me a really big transcendent moment, I had experienced one for the books. And I even had professional photos from George to serve as a reminder.

CHAPTER 16:

A Guide to Bliss
and Magical Me

"All that counts in life is intention."
—**ANDREA BOCELLI**, Italian opera singer, song-
writer, and record producer

Working with my editor and cousin, I submitted the proposal for *The Magical Guide to Bliss* to Hay House and with it a chance to win a publishing contract without having to get an agent. Following the editor's advice, I had two separate books now: *The Magical Guide* was a book of insights and *Butterfly Awakens* was my memoir still in progress.

As I awaited a decision, I continued to work on editing what had become a guide written to empower and inspire me to create the life that I have always wanted by following my bliss. Over twelve months, I followed a journey of belief and possibility beginning with the concept of "Carpe Diem: Seize the Day" in January and culminating with "Awe-Inspiring Magic and Miracles" in December. My intention was to use the keys to open up to incredible opportunities once I identified— and followed —my passions.

Less than three weeks later, in December of 2014, I learned I hadn't won. Feeling clarity around self-publishing it, I happily moved forward without delay. Night after night, I worked on editing over four hundred pages. Now working an eighty percent schedule, I got home early enough to take care of my family at a reasonable hour. Then I spent time until the early hours of the morning reading through my book to cut and add where necessary. Sleeping very little, this time not due to insomnia, I sent the book off for final line edits in June of 2015. Now I had to sit and wait for those edits to come back to see what happened next.

In the interim, in September I traveled to the Omega Center in upstate New York with my best friend, Lisa, for the Being Bold, A Women and Power retreat. There we met female trailblazers: Omega co-founder Elizabeth Lesser, Olympic medalist Bonnie St. John, and Voto Latino president Maria Teresa Kumar. And, as an added bonus, we were at the first screening of the 10,000 Maniacs lead singer's documentary, *Wonder: Introducing Natalie Merchant*. Sitting next to the artist and listening to her song of the same name, I recalled the words of my soul sister and smiled as I thought, *Who would have imagined this? I guess this is the universe's sign that I'm making my way!*

When I returned to Miami, I received the author's copy of my book from the printer. I was so excited. Like the name of one of my father's favorite songs written by the Hollies, on the cover appeared a long cool woman in a black dress holding a wand-like key and three bedazzled butterflies located at various points. When the first edition was published on October 8, 2015, the guide I had prayed for was a reality. Channeled wisdom from my mother readily at hand, I now intended to follow it and see where it would lead.

After over six months of preparation, at the end of October, exactly a year to the day that Oprah came to Miami, I organized a committee and chaired our first S.H.I.N.E. networking event to a sold-out audience. S.H.I.N.E. stands for Spirit, Hope, Insight, a Networking Event where we invited guests to claim their tiaras and crowns and designed the day to continue the uplifting vibe from the Life You Want Weekend, creating an opportunity to reunite with friends and meet new people connecting in a positive way. We encouraged collaboration.

Followed by two incredibly successful book launches in Miami and Orlando, I was well on my way. After a radio interview on the podcast called *Intrepid*, I received my first review from *Kirkus* that praised my book as "a successful, progressive daily handbook about awareness, creativity, gratitude, and fulfillment." It felt so good.

From January on, it seemed like my vision board was on fire. In February, my first televised interview entirely in the Spanish language aired on *CNN Español* with the estimable Ismael Cala introducing me to an expanded market in the Americas. In March, I was invited to speak to the Women's Leadership Committee with the Florida International Business Association, introducing my approach to bliss to the Miami business community and expanding my own network. In April, at the beginning of the month I traveled to Los Angeles for an amazing experience with one of my favorite sidekicks Paulina De Regil, a former legal intern and now a good friend. We were going there to attend Oprah's Super Soul Sessions on the UCLA campus. Twenty-five years earlier I had been in Los Angeles with my college roommate where I spun a dollar on the famous *Price is Right* wheel; I had thought that was my fifteen minutes of fame. Returning there again, I knew that most of my success over the years was not worn on the outside for all to see but was an internal spiritual badge of enlightenment getting stronger each time I stepped outside the box of a safe existence.

From the beginning, trust in the journey guided our way as it started out as an adventure. I discovered the night before that my original hotel was over an hour away from where we were supposed to be, but I had enough time to make a change to the Beverly Hills Hotel without penalty. Leaving for the airport with what we thought was plenty of time, we got stuck in traffic and experienced a two-hour delay. Worried that we would never make it, we saw a gap in the orange tubes that separated the carpool lane from normal traffic flow.

"Get in there Meg!" Paulina (Pau) screamed out.

"I'm scared—I'm gonna hit it."

"You gotta go, or we're going to miss our flight."

"Ugh! Here goes nothing—you're corrupting me!" I belted out as I swooped into the open lane and continued on our way, both of us laughing and feeling the adrenaline pumping.

Though we made it to the airport with time to spare, we got lost in conversation. We could talk for hours. Curious as to why we did not hear our flight announced, we walked up to check in at the gate. The attendant said, "We called for final boarding five minutes ago."

She grabbed her colleague to stop her from closing the doors so that we could run and board the plane. Four years ago, my anxiety would have been through the roof. My tinnitus would have been screaming out of control. Whenever something like this happened, I used to feel like I would die; the fear might even have stopped me from traveling. Not today. We were laughing about it and spent the entire five-hour flight there dreaming out loud. This to me was a huge success.

There, Pau and I visited all the famous tourist attractions like the Mann's Chinese Theatre, the Hollywood Walk of Fame, the Los Angeles County Museum of Art, and even the lesser known Café Gratitude. Even after meeting Oprah's doppelganger, author Cheryl Strayed, and inspirational speaker Mastin Kipp, the best part of that weekend was how much fun I had with Pau.

Knowing that the anniversary of my mom's passing was in April and my life would never be the same as it was when I first came to LA at twenty-one, I was blessed with the opportunity to create anew and stop trying to rebuild what was. I was so different now. No longer star struck by fame, I basked in how much more delight I gained from connecting to another soul sister. I got lost in laughter when at one point in time laughter was lost to me and felt alive in the conversation again as I got to experience what I had with my mom on a greater scale.

Returning to Florida, as we drove home from the Ft. Lauderdale airport back down to downtown Miami, Pau and I were singing like teenagers going on a joy ride—with the sun roof opened and both windows down. At the top of our lungs with a renewed exuberance, listening to the version of the song "You Don't Own Me" by SAYGRACE, we declared to the universe, taking back our power, "Just let me be myself, that's all I ask of you."

I embraced the dreamer who lives to inspire others to dream. Even if my dreams are different now, moments like this continued to tie together what makes a life. I wanted to be sure to share this with others as well. At the end of the month, I was going to relay this message as I ended April on a high note, headlining my bookstore debut at Books & Books, the famous local independent bookstore and Miami landmark that boasted book events featuring presidents, Nobel prize winners, athletes, artists, celebrities, poets, and now me.

That previous February, I met with Hector, the artist who painted the butterfly while I read from *The Magical Guide* at my book launch in December, to collaborate once again. I enjoyed working with Hector as he was kind, passionate about his craft, and possessed an incredible eye for color and creativity. When I told him I had scheduled the evening at Books & Books, we came up with the idea to create an evening of engaging the senses. Expression through words, music, painting, aromatherapy, and sweet wine and dessert, we called it La Dolce Vita, inspired by the search for the sweet life in Fellini's film of the same name. Hector painted a portrait of Anita Ekberg who portrayed Sylvia in the film *La Dolce Vita*, while his daughter's band, called Columbus Avenue, played jazz tunes in the background.

I, with my husband and kids, drove up to the exquisite 1927 building listed in the Coral Gables Register of Historic Places and found metered parking close to Books & Books. My six-year-old daughter ran out of the car and pointed at the storefront window.

"Mommy, Mommy, look! There's your book in the window!" she screamed out with excitement.

At the entranceway, the placard announced in purple and yellow fluorescent chalk:

TONIGHT @8PM MEG NOCERO
THE MAGICAL GUIDE TO BLISS.

I felt giddy. All that work, all those late nights—this was the reward for persistence and never giving up on my dream. We unloaded the books and banners and made sure Hector had room to paint, the band knew where to go, and my friend Stela could display her aromatherapy products, with thirty minutes to spare.

It was a perfect Miami evening in April—a fresh and crisp seventy degrees, the kind of weather we yearn for when living through those unbearably hot and humid summer nights. We chose an outside table in the center courtyard between the restaurant and the bookstore and ordered a bottle of champagne to celebrate this momentous occasion. My friends Denise (a Judge with whom I worked with and had become close friends) and Hector joined us in a toast.

The Books & Books manager greeted us with, "Are you ready?"

"Yes!" I replied.

"I will introduce the event and invite Denise to the stand to say a few words."

"Great."

"The livestream will begin at eight and go out to the bookstore's webpage for customers. When the evening is over, I'll send the link to you to share with those who were unable to join the fun. You'll sign books after everything is done. Any questions?"

"No, thank you so much."

When we all congregated where the presentation would take place, at least sixty people showed up. Many of my friends came over to hug and congratulate me before they took their seats. At eight o'clock precisely, Denise, decked out in one of her black, always stylish leather outfits, was invited up to the front of the room to begin. She had done a great job giving a testimonial at my first S.H.I.N.E. event. I knew that she was the perfect person to introduce me that night.

"Good evening. Welcome to a magical evening of bliss. I am so honored to introduce Meg Nocero and *The Magical Guide to Bliss*. Meg has asked me to give a brief description of my life. I have led an amazing life with amazing experiences and successes. However, for the better part of my life, I worked hard to have a relationship and seek acceptance and love from someone who was never going to give it. So I would wake up every morning to a void. Sometimes, I was in a room of people and I would feel lonely because of that void, and I knew something was not right. Then I met Meg, and I connected with Meg and her energy. And then I followed Meg on the journey to bliss. And now I do live that sweet life. I do live a life of bliss. I wake up every morning with joy and with intentions. So I encourage each of you, when you wake up every morning, to wake up with no regrets. To love the people who treat you right, to forgive the ones who don't treat you right, to believe that whatever happens, happens for a reason, and to enjoy your view."

Everyone applauded.

"Now to the reason why we are here. Meg and I are dear friends. In connecting with Meg, I can unveil myself to her with no thought. I can surrender my soul to her with no judgment. I love her smile. I love her energy. I love her wisdom, and I love her insight. She is pure magic to me, and she really shines. I strongly encourage each one of you to wake up every morning and read the daily guide insight from her book, *The Magical Guide to Bliss*. Because if you do, you will have a blissful, sweet life. Now I am going to ask each one of you to stand up and give a rousing round of applause as we welcome Meg to the stand."

And they did. They all stood and applauded while I walked to the front of the room to hug Denise in gratitude for her friendship and such kind and loving words. Really hearing what she said about me, I was happy that this amazing woman was a part of my journey. Then I turned around. Dressed in one of my mother's classic black wraparound dresses accessorized with a single strand of pearls, I thanked the audience, mostly made up of good friends who stood by me through the truly challenging times of my grieving process. As I announced that it was time for them to claim their tiara, I held my head high and said, "If you don't mind, it is a little helpful for me to put on my tiara tonight before I begin. Thank you very much."

As I placed my sparkly rhinestone tiara on my head, the audience applauded.

"You know I am a dreamer. I live by a mantra: Magical work for magical pay, magical service every magical day. As such I look for others in the world who are dreamers too, so I can follow them toward greater bliss. And like all great dreamers in history, we seek to inspire others with a wondrous story to tell. For once upon a time, I was a little girl with a great big imagination, and now I get to share it with all of you."

The artist painted as I, the writer, spoke about my book of finding magic in everyday things. Then I lost myself in that magic while telling my story. When I was finished, the artist encouraged everyone, "Find the child inside of you."

When I invited questions, a young girl in the front row, a child compared to the rest of the audience, asked, "When did you know your journey began?"

I stopped and really thought about that question. She was so young to ask such a wise question. I thought, *When did I become conscious?*

I replied, "I was not fully awake for a long time. Perhaps, it was when I lost my mom at forty-one. I had a choice to numb myself out or wake up. The tinnitus forced me to choose to wake up. Lots of different chapters to my story—I hope to have many more. Some I remember well, some I want to forget. But from all my life experiences so far, I have learned so much. And while I have not always enjoyed the journey, I have gotten more grateful for the awareness that the path brings me."

I looked at this young girl and said, "You know, you are very lucky to be so young and so wise to know to ask this kind of question. You are definitely ahead of where I was at your age."

She looked at me and smiled.

"Thank you for giving me hope for the future."

At the end of the evening, Hector's daughter Val sang and played my favorite song in the universe, "Yellow" by Coldplay, on her ukulele. It was my inspirational lullaby. It was what I listened to when I needed to cry. It gave me hope when my spirit wanted to die. It was the perfect song for butterflies who believed they could fly.

As I signed books and handed out yellow roses to all my guests, I was surrounded by creative energy. This evening marked an incredible moment for me that I hoped would lead to so many more. On this, my hero's journey, I was so grateful that I woke up to the call to live a more authentic life surrounded by music, color, good scents, good food and wine, and most of all—good people. With *The Magical Guide*, it dawned on me that I had just written the outline for an incredible future. I was excited and curious to see how the rest of this chapter would unfold and who would show up on the path. This evening was pure perfection, from beginning to end.

And in May, more excitement was on the horizon as I traveled to Tampa to participate in the Oxford Exchange Book Fair, where I was able to mingle with the literary community and meet some incredible fellow authors. In June, after submitting *The Magical Guide to Bliss* to President Obama, I got an invitation to tour the East Wing of the White House with my family. In July, I participated in the American Library

Association Conference in Orlando. In August, *The Magical Guide to Bliss* appeared in *Boston College Magazine*'s (my alma mater) "Class Notes." In September, I spoke in Tampa at the 2016 On Pointe Book Fair. And in October, with a bigger team, I chaired S.H.I.N.E. Miami 2016, Journey to Bliss, this time as a nonprofit providing educational scholarships called S.H.I.N.E. Ambassador Awards to two young innovative leaders in our community who are making a difference locally and beyond. And in November, I ended the year showcasing *The Magical Guide to Bliss* at the Miami International Book Fair.

I was working very hard to make the shift away from my day job. But even with all the above, I was investing and spending a lot of money to get publicity and not nearly breaking even. I was so grateful for the support, yet I felt a bit down. I was reminded of the wise words that my mother must have said over and over: everything you go through has a reason. I had to trust the process. But in the quiet of my closet, where I hid away, my patience was waning. I was experiencing a never-ending learning curve and growing tired of stumbling along the way; I desperately wanted someone, an expert in the field of publishing to *help me*. Believing in the magical, I would never throw in the towel on my dreams. I forged ahead.

CHAPTER 17:

We Plan, God Laughs

"We must let go of the life we have planned, so as to accept the one that is waiting for us."
—JOSEPH CAMPBELL, 1904–1987, American author and professor of literature

Remember, even though I wanted change, I hated the thought of losing my way. After my mom died, because I was forced to let go of so much, I stubbornly held on tight to what remained. Yet change was coming, and I knew it. Picture this: In *Mary Poppins*, Bert, the lovable chimney sweep, entertains the locals with his one-man band. Everyone is singing and dancing joyfully, clapping their hands. Suddenly Bert stops playing, the sky goes from bright and sunny to dark and foreboding. When he looks up, he says, "Winds in the east, mist coming in, like something is brewin' and bout to begin. Can't put my finger on what lies in store. But I fear what's to happen all happened before."

When the stormy winds of change came blowing through my life, I too had no idea of what lay in store. Feeling increasingly uncomfortable where I stood, I faced two choices. I could stay where I was with what I knew and slowly grow numb, physically there but spiritually fading away. Or I could let go and move on because the pain of holding on was far too great. When I finally made the difficult decision to move on, I was terrified of what would come next.

Dragging my feet in the sand, I was literally pushed out. My professional plan did not include working for almost twenty years, giving it my all, my heart and soul, and in the end never advancing. And while I decided when to go, I felt rejected, unappreciated, and dismissed in the end. This came hard, especially when at the beginning of that professional chapter many years earlier, I felt like I had finally arrived.

May 24, 1999: My First Day at INS

My career as an attorney with the federal government officially began on Monday, May 24, 1999. I confidently walked, briefcase in hand, into that dilapidated eleven-story building on 79th Street and Biscayne Boulevard that housed the District Director in charge of Operations and the District Counsel in charge of the attorneys for the Immigration and Naturalization Service. After I eagerly produced my identification and announced to the security guard on the first floor that it was my first day there, he called to verify my information. Then I went through the metal detector, retrieved my things, and waited for one of the three elevators to take me to the eleventh floor.

The elevator arrived, the doors opened, and my happy eyes linked with those of the receptionist who was expecting me. She motioned for me to take one of two chairs on the opposite wall. It was pretty dark. I don't remember if there were any windows in the lobby. I noticed that the decor hadn't been updated since the 1960s. There were fake wood panels on the walls. The carpet was dark blue and worn, and the corridors leading to the internal offices were pretty narrow. I arrived early for one of the first times in my life, smiling with a big toothy grin at anyone who passed me by. I'd thought I would be the only one to start that day; they hadn't given me any information other than where and when to show up. But not even twenty minutes later, another woman in her late twenties, dressed in a conservative blue suit, arrived just as eager and excited to begin this new job as Assistant District Counsel with me.

We introduced ourselves and provided some background on who we were.

I told her, "I'm so excited to begin. The background checks took forever. I worked here as a legal intern during my last year of law school. After almost two years in the private sector, I'm overjoyed to come back."

"I feel the same way," she replied.

I truly felt like I'd won the "golden ticket" of legal jobs when I received an offer to return. It was a dream of mine to work for the federal government. And for years and years, I listened to the stories told about my Italian American grandfather who represented New York in Congress in the sixties. I was star struck by the photos that used to hang on the walls in his home on Pelham Parkway in the Bronx—photos that showed him campaigning with President John F. Kennedy at Lucky Corner, shaking the hand of President Lyndon B. Johnson outside the White House, and sitting with the famous Italian actress Sophia Loren at a private function. They amazed me. These were big shoes to fill, public service as a banner of the highest achievement in my family. As I sat there in that small, dark lobby, I smiled as I recalled that he even handled immigration legislation on the Hill, and here I was starting out as a federal immigration attorney.

On the night before I started, I had talked to my mother about this opportunity. She and my father were so proud of me. When I stood to take the oath of federal office required for all civil servants, I raised my right hand with great pride myself and repeated, truly enunciating each word as follows:

> *I, Meg Nocero, do solemnly swear that I will support and defend the Constitution of the United States against all enemies, foreign and domestic; that I will bear true faith and allegiance to the same; that I take this obligation freely, without mental reservation or purpose of evasion; and that I will well and faithfully discharge the duties of the office on which I am about to enter. So help me God.*

Just like the badges characters in movies like *Men in Black* pull out of their jackets to announce themselves, I had an official federal credential, a badge with the bronze INS emblem and the United States seal. I was well on my way to getting closer to that ethos of perfection that was passed down to me from earlier generations. At the end of that first day, I promised myself that I would do my best, maintain my integrity, and serve my country with distinction, upholding the laws of the US Constitution, as my grandfather had. I would show everyone what I was truly capable of accomplishing. I wasn't going to be an embarrassment to the family after all.

August 2011: Pact of Los Tres Magos

Fast forward nearly twelve years to August of 2011. All the possibility I had felt on that first day had slowly leaked out from my experience there, like a worn-out tire losing air. I was ready to quit. In fact, I had declared soon after my mother died in April of 2011 that I was desperate to do something different. She was the one who told me, "Meg, stress will kill you and have no regrets!"

Reflecting on my current crappy situation, I was physically and mentally exhausted. I missed my mother terribly and realized that nothing could truly fill the gap that she left behind. I was stressed juggling my family and a full-time work schedule. Running back and forth to immigration court, having no professional freedom to be creative, I couldn't imagine that this was the pinnacle of my career. Life happened. I had a second child, my mom got sick, and then she passed away. Things were not unfolding as I had planned. Searching for peace in my chaos, I was ready and willing to break out of the traditional career path that had been offered to me as the only option. Knowing as well that I had responsibilities of my own, I needed to get paid for work in an area that was more professionally satisfying. I recently read Bronnie Ware's, *The Top Five Regrets of the Dying*. In this book, she sets out the five top regrets, but this one spoke to me the most:

> *I wish I'd had the courage to live a life true to myself, not the life others expected of me.*

So keeping this in mind, on an auspicious day in August, after handling a fifty-case docket on an immigration court calendar, I had spoken to Richard, one of my closest friends at my office, about the regrets I had and started a conversation about what we would do if we resigned. He, an incredibly introspective person, was an avid lover of cooking and all things healthy. He made the most delicious gourmet meals. Looking at perhaps becoming a chef, open to possibility, and forever seeking a path that would keep his third eye expanded, we imagined that he had a successful cooking show. After it launched and aired, he would open up a full-scale spa in Curacao where he could bask in the beauty of the islands and write his books. We started to get more excited as we visualized what the realization of this incredible dream would look like. Perhaps after a yoga class and meditation, he would retire to his beautiful Caribbean resort to enjoy the ocean mist on his face and the gentle breeze blowing through his hair.

Wanting in on this incredible vibe, I, then, shared my dream of having a talk show where I could help inspire other people to figure out how to come alive to the beauty of their dreams. I would write inspirational books and travel to meet different people as a student of the world, making as much of a positive difference as I could. I would have more time to take care of my two-year-old daughter and eight-year-old son and teach them what I know.

About twenty minutes later, another colleague passed by, heard some of our conversation, and out of curiosity sat down and inquired what we were talking about. We explained that we were plotting our escape from what had started out as the best opportunity that ever happened to us, the "golden ticket" that had turned into a life-sucking job earning us material comforts, the "golden handcuffs." I have heard it said that working a job you strongly dislike is like driving a car with the emergency brake on. It will move, but a lot of energy is wasted in the process, and soon enough, the car is going to break down. We did not want to break down.

Looking for an outlet to express our creativity, the three of us made a pact. We set out terms and thought six months would be enough to see some forward movement. We circled January 6, 2012, and called our pledge the pact of *Los Tres Magos*, the Three Wise Ones, since it fell on the day when the three royal magi arrived at their destination bearing gifts after traveling under the guidance of a bright and brilliant North Star.

January 6, 2012, came and went. As life events unfolded around us, all three of us had lost sight of our arbitrary deadline. Yet, nearly five years later, the pact of *Los Tres Magos* would resurface when the next three events would synchronistically lead up to a big change on January 6, 2017. The question remained, would these events lead to similar gifts?

CHAPTER 18:

The Trifecta—I QUIT!

"In three words, I can sum up everything that I have learned about life: It goes on."
—ROBERT FROST, 1874–1963, American poet

Pay attention to "the rule of three" (in Latin, *omne trium perfectum*). Most times this rule ushers in more blessings than I can keep track of. This time, starting on November 6, 2016, a trifecta unfolded that led to one huge, life-changing decision. And when the rumbling began, I didn't know if it would ultimately be a good thing. But I held on to the belief that the emotional avalanche I was about to unleash wasn't an ending, but instead forced my hand to make choices that would lead to a vital new beginning. I had to surrender and let some dreams go so bigger ones could start to unfold.

Election Day in the United States of America, November 6, 2016: 1 of 3

I had a fixed routine each weekday morning. I would wake up at five thirty, go to the gym located on the ground floor of our condominium, and ride my favorite, beat up yet reliable stationary bike for thirty minutes. And, at the same time, I would read something inspirational while writing out the insights that made up the pages of my blog. However, on November 6, 2016, I slept in feeling achy and ill. When I finally dragged myself out of bed, I went into the bathroom to brush my teeth and wash my face. I had a dental appointment scheduled later that morning. Because my throat felt scratchy and I felt like I was coming down with a cold, I decided to cancel it. I was supposed to go into work later that day, so I got out of bed to take a shower and see if I felt any better afterward.

Today was Election Day. We would finally find out who would take the mantle as the new president of the United States. It had been a long election campaign cycle, with a great deal of fearmongering by one of the candidates, especially around immigrants. It had gotten to a nauseating level of nastiness and mudslinging. The political ads couldn't get any worse; you couldn't turn the television on without being subjected to a new low. The negativity that the candidates spewed affected many of us.

Friends angrily attacked each other via text, tweets, and, as evidenced in many places, actual physical violence. This time, one of the main candidates was base and vile with his rhetoric, falling to low levels and welcoming a "reality-show style" of reprehensible conduct. In my opinion, he was an unqualified narcissist who thought it appropriate to continuously use derogatory remarks against the disabled, foreigners, and women. His candidacy was juxtaposed against another prospect who, while qualified to do the job, had a huge problem with likability, not to mention an email scandal hanging over her head. I kept thinking, *Whoever wins, that portrait will hang in our office for all to see for the next four years.* That would essentially be my new boss, and their policies will dictate how I get to do my job.

On this Tuesday morning in November, I was glad that it would be over soon. I felt physically depleted, staving off a cold. Standing under warm water, I grabbed my peppermint body wash hoping that the fresh scent would get me going. After rinsing with cold water, I toweled off and sat down to blow dry my long hair. My cell phone rang. I looked at the screen, and to my surprise, it was the head of the Miami office. I let it go to voicemail, then turned the speaker phone on and pressed the arrow to play back the message. Sounding a bit nervous, he asked me to return his call at my earliest convenience. I knew in my gut that it had to be about a promotion I'd interviewed for six months earlier, and I would have preferred to find out face to face and not over the phone. In that vein, in my experience bad news in my office was never delivered in person, and I sensed that what he would have to say was probably not favorable.

After many years of little opportunity to move forward in Miami, the tides of change had swept through in full force at the beginning of 2016. A new head of the office was finally appointed after an extended vacancy, and the powers that be received the go ahead to hire after years of understaffing. We also received notice that they were looking for three supervisors as well. I applied again. Third time's a charm.

The first time, in 2005, my application had been rejected as incomplete. In July of 2009, second time I applied, I met with a panel of three, the Principal Legal Advisor, the Deputy Legal Advisor, and the head of the Miami office. After a tough, stressful interview, I did not get the job in Miami, but because I was deemed an exceptionally qualified candidate, I received an offer to be a manager in Orlando instead. If I wanted to move up, I had to move out. Never an easy choice, I weighed the pros and cons. My husband would have to find a new job; my kids would have to start at a new school in the middle of the year; and at that same time, my mother's cancer returned adding to an already complicated situation. I really wanted to move my career forward and serve in my agency as a leader, but as bad luck would have it, I knew I could not this time around. Returning to work on Monday morning, I reluctantly and politely declined.

Fast forward six years, I applied again. As this was my third time, I put it all out there and left everything on the table: all my accomplishments, in court and otherwise, my writing successes, my ability to effectively hire, train, and manage over three hundred law students for over sixteen years, and my skill in managing challenging interns. Also, I was a certified mentor with ICE Mentoring, a certified instructor for the Federal Law Enforcement Training Center (FLETC), and I had received extensive training on how to effectively support, develop, and build interoffice morale—this seemed to be a persistent problem for the Department of Homeland Security (DHS). My resume was even better now, and I was more qualified. In my opening paragraph, I set the tone for the kind of leader/supervisor I hoped to be:

I am a people person who has over eighteen years of experience in all facets of immigration law. . . . My greatest strength is inspiring others to fulfill their utmost potential. I know actions speak louder than words as I follow closely the wisdom of Maya Angelou who said, "I've learned that people will forget what you said, people will forget what you did, but people will never forget how you made them feel." As such, I have always done my best to choose actions that uplift and encourage in my various roles both professionally and personally. If given the chance to work as a Deputy Chief Counsel, I would bring a positive culture of service that focuses on motivating my colleagues to confidently use their strengths to support the agency mission to protect the homeland. This positive culture would be the basis for diligently litigating cases while adhering to the highest standards of professional conduct as well as providing timely and accurate legal advice.

After I'd dotted my *i*'s and crossed my *t*'s, but before I sent it, I set an intention to the universe and said out loud, "God! Are you listening? Here I go again. I'm putting it out there. If I get it, I stay. If I don't, I leave."

On April 27, 2016, I interviewed with a panel of three. Wearing one of my favorite black suits, I entered the room and shook the hands of both men present while waving to the one on the video teleprompter. The conference room had a beautiful view overlooking the Miami River. As I took my seat at the table, I admired the yachts and commercial liners passing by on this gorgeous spring day. I placed my portfolio on the table and prepared myself to answer questions. Making small talk at first, I wanted to get a feel for the energy in the room.

From the beginning, I had my concerns. While I believed that seniority in my office did not count for much, here I was once again having to sell my past performance to an unknowing audience. While I had received a previous offer and achievement awards for my quasi-management position the entire time I worked there, I knew I should have had an excellent chance. Yet, based upon their questions, I wasn't sure if they valued what I brought to the table, or had even fully read my materials. Furthermore, while I had experienced this agency's toxic work culture firsthand over the years, I hoped that by throwing my hat into the ring, I could make a difference and bring more transparency. Sitting in that room, I was uncertain whether this head of the office could change the patterns and practices already sewn tightly into the fabric there. I was interviewing them to figure out which direction he would go and what kind of vision he had.

Every year since I could remember, DHS sent out a federal employee survey to determine the employees' perceptions of workforce management, agency goals, leadership skills, and ability for communication. And every year, the results showed that DHS rated among the lowest for morale and senior leadership. I saw favoritism as rampant, the higher-ups promoting their friends rather than hiring based on merit. It felt like management looked down on the line attorneys as only necessary warm bodies to handle a huge workload where burnout was not far behind. I felt that once a person was welcomed into the inner circle of management, there was an intoxication of professional freedom and power that they continued to protect, to the detriment of the line attorneys. New attorneys would not be aware of this, but those who had seniority saw it over and over again.

Knowing the current low morale in our office after so many events had shocked our conscience over the past several years, I wasn't convinced that the current head of office, who was an external hire, understood our office's history. Several colleagues had disappeared without a reason. And two employees, who were beloved and the heart and soul of that place for years, had passed away suddenly. This head of office seemed to rely on the other managers, who I felt showed clear bias toward promoting their own people.

Understanding this office and that we were among the best and the brightest, I knew the candidates presented were vying for recognition in a small box. While my resume and performance should have spoken for themselves, I probably needed to play the game and get someone to champion me. But once again, that's not how I roll. When the interview concluded, I thanked them, got up, and left sensing my vision was not aligned with this promotion. I had a premonition that they had already made their choice, and it was time for me to move on. I would have to wait and see what would happen next.

Sitting on the ledge of my bathtub that morning, I remembered the prior Tuesday, when the director of ICE had visited the Miami field offices to speak to the attorneys and support staff. When I heard her speak at a detention conference in Washington, DC, in June, she shared her gratitude for the support she received after the recent loss of her teenage son. Hearing this, I mailed her a copy of my book in hopes that it would help her with her grieving process. After her presentation in Miami, I went up to her to introduce myself and to see if she received it. She acknowledged it and took me aside to thank me. I felt appreciated, and we had photos taken together in front of the American flag, the DHS emblem, and a photo of President Obama.

To top off an already amazing day, when I arrived at home, I received an envelope addressed to me from the Richard Rodgers Theater in New York City. Opening it, on the front was a photo of Lin Manuel Miranda, the creator of Broadway's *Hamilton* musical. On the other side, the top read *From the Desk of Lin Manuel Miranda*. Underneath, he had written about *The Magical Guide to Bliss*:

Dear Meg,
It has been a real treat flipping through your book to find wisdom
for the day. You clearly worked extremely hard on it and deserve
praise. Thank you for sharing your work.
Siempre, Lin

I was jumping up and down, joyful that someone I highly respected validated my work.

Now, one week later, I had a feeling that it would be a different kind of day. I took a deep breath and pressed redial, ready to accept my fate.

"Good morning, it's Meg Nocero. How are you?"

As if following a script, he began, "Good morning, Meg. My apologies for delivering this over the phone, but unfortunately I need to tell you that you did not get the deputy position in Miami."

"Okay." So much for small talk, I replied, "Can you explain why not?"

He said, "While your people skills were off the charts, we made the determination that you were not technically qualified to do the job."

I asked him again, "What exactly does that mean? Not technically qualified?"

He replied, "We made a determination based upon your interview and resume that you lacked the technical skills for the job, I'm sorry."

"Okay, but what does that mean? And if I may ask, who got the job?"

He did not address the former and replied to the latter, "That will be announced later today in a formal meeting."

"Okay, but if it's all right, I'm not coming in. I'm not feeling well." I felt sick to my stomach.

"That's fine, I'll let your supervisor know." Then he hung up. *Click.* I broke down in tears.

I was mortified because he kept saying I wasn't technically qualified and couldn't explain what that meant. I felt I deserved that much. And truth be told, after weeding out who did not get the job to determine who did, I was surprised. As the news sunk in, I slumped down from the bathtub ledge on to the mat and lay down on a heap of towels feeling sorry for myself and demoralized. My ego was bruised. I got my answer: no promotion, time for a new ladder, time to go. I sat there in my robe, wondering what I was going to do now. All I knew for sure was whatever was next, it was not this!

Since I have always believed that bad news comes in threes, turning toward the news about the election, a sense of impending doom came over me. The results would probably be unfavorable there as well. And two thirty the next morning, in one of the most shocking US elections in modern history, I watched the Associated Press declare that Trump was the next president of the United States. What just happened?

I remembered feeling so hopeful in November of 2008. I called my mom to celebrate, crying tears of joy as we found out that the first African American had been elected president of the United States. Now I was crying tears of sorrow and I didn't have my mom to turn to. Nothing made sense. Trump treated women with disrespect, he rallied people through hate that spurred on a further divided nation, and he got caught in lies over and over. Reality struck and overwhelmed me. Over the course of just twenty-four hours, life as I knew it was over. Change was coming my way, and I was scared, not sure I was ready for it. Exhausted and still not feeling well, I fell to my knees and sobbed. I was about to walk away from a federal legal career that I worked so hard to build, all the positives about my country could be jeopardized, and I had no idea what I would do next under this new reality.

Leaps of faith are a tricky thing. Once you grab on to hope and pray for a just result, when the outcome is not the one that you thought you were looking for, disappointment and another period of grieving begins. I wondered under this new administration, *What will become of this country*? The world you woke up to the morning after is somehow very different than the one you knew the night before. How do you then hold strong to hope, to all that you believe in when you face feelings of despair? Grieve it, then move on to the "what next?" right around the corner. I knew I couldn't stay where I was. It was time to come up with an exit strategy of my own. I needed to leave before the new administration got their act together and replaced Obama's photo with Trump's.

Quite simply, the universe was pushing and squeezing me out the door, knowing that I would never want to work for or align with someone whose vision of the world I did not respect. But before that happened, I resisted making a move and ignored the call, at least until my circle of safety and influence started to fall apart.

The End of the Dynamic Duo, December 2016: 2 of 3

When my friend Richard told me that he was leaving the agency on January 6, 2017, the day of *Los Tres Magos*, I was happy for him to move on, but sad that I had to stay behind. I'd met Richard fifteen years earlier when I hired him to work with INS and had instantly liked him. He was smart, but more importantly kind. While he did a great job as a government employee, he marched to the beat of his own drum and continued to do so when he signed on as an attorney with the office in 2004. Sporting a faux hawk and always stylishly dressed, he most certainly brought a distinct uniqueness and class.

After only a couple of months officially on board, I brought him onto the intern team, and we worked together for over thirteen years. We were a dynamic duo. We spent a lot of time together, talked for hours, and dreamed, as evidenced by all the places and people we got to know. We engaged in spiritual inquiry as often as we traveled to various universities at least four times every six months to see what special talent we could recruit. I loved those rides. Though some in our office sarcastically called them "boondoggles," their suppositions could not be further from the truth. We essentially weeded out the stars locally, trained them well, and readied them to eventually come on board as a part of the staff.

While I introduced him to the teachings of what he called my many "holy healers," he poked fun as we laughed and sang to the 1978 Euro disco hit song by Boney M., "Rasputin," the semibiographical song about Grigori Rasputin, the mystical healer, political manipulator, advisor to Tsar Nicholas II of Russia, and "lover of the Russian queen." Always open to new ways to raise the vibration in our office, he brought to my attention efforts like Will Bowen's *A Complaint Free World*, suggesting that everyone try for twenty-one days to break the habit of complaining. On my own dime, I purchased over a hundred purple rubber bracelets for my office as a tool each person could use to help them stop being so negative. Each time a person complained, they would have to move the bracelet from one wrist to the other. I challenged each participant in my office to see who could go the full twenty-one days without a complaint and to find out how they would feel once they accomplished this great feat.

We loved the staffs at the career placement offices at all the local law schools as we got to know them well over time. It felt like a celebration when we came on campus. We had a reputation for the most enjoyable interviews as well as the best internship experience. When Richard told me he was leaving, I knew no one could replace him. But when my supervisor chose his replacement without asking me, I saw the writing on the wall.

On January 6, 2017, we were scheduled to gather for Richard's farewell breakfast at eight o'clock in the big third-floor conference room. I dreaded going to work that morning, but they asked me to say a few words about him. How could I say no and not go? At 7:45, I sat in my car in the parking lot trying to get it together, feeling very sorry for myself, tears streaming down my face and slowly ruining my makeup. I had no idea how I would be able to speak in front of the whole office.

I got out of my car and walked through the gate onto the street across from the federal immigration building where the homeless sleep at night.

I thought back to about two months earlier when Richard and I came back from a day of interviewing. We were greeted by yellow police tape and two officers covering up the body of an overdose victim.

Shocked, I remembered Richard saying to me, "We need to get out of here!"

Horrified, I replied, "You think?"

Now Richard *was* getting out and I was running late. I hurried across the street, showed my credentials at the front security, and finally arrived at the third floor. I dropped my purse on the floor and, still wearing my coat, walked into the conference room filled with people. My supervisor immediately approached me and asked me to speak.

Through tears, I began: "Rich, I'm so proud of the attorney you have become. This is a big loss for this office, but I'm sure it's the best decision as many opportunities await. I know that I'll miss you dearly. You're an excellent colleague and even better friend. I'm so grateful that you were my partner for thirteen years on the legal intern team. We really created something wonderful here. You're family to me. I know that we all wish you the best of luck and every possible success."

We all applauded him, and our supervisor presented him with the customary DHS plaque in appreciation for his years of public service as well as a DHS emblem signed by all of us on staff.

As I was about to go back to my workspace on the second floor, the head of the office approached me. I was sad and in no mood to make polite conversation, but it looked like he had something to say to me. I did not want to be rude, so I stayed to find out what it was.

"Good morning, how are you?" I asked.

"I'm good. It seems we are losing a good employee," he answered.

"Yes, we are. It's too bad for us, great for him," I replied.

"I did tell him that the door was always open if he wanted to come back."

"I'm sure he was happy to hear that," I replied.

He continued, "So I got off a call this morning with the head of the Executive Communications Unit in DC. Good news, they picked you for the temporary detail. Once they get things organized, probably at the end of the month, you'll fly up for a training week. Does that work?"

Shocked and happy to hear this, I replied, "Yes, of course."

He finished, "Then you'll even be able to telecommute for the time period that you're with them."

On Richard's last day, *I* was getting out too. I was relieved and pleasantly surprised. I had no idea when I applied that I would be able to work from home. Perhaps this was the perfect transition that I was waiting for.

I answered, "Thank you, that is such great news. Just let me know who I have to get in touch with to arrange everything."

A door was finally opening, movement was happening for me, and I was going to walk through ready for what awaited me on the other side.

Ladders and Doors, January 2017: 3 of 3

In light of how my professional path was unfolding, I contemplated the concept of ladders and doors as I wrote in my blog:

Ladders all around, which one do you choose? Choices to be made, there is no time to lose. The weather is stormy, no time to be confused. All the trickery aside, your life is not a ruse. Tomorrow is not promised; you must do this today. You made it here so far, your higher power will guide the way. You are a beautiful soul, you magical one. Your destination awaits, it is all a part of the fun. If you stay and do nothing, you waste such a chance. This golden opportunity, this once in a lifetime to dance. The journey is the reason, but you must walk to meet your fate. Go now, embrace it, before it's too late.

Which direction beckons to you, which cajoles you to rise? It is a ladder you must take, at each rung awaits your prize. My dear, my sweet dear, please I implore, those lessons hard earned, prepared you for what is in store. The magic, the miracles, you know where you need to go. Go for it now, the sky is the limit you know. Start to see clearly, eyes closed and all. Trust your intuition, I promise you will not fall. One by one, up you go. Even in the darkness, the clouds part and you will know. A bright beautiful world, it is there, today's the day. Start NOW my dear child and your inner light will guide your way.

Then a quote from Joseph Campbell came to mind: "Follow your bliss and the universe will open doors where there used to be walls." As I chose a different direction following my bliss, there were two doors that opened for me that made it easier to close the third.

Door #1: Executive Communications Unit (ECU), Washington, DC

In May of 2016, I was contacted by one of the managers to assist in providing information that I had compiled over the years for a cohesive national intern program. I enthusiastically sat down with her to go over what worked and what did not. I hoped that this was an opportunity that could lead me into something better. Developing young minds was certainly a passion of mine.

After I gave her the information she'd requested, and she thanked me. I got up to go, but then stopped, turned around, and asked, "Do you think that I could play a role in this? I want to do something else here. I'm so frustrated. I couldn't have missed my chance. I applied to be an instructor for FLETC. I'm a mentor, I even applied to head the training committee. And I'm waiting to hear back on my application to be a supervisor; I could do that job along with this. This is perfect for me. Can you help?"

I felt a little uncomfortable asking. I hoped that she would offer me guidance, but it was hard to know. I had helped her before. When she came to me years earlier about her own unfair situation with management, I spoke up for her even when it turned out to hurt my prospects in the end. She got the promotion and her career advanced in Miami while mine went nowhere. I hoped she could put in a good word for me with headquarters. I felt like no matter how innovative or successful my program was in Miami, there seemed to be a wall around that office where only the select few could break through. I needed her help and assistance now. My career there had stalled out.

She replied, "I get it. Let's go to dinner."

We decided to go to La Mar, a chic Peruvian waterfront restaurant close to our office and located on the same island where I lived. After we ordered our entrées, I finally broached the subject of potential opportunities. Right to the point, she commented that I may not have had enough external experience for the supervisor position that was still pending. This perplexed me.

"How is that possible?" I asked, "I was offered the position before when I had less experience."

I knew the names of those who were a part of the applicant pool, and my experience managing people certainly surpassed others.

Then I asked, "Who else in the applicant pool has the management experience that I have? What more are they looking for?"

As we continued to talk, she didn't address my questions, but encouraged me to apply for opportunities outside of Miami and suggested the detail at ECU. Presuming that she had the inside scoop, it became clear to me over the next hour that another attorney in our office was most likely slated for the promotion. At the end of the evening, we started to talk about ladders as I soon realized a door of opportunity was about to close.

"Meg, really think about where you want to put your ladder going forward," she said. "You don't want to make the wrong move and have to climb back down. Maybe the next ladder is one you never even considered."

Fast forward. After I did not get the promotion in November 2016, I took her advice and applied for the ECU detail in December and left for Washington, DC, in January of 2017. After a week of training at headquarters, I returned to Miami where I worked remotely from home. This was a new ladder I needed. I could feel it. Exploring a whole new area in this agency, I gratefully jumped outside the fishbowl of the Miami office to seek out opportunities to grow.

I started my new position the Monday after the inauguration of Trump's presidency, and I could already feel tensions rise around immigration policy. During his campaign, this president set his sight on immigration reform, talking about building the best wall along the border and keeping out all illegals, the "bad hombres" and rapists. Up to that point, I had worked under the administrations of both Democrats and Republicans: Clinton, Bush, and Obama. This changing of the guard felt very different. With the crowd size controversy on the first day as the president obsessed over his inauguration and "fake" media reports of low turnout, no one at my agency really knew what to expect moving forward. While the president's first few shots heard 'round the world were directly counter to what the poet Ralph Waldo Emerson meant in his poem as movement toward democracy, his first executive orders, the so-called Muslim bans, I felt challenged American values and set an isolationist tone for the future. While I recognized that there needed to be a balance between enforcement and benefits, this administration was crossing constitutional lines, and I was concerned that some policy decisions might not be consistent with my values.

Establishing a good routine and learning my new job quickly, I excitedly took on this new challenge. With deadlines, follow-up, and a calm customer service tone, I worked late into the evenings, sometime staying way past closing time. ECU compiled and finalized the Office of Principal Legal Advisor (OPLA) division responses and forwarded OPLA's advice to the Office of Policy, Office of Public Affairs, and Office of Congressional Relations. ECU was responsible for handling issues regarding regulations, governmental audits, and congressional matters. ECU attorneys interacted with OPLA senior management on a regular basis. And at the end of the day, while this was still not my dream job, it was a good change.

On my days off, I put my energy into marketing my book. The detail was only for a short time, initially for three months, happily extended to five. If I did not have a plan by the end of May, I'd have to physically return to my office in Miami. Knowing this, I would send my book out to influencers who resonated, hoping that the stars would align to attract more attention.

As a big fan of the British alternative rock band Coldplay, I went on their webpage to see how I could connect. I knew they were coming to Miami for a concert, and I was hoping somehow I'd be able to meet them and hand Chris Martin my book to thank him for all his inspiration. I listened to all their albums over and over for years, and their music was the soundtrack that gave me hope at the onset of the grieving process. Songs like "The Scientist," "Fix You," and "Us Against the World" really got me through a very dark night. Especially "Yellow," when I retreated to my closet for safety. I played this song repeatedly, imagining that my mother would speak to me through those lyrics. I felt her telling me that she loved me and thought I had turned into something beautiful. This was something that I'd desperately needed to hear.

I couldn't wait to go their concert. On their webpage, the latest album, *Head Full of Dreams,* and tour dates appeared front and center. When I clicked on the Events tab to see about getting tickets, a photo of Super Bowl 50 popped up where the crowd spelled out "BELIEVE IN LOVE" against a multicolored background. Chris Martin wore a LOVE button. It resonated with me, so I clicked on the link that took me to a page for The Love Button Global Movement. On the bar at the top, I noticed Live.Love.Laugh, the same words my family placed on my mother's epitaph.

All of this reminded me of the Give Love Project that I'd started with my kids. In 2012, the sparks of light from joy and hope reawakened my own attitude of gratitude for life's blessings. In order to express my appreciation for the crucial love that had propelled me out of the depths of depression, I wanted to give something back to the world. Moreover, I wanted to demonstrate to my children, Ava and Michael, the power inherent in simple gestures of love and provide them an opportunity to exercise their ability to make such gestures and an outlet to do so. Since my children and I enjoyed arts and crafts, when the idea arose to make Give Love Rocks, as they came to be known, and give them to others as a tool by which to spread love, we all pursued it enthusiastically. Indeed, they served as a reminder to spread love, which can make a difference to a person experiencing hardships in life.

I wanted to share my project and book. I clicked on the Contact Us link and sent an email:

> *I wrote a book called The Magical Guide to Bliss. Inspired by my mother who passed away in April 2011 after a battle with breast cancer, her motto was Live Laugh Love. I saw that this was on your website. So many wonderful synchronicities! I'll be at the Coldplay show at the Hard Rock stadium in Miami—I am a big fan. I would love an opportunity to thank them for the incredible insight and inspiration!*

I included the link to the livestream video of my book's La Dolce Vita launch sharing about being a dreamer, and I left my contact information. That was on a Sunday at the end of March 2017.

As I sat at my computer working on my daily taskings on the ECU board, Coldplay's "Something Just Like This" played in the background. I danced in my chair and sang the lyrics at the top of my lungs, screaming out to the universe and asking for my fairytale bliss. Then I got an email asking, "Meg, when are you scheduled to return to our office?"

Having no desire to return to where I felt unappreciated, I wanted to write back "NEVER," but instead replied, "I'm uncertain. I believe that ECU was going to request an extension."

"Let me know as soon as you do."

As I was just one of many, I assumed he was looking at the numbers and needed to plan to put me back on the court schedule. I probably could not get another extension and postpone returning any longer. After that brief exchange, I was instantly sad and wanted to clear my head. I needed a break, so I signed off the board for an hour.

Grabbing both my dogs, I headed out to the local market at the bottom of the hill to get as much fresh air as I could. Just thinking about returning to my old office made my whole body tense up. I sat at a corner table outside of the café, running my hands nervously through my hair and contemplating what the hell I was going to do next. I could apply for a permanent position with ECU and stay with DHS, but I would have to relocate to Washington, DC. And, once again, my husband wasn't going to move with me, and I wasn't going to leave my family behind.

Feeling stuck and frustrated, I turned to God:

I want to quit. I have no other solution. Why can't this be easier? I'm terrified. I still don't have a back-up plan. Frank does not support my leaving. In fact, he doesn't even want to discuss it. He made it clear to me that I needed another job before I could go. I told him I'm done. I'm jumping out of my skin. What am I going to do? I need help. It looks like I can't figure this out on my own. I need a sign. Please send me a sign as to which direction to take. I am going to trust You and let it go.

With that, I grabbed my dogs and walked back up the hill to my condominium. Arriving, I resumed my work. I hoped that my prayers would be answered sooner than later, and most importantly, that I paid enough attention to get the message when the response came.

Door #2: Love Button Global Movement

Two days later, I rolled out of bed at eight, took a shower, and got ready to tackle my to-do list. It was my first day off in a while and I was going to make the most of it. Before I left the house, I received a short text message from a gentleman named Dr. Habib Sadeghi from the Love Button Global Movement. He asked if he could call me at 8:47 Pacific time, that would be 11:47 that morning Eastern time. Excited and curious, I immediately replied, "Absolutely, yes!"

Wanting to know more before we spoke, I ditched my plans so I could search the internet to find some information about who he was and what he could possibly want to talk about. When I googled his name, I pulled up his presentation at the 2014 TEDx Austin Women Conference. I sat there and watched this delightful man full of love and gratitude tell his story about a journey from cancer diagnosis to a rich soulful belief that anything was possible. In the nineteen minutes that it took for him to relay how emotions and thoughts affect our health, I wished that he could have helped my mom.

When he called at exactly 11:47 Eastern Time, I noticed the numerology 11:11, a symbolic wake-up call, the universe sending a signal that the energy gateway had opened up for me. I was really paying attention now. After initial introductions, some of his first words to me were, "I saw your beautiful video. I'm so proud of you. How can I help you?"

Skeptical, I didn't trust anybody at this point. I asked, "I'm sorry? Help me? What do you mean?"

"What can I do for you? You wrote me sharing your book and your video about dreams, and I was very moved by your message. How can I help you?" Dr. Habib asked again.

I asked, "Are you serious? I don't know what to say. No one has ever offered me unsolicited help, especially someone I never met before."

We talked for over an hour.

He ended our conversation as follows: "I want to invite you to our Love Button fundraiser in May; you and the woman in your video can be my guests in Malibu. I'll send you the information. Then send me your book and let me see what I can do."

My mouth dropped open. I sat on my couch thinking about what just happened. I actually took notes to be sure that I had not made it all up, it seemed so crazy and hard to believe. He'd just invited me to join him in Malibu, California, on May 20, 2017, for an exclusive fundraising event with special performances supporting the Love Button Global Movement. I was so beyond excited.

So at the end of May, my husband Frank, my good friend Denise, and I traveled to Los Angeles. After a beautiful drive up the Pacific Coast Highway, we arrived in Malibu at dusk on a perfectly gorgeous California evening. The night air was a cool and crisp sixty-five degrees with low humidity. Excited, Denise and I both were dressed to the nines. We had gone all out and gotten our hair and makeup done to match what we believed would be the perfect outfits for a magical celebrity-style evening like this. Denise was wearing a low-cut black jumpsuit with a multiple strand gold bead necklace, her hair pulled back into a long ponytail, with red lipstick and eyelashes to die for. I wore a low-cut, black-and-white striped maxi-dress with a hot pink sash and a single strand of white pearls, and pink lipstick. Frank wore a casual blue blazer and a white button-down shirt.

When we arrived at the address on the invitation, we joined a long line of cars and waited our turn to hand over our keys to the valet. At the front of the walkway that led up to the house stood a gray wooden sign with the words "Magical Kingdom" and covered by various colors of butterflies and tropical flowers. Turning toward the entrance, we walked under a trellis whose lighting boasted bright charming flowers against the lush greenery. We were giddy, taking as many photos as we could to remember the evening.

At the check-in, we each grabbed a handful of Love Buttons and handed over our telephones, as photos were not permitted. We gathered excitedly with the other guests on a tennis court that had been transformed into a Magical Bazaar. At one end of the courts, a table was set up with all kinds of Middle Eastern food and specialty drinks: pita, grilled vegetables, falafel, hummus, lamb, and chicken skewers. The rich smells of herb-infused cuisine penetrated the air. At the other end, a makeshift stage awaited the appearance of the main act. In front of the stage, colorful throw pillows were available for seating. Behind them, picnic tables lined up in a row. All around were decorative hanging lights and sporadically placed heaters to warm the guests.

In the midst of the fanfare, I saw Dr. Habib with his wife talking to various individuals. He was one of the happiest human beings I had ever seen. So much loving energy, you knew he had to be the real thing. Even I, the most skeptical person around, felt the high vibration surrounding him. I went up to him to introduce myself, Frank, and Denise. When he saw me, he enthusiastically said, "You're here. I can't believe you came all this way."

I replied, smiling from ear to ear, "I'm so excited to be here—thank you so much for your invitation."

"Picture, we all need a picture." He waved over the photographer. I smiled; at least I would get one photo of all of us together.

Frank went to get us drinks as we stood in line chatting with the others. We recognized a few A-list celebrities including Orlando Bloom and Kenny G. Sufi whirling dervishes, dancers who performed a twirling ritual as if in a trance, delighted the group accompanied by typical instruments. After Dr. Habib thanked Coldplay's Chris Martin for hosting, he shared a few words about his nonprofit Love Button and its mission to promote a culture of love by inspiring others to act with loving kindness in their daily lives. He then showed a video highlighting the educational and humanitarian programs Love Button supports locally and globally.

Then Dr. Habib invited the musicians who played the string instruments to join Chris on stage to perform. Without further ado, Chris began with his first song, "Yellow," the same one that we'd played at my book launch. So happy, I looked back at Frank who was sitting behind me. He placed his hand in mine. I wanted to pinch myself to make sure that I wasn't dreaming all of this. Looking over at Denise, she radiated pure joy and was smiling from ear to ear. Chris invited Kenny G on stage to play a Pink Floyd song in a tribute to the band Soundgarden's lead guitarist, Chris Cornell, who had passed away that week.

Then we were all invited to come up to the stage. Denise and I joined Dr. Habib and his wife, Dr. Sherry, in front and danced to Coldplay's "Sky Full of Stars," laughing and singing along. At the end of this glorious night, we thanked Dr. Habib and his wife for such a lovely evening and said goodbye to our new acquaintances. Such a wonderful night—I thought no one would ever believe any of this happened; even I barely did. Before flying back to Miami, Frank and I said goodbye to Denise. "I'll call you tomorrow after work."

"Safe travels. Love you guys!" she answered back.

"You too."

I felt that the whole experience was a dream come true, and I was ready to discover what more the universe had in store for me.

Door #3: Miami Immigration Court

After receiving an exceptional performance review from ECU for my work and leading and monitoring the legal intern program without missing a beat over the past six months, I contacted my supervisor and asked to be nominated for the DHS Secretary's Award for Diversity Management. Confident that my contributions to this agency certainly proved worthy of this recognition, I attached the justification in support. I had effectively led and empowered a diverse group of up-and-coming DHS recruits. My innovation and leadership in this arena had produced outstanding results expanding diversity representation while successfully providing a workforce to assist with managing a voluminous caseload. And I'd enhanced community relations and elevated the agency presence as supporting diversity at the local and national law schools.

In reply, my supervisor stated that he looked forward to reexamining and rejuvenating the program with the new team and would wait for a year to recognize any anticipated success. In sum, he wasn't even going to elevate it. After I'd vetted and trained so many, I asked that he would promote what I did for my program on a national scale. Recognition was a huge part of moving forward. I wasn't going to play it safe and stay until next year to see the outcome. I wanted some control over my future—I felt like I had been patient waiting for my chance to move up. Now, I wanted to see what more I could do—to see my gifts put to good use. I just couldn't waste any more time in a place where opportunities and acknowledgment appeared to be saved for the chosen few. With this development, I promised myself that I was done here.

To add insult to injury, during my detail with ECU, he requested a full report from me listing the names of all past interns and subsequent hires since I started in 2000. Then he asked for all the best procedures that led to our successful recruiting and hiring.

I gave it to him after inquiring why he requested it now. I sent it and said:

> *Not quite sure why you wanted this information. Actually having to compile it, bringing to light the faces over time and the friendships established, it proves once again that this program is by far the contribution that makes me most proud during my tenure with this agency. In my opinion, the intern team deserves more recognition than an honorable mention. Each person who has dedicated their time and truly heart and soul to this program has made the Miami OCC better for it. Look at all the qualified hires brought on board because of it.*

Too trusting once again, it turned out to be a stupid move on my part. I kicked myself. Now that he had the historical information he'd asked for, I felt that he no longer needed me. For all intents and purposes, it felt like he took over the lead of this program, and I felt demoted on a committee that I had created and run successfully for many years. I wished I were still in Malibu; it didn't take long for the magic of that incredible weekend to disappear now that I was back in Miami dealing with all of this again. I made up my mind I was going to resign in August.

At the beginning of June, I returned to the Miami office. As a union representative, I met with the head of my office to discuss certain issues that negatively affected some of our senior members involving office space. During this conversation, I communicated to him my own experience and opinion that seniority in this office had to count for something. So many new people had started and did not have the know-how and expertise. I felt like the old guard was being replaced with the new. I encouraged him to recognize those on his staff who knew where the proverbial bodies were buried and knew the history of the organization to get things done. I communicated that, in my opinion, for quite some time, leaders in our organization were not approachable and it felt like they did not support employees who were overwhelmed with the caseload that led to burnout. I had shared with him what my colleagues were afraid to express: the office needed a boss who reached out to employees and discovered what they needed to continue to do their job well. Instead of relying on the managers who were happy with the status quo, I encouraged him to talk to the attorneys who were in the trenches every day. Until he sought to understand what needed to be done, the office could lose the overlooked experienced ones, as they would leave to seek professional advancement and better opportunities elsewhere.

In that vein, I added that I would be resigning at the end of the summer. He nodded that he already knew. Even still, he seemed like a really nice guy. I was grateful that he did not stand in the way of the ECU detail—I suppose he could have. And, to his credit, he listened and thanked me for my input. But, I just saw no future there for me; there was no turning back now. Subsequently, I wrote the best blog post of my career entitled, *Final Mission Statement: I Quit.* It must have resonated. It got over ten thousand hits. I started it off:

If I stay, I am guaranteed that nothing will change, but if I go the possibilities are endless. . . .

I consciously made the decision to close this door and place my next ladder on a new wall. I was tired of seeking approval from those who did not see my potential. And moreover, I was tired of looking for my own self-worth externally. I'd already stayed longer than I should have because I was afraid to venture out. Now it was time to quit and take a leap of faith outside of the proverbial box. While I was terrified, I felt empowered for the first time in quite a while. I spoke my truth, even when my voice shook. With a defiant spirit, I was choosing not to settle. I was choosing to bet on me. When I told my husband I was resigning from my job, he was so angry with me. Making the decision that I could only face one huge hurdle at a time, I knew that either I could choose to stay at the job and leave him or leave my job and work on us. Because I loved him and my family, I chose to stay with him. If he could not handle it, I asked him to give me three months to get on my feet and set up my business so I could support myself if he decided to leave me.

After such a wonderful experience, feeling on top of the world, it looked like I had to face some significant music—it was in this moment that I remembered my father playing opera for us when I was younger. It felt like one of the greatest composers of Italian opera, Giacomo Puccini, was taking me on an emotional crescendo in *Tosca*. Resigning herself, the main female protagonist Floria Tosca sings her beautiful aria "Vissi d'arte," ("I lived for my art") following significant life-altering emotional peaks where she feels that God has abandoned her. Whether it be my relationship or life purpose, it was safe to say that I did not have any idea what the future would hold on the other side of this journey. I just had to keep walking. I certainly appreciated inspiring music to move to.

Part Three:

A Leap of Faith to Fly!

"We are travelers on a cosmic journey, stardust, swirling and dancing in the eddies and whirlpools of infinity. Life is eternal. We have stopped for a moment to encounter each other, to meet, to love, to share. This is a precious moment. It is a little parenthesis in eternity."
—PAULO COELHO, The Alchemist, Brazilian novelist

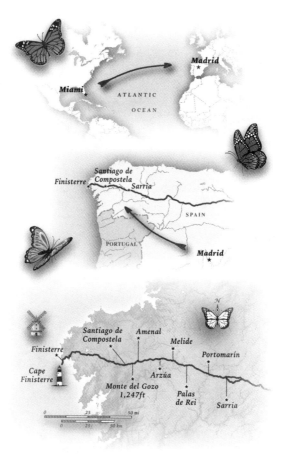

From Miami, Fl to Northern Spain-El Camino de Santiago de Compostela

CHAPTER 19:

Live, Laugh, Love—Beginning
the Journey to Bliss!

*"Life should not be a journey to the grave with the intention
of arriving safely in a pretty well-preserved body, but rather
to skid in broadside in a cloud of smoke, thoroughly used up,
totally worn out, and loudly proclaiming "Wow! What a Ride!"*
—**HUNTER S. THOMPSON**, 1937–2005, American journalist

Time to Move On

This quote is on a plaque underneath a mirror on the front wall of the
office that I had taken up residence in for the better part of my legal
career. It hangs by the entrance near a portrait I drew at a paint party that
reads "A Girl Should Be Fabulous." All around my office were symbolic,
inspirational tokens strategically placed to remind me to dream, to follow
my bliss, to not give up hope, and to be grateful for the opportunity
of this once around. And over the last twelve years, since 2003 when
I moved in, this particular corner office that was my home away from
home served its purpose as a little fortress, my work closet, the place I hid
myself away. Slowly getting stuck year after year, I did not know when to
cut loose from the gilded cage. I became more fearful of breaking out of
the safe routine that I found myself in. I hit the metaphorical glass ceiling,
that is until I took the detail with the Executive Communication Unit at

DHS Headquarters. I could be of value somewhere else. That experience confirmed my decision to leave. Now I was not scared anymore.

Because I made things too comfortable, it became very difficult to move. Perhaps I feared that this was as good as it gets. Perhaps growing older, I became more risk averse and less willing to compromise the status quo to see what more life had in store. Fixed in my ways, stubborn to change, I traded excitement for security. However, by choosing conservatively, I knew that I denied myself growth. Now I felt my inspirational hideaway lose its hold on me. I was ready to take a chance to do something I loved. And, gratefully, I became aware of this while I was still young enough to recreate myself as a forty-something entrepreneur. Besides, the universe was about to squeeze me out of my comfort zone anyway. For at the end of June, when I returned to my old office at the Miami Immigration Court, the new head declared that he wanted to move the part-timers out of their private offices into shared doubles regardless of seniority or the number of days that they came to work. Even though I worked more than an 80 percent schedule, that group included me. I promised myself that if I moved, it would not be to another office, but out of there.

The comfort I thought I had created wasn't so comfortable anymore. Old friends who'd been constants for many years had already moved on. Many new attorneys began work, eager to impress. There were no more options for advancing my career path with the federal government in Miami. I had nowhere to go there but back to court, and I knew that I didn't want that. The next obvious step as a manager failed to materialize. Those who stood in the shadows for years, bolstered by close insiders, came out just in time to make a claim. And worse, after sixteen years, I had been essentially demoted in the program that I created.

The "what ifs" of leaving a routine that had gotten me so far no longer threatened to hold me in a pattern. Staying there was far more painful than venturing into the unknown. And the unknown, even though it could be a stressful proposition, felt somewhat more satisfying than giving up on myself before I actually began. Besides, I'd already declared that I'd had enough. I knew that there had to be more, and I was about to set out to find it. Excited, looking back with a smile, knowing that I could never return from whence I came, a new journey was beginning.

This process was built on faith, perhaps a little bit of egoic desperation, and a whole lot of proclamation. I was forever grateful for the angels along the way who showed up when I needed a bit of "living" inspiration to remind myself, even if I temporarily forgot, who I was becoming. The encouragement came as I stopped focusing on the safety of an office with a plaque on the wall that holds these words, "Wow what a ride!" and instead took the suggestion to heart and got ready to get out there to experience more of life. Get out there and skid broadside. Take the leap of faith and fly, doing things I never thought I could do.

Before I could take the final step and submit my resignation, officially ending my career there, I wanted my dad's blessing—the parental thumbs-up—that if I moved on, he would stand by me. Terrified, as I dialed his number, I reverted to when I was a little girl seeking my parents' approval. Knowing he had not supported me when I first broached the subject of leaving a safe and prestigious government career after my mom died, I worried that his possible disappointment would lead to a disavowal of me as his child now. But I, as a grown woman, had made my decision. There was no turning back, even if he was not on board. I held my breath as the phone rang, and I waited for him to pick up.

"Hello," he said.

"Dad, its Meg."

"Meggie, how are you? What's up?"

"Well," I nervously began, "I have something to tell you, and I'm not sure you'll like what I have to say."

"Okay, go on."

"I'm resigning from my job. I've had it. It's just one thing after another. I didn't get promoted. In fact, they demoted me on my own committee, and now they want me to move out of my office. I'm not happy here anymore. And this administration's toxic immigration policy is the final straw."

"You know, Meg," he paused, and I held my breath. Here it comes. "Screw them!" *What did he say?*

"Seriously, Meg. Go, if you think it's time to go. You're smart. I know that you're making this decision having given it much thought. Look, after forty-four years of working with a practice, I'm starting all over. I'm not ready to retire. I still want to be of service in a field I love. This is the best thing that could have happened for me. I should have done it sooner. I gave my everything to that practice, my blood, sweat, and tears. Now I get to treat my patients on my own terms. So do what you have to do!"

I couldn't believe my own ears. He continued, "You know the Latin phrase, *Illegitimi non carborundum*? You know what that means?"

"No, what?" I inquired, still in shock.

"Don't let the bastards get you down, Meg! You have my blessing. You hear me? Do what you have to do. I love you!"

Relieved, I replied, "Thank you so much—you have no idea what this means to me."

He reminded me, "It's never too late to start again."

As Merlin encouraged Arthur to pull the sword from the stone and answer the call, my dad gave me the encouragement I needed to start an adventure as a writer and motivational speaker, taking my place in this world. He gave me permission to create a better legacy, one that aligned with my purpose. The heaviness of having to go it alone fell away. This time when my old friend Fear materializes, like Rumi's poem "The Guest House," suggests, I'll close my eyes and visualize inviting her for tea. And the conversation would ensue:

Meg: *Here we are old friend.*

Fear: *Please don't do this, it's so painful to draw attention to us—to be out front for all the world to judge us. Stay in the shadows—it's safe there.*

Meg: *It may be safe, but how will we grow? We have come so far and made some big choices. Let the wounds heal, it's time.*

Fear: *I'm too scared of the pain of the past from words of ridicule and mean-spiritedness. What if they say we are an embarrassment or even worse a hypocrite? What if they judge us?*

Meg: *And what if they do? To not do something because of another's opinion is no way to live. We survived what we thought would kill us. It's time we believe in the beauty of our life and remind others of the same. It's time to give ourselves the approval that we have sought for so long.*

And on July 10, 2017, I printed out my letter of resignation. While short and sweet, I found the perfect words that summed up nearly two decades of my professional life, as follows:

This letter serves to inform the Miami OCC that my last day with this office will be August 4, 2017. It has been a distinct honor to serve the federal government and this country in my capacity as an attorney with INS and ICE for nearly twenty years. I will always be grateful for the opportunities that I have had to not only hone my craft as a litigator, but to train and mentor so many individuals during my tenure with this office. Of all my accomplishments during my career with this agency, the establishment of a well-respected and successful Miami OCC Intern Committee, together with the relationships and connections made will continue to be some of the greatest highlights for me.

I will always be grateful to be a part of DHS/OPLA, as this place will always be more than an office to me; it has been family.

Nervously, I signed a copy and walked up the stairs to the third floor to deliver it. I was hoping to just leave it on my supervisor's desk so I would not lose my nerve. While resolved to move on, I did my best to hold back tears as I felt the enormity of this decision. This wasn't the way I thought my career with the federal government would end. I'd had such high aspirations to make a positive difference moving up this ladder. I resolved that it was not going to happen.

Turning the corner, walking to the end of the hall, I saw him return to his desk. When I got to his door, I politely knocked to get his attention. He looked up.

"Do you have a minute?"

"Of course, come in," he replied. I sat down, mustered all the courage I could and with my head held high, I handed him my resignation.

He took it from me, looked at it and said, "You're sure about this?"

"I'm sure."

Then he asked about my plans. The realization sunk in that I did not have anything finite. The only thing I knew for sure was that he had my resignation in hand. I was walking away from the security of this job, along with the retirement and healthcare benefits it offered. While I was aware of the uncertainty that leaving presented, I knew staying there would be worse. I'd had enough of sitting by as other people got opportunity after opportunity. I did not have the energy to start proving myself to a person who saw my resume and still said I was not technically qualified without giving me any basis for this conclusion. And, while I was proud to have served my country for nearly two decades, I was embarrassed to even remotely be associated with the xenophobic immigration policies emerging from the current White House. It was time to move on.

Speak Your Truth, Even If Your Voice Shakes

While sightseeing that previous February in Philadelphia, "the City of Brotherly Love," my family and I walked through a Holocaust Memorial Park downtown. At the end of a lighted path, there stood a large gray slab marked by a quote from German Lutheran Pastor Martin Niemöller (1892–1984), an outspoken public foe of Adolf Hitler. It read:

> *"They came first for the Communists, and I didn't speak up because I wasn't a Communist. They came for the Jews, and I didn't speak up because I wasn't a Jew. Then they came for the trade unionists, and I didn't speak up because I wasn't a trade unionist. Then they came for the Catholics, and I didn't speak up because I was a Protestant. Then they came for me, and by that time no one was left to speak up."*

In light of the tumultuous political climate in the United States after the 2016 presidential election, these powerful words really impacted me. I questioned whether history was repeating itself. Clearly this could happen again where people stay silent as they see many wooed by the evil rhetoric spewed with such determined aim at the perceived weakest members of society—nationalistic ideas defined by race and rooted in a disdain for foreigners here and around the world. How could the United States have a leader who not only amassed power for his own personal gain, but espoused policies like the Muslim ban, the border wall, and family separation? As a third-generation Italian American, there was no way I could support a xenophobic policy or work for an executive branch that played to the worst aspects of humanity. What happened to substance, rational sound values, and policies meant to unite a divided nation?

We were already a great country made up of a beautiful and diverse citizenry. From the words of Lin Manuel Miranda's *Hamilton*, I couldn't help but think that to maintain the integrity of this American experiment built upon the rule of law, it's true that "history has its eyes on you." I am certain that our forefathers and foremothers would hope the answer would be to build on an American dream that was envisioned long ago and improved upon with time, not destroyed.

The week after the results of the presidential election, a friend of mine, who was inspired to do something when her son told her "Mommy, the bully won," called for a community meeting as a call to action at a local establishment. That gathering was the beginning of a new grassroots group that would be called the PerSisters. About twenty of us showed up, desperate to stand against hate and organize to protect our democracy. Starting with the peaceful Women's March on January 21, 2017, our group, instead of staying silent, chose to stand up, for not only women's rights and immigrants' rights, but for human rights here and around the world. Preparing a strategy of canvassing, voter registration, and supporting candidates in line with our beliefs, we as a growing group decided against apathy to fight for what made this country great in the past and present.

In September 2017, a month after my resignation, I was asked by a fellow PerSister to moderate a discussion of immigration on a panel of three entitled "The American Dream, Whose Is It Anyway?" following a play called "Building the Wall." Brought to the Adrienne Arsht Center for the Performing Arts of Miami–Dade County by City Theatre, Pulitzer Prize and Tony Award-winning playwright Robert Schenkkan's play was presented as a response to Trump and his anti-immigration campaign rhetoric. Revealing a scenario of how campaign promises becoming law might lead to a terrifying, seemingly inconceivable, yet inevitable conclusion, the drama was set in the very near future, after the election, as a Trump administration carries out its promise to round up and detain millions of immigrants, following a terrorist attack in Times Square. This illuminating drama delivered a powerful warning and put a human face on the inhumane, showing how the inconceivable becomes inevitable when personal accountability is denied. Leading a panel of two immigration lawyers and a professor with a question and answer follow-up, I was ready. About to be liberated to speak my truth, this would only be the beginning.

CHAPTER 20:

Dear Uncle Sam...

"There is always so much ahead, and it is so clearly seen. . . ."
—**DOROTHEA BRANDE**, 1893–1948, American writer

August 4, 2017

A final glance around the room taking in the love gained from years of serving together. One last opportunity to express my gratitude for this part of my journey. One last sentiment of profound appreciation for the honor and privilege to see this dream of public service unfold. One last smile acknowledging the lessons learned and the friendships made. This morning, many members of my office, both attorneys and support staff, gathered in the conference room on the third floor for my final breakfast farewell.

I had visualized what this would look and feel like for quite some time. One of my closest friends said a few words and gave me a framed poster that read "It Always Seems Impossible Until It Is Done." Another one dear to my heart showcased her creative edge when she presented me with a giant replica of my face made out of candy. Because I made my interns put their intentions for the summer on butterfly cutouts that I taped to my door, they presented me a butterfly diploma from the imaginary Farfalla University signed by all of them. How appropriate; I felt like I was graduating.

"What are your plans next?" This was a repeated question.

I had a visual, nothing concrete. Was I crazy that I trusted that I would figure it out and find my way? I replied, "Marketing my book and actively writing to finish the next one. I'm giving myself a break from the practice of law for now, taking a sabbatical, and planning for my nonprofit S.H.I.N.E. in October. Come and join us!"

When the breakfast was winding down, my supervisor took the stage. This was it, this was the moment that would mark the culmination of nearly twenty years of service. Excited to hear what he had to say, I was also looking forward to receiving the traditional DHS plaque commemorating my service with the government.

He started, "With these final parting words, we wish you well and thank you for all that you have done for the Miami OCC. Your contribution with the intern program, as its first legal intern coordinator, was key to sixteen years of development and employment of many exceptional former interns who now work for OPLA. We hope you realize your dreams and will miss you as you embark on a new path." Then he looked at a piece of cardboard embossed with the DHS seal. "Many at the satellite offices still want to sign this, so once we give them a chance, we will send it to you. Good luck Meg!"

"Where is the plaque?" I whispered to myself. I was grateful, but I thought, *That's it, no plaque? Everyone gets one when they leave, why not me?* At first, I thought it was an oversight and asked the HR person what happened. She didn't know. She said my supervisor was responsible for requesting it. I was embarrassed for having said something. I got angry at myself for expecting more. But it was very important to me; it would have meant a lot. Symbolic perhaps, proof that I spent nearly twenty years there. I was so disappointed. Heartbroken really. In their estimation, after all my hard work, I wasn't even worthy of a plaque. A perfect end and one final push on that door forever shut. No turning back now. *Dear Uncle Sam, it was a pleasure to serve, but Lady Liberty is calling my name.*

And before I closed the door one last time to Room 256, my corner office since 2003, I looked around, breathed deeply, and took it all in. The walls that once boasted my diplomas and colorful Romero Britto paintings now were bare. The tops of the bookshelves that displayed photos of my loved ones and friends and the chairs that provided comfort for the lively conversations over various topics all sat empty. And the desk that used to be covered with my files and papers lay clear, waiting for its next occupant. Other than a tiara left on top, there was no other evidence that I had ever been there. I smiled, knowing full well that a chapter of my story had ended, and another was just beginning. I felt like Mary Tyler Moore did as she closed out the last episode in the final scene of her groundbreaking show. Just as a very emotional Mary looked back, I leaned my head against the door, taking in one last moment on that steamy August afternoon. I held back tears and closed the door. At the same time, one of my friends called out to me, "Don't be late for your own celebration!"

I replied, "I'm coming!"

I looked at my name plate one last time. As I left the building, I noticed the inspirational magnets I gifted to my coworkers, coined as "megnets," that were still there. How appropriate that Henry David Thoreau's quote was the last one I saw, "Go confidently in the direction of your dreams! Live the life you've imagined."

All around me, I hear stories of people's lives undergoing big changes, leaving jobs, relationships, places, or habits that no longer serve them. *"I left my spouse," "I left the corporate world," "I spoke up for myself,"* or *"I moved to a new place."* Many no longer suck it up or tolerate the hand that was dealt to them. They stand strong and make the decision to quit and move on. Now I was one of those people, hoping there would be much that lay ahead and a clarity that is finally seen.

Memories. The words of the poet Etienne de Grellet spoke to me: "I shall not pass this way but once; any good that I can do or any kindness I can show to any human being, let me do it now. Let me not defer or neglect it, for I shall not pass this way again." I did my best to be kind to those with whom I interacted. During my long career, one such case I will never forget involved a young girl with a hemangioma, a bright red birthmark that covered the right side of her face. Her mother was seeking a form of relief called cancellation of removal from the United States. In support of the application, the fifteen-year-old, as the qualifying United States citizen relative, testified on her mother's behalf. I was so impressed with how courageous she was to share how painful the surgeries to correct her defect had been. She talked about the harassment she suffered at the behest of the other children. She told the court how important it had been that her mother championed her every step of the way. She openly unveiled the vulnerability of her story for all to hear.

At the end of the hearing, I asked opposing counsel if I could address the young girl. He looked to his client and she nodded yes. I grabbed her hand and looked her in the eye, remembering how she said that the other children bullied her incessantly.

"I see you, and you are a beautiful girl. So brave and courageous! Please never forget these words, you're special and will make a difference in this world. I know it. Look at what you did for your mother. I'm so proud of you."

There were many instances where I felt great pride in my work. There were many times when I met the government's burden of handling the prosecution of criminal cases where the respondents had hurt other people, stolen, or lied, and did not merit relief. And there were many times when I exercised discretion in favor of giving a second chance. I was fair, respectful in court to all parties concerned, and proud of my work there. Despite how let down I felt by him, I emailed the head of the Miami office before I left:

> I wanted to wish you well for future success for both you and your family here in South Florida. Paths always cross for a reason, I'm very glad to have made your acquaintance in the short time you were with the Miami OCC. Until we meet again, best of luck, and I hope that your vision and leadership inspire others to bring their talents to the table and propel all your employees to see their own greatness, thus encouraging them on past their comfort zone to great things.

I did not know him. He did not know me. I only spoke to him a handful of times. He happened to be the messenger. He was the deliverer of the final decisive blow that allowed me to choose a different path, close a door, and climb up a different ladder. I supposed I should be grateful.

After all, this door closed was what I wanted now, but still my precious ego took a serious hit. I had no idea who I was without this job.

As I placed the rest of my things in the trunk of my SUV, I turned around to look at the building one last time. I made a mental note that the only leaders who ever showed any interest in my professional development in this agency were women. Two senior, female mentors who actually cared about my career there, appreciated my talents, and supported my endeavors. They empowered me to want to do a better job and keep going. And through their examples, I did the same with the people I mentored. They were the ones who inspired greatness in me and encouraged me to use my talents as a leader. One went above and beyond to offer me an opportunity. I remember her words to me when I had to decline it:

Please keep up your interest in management. I think that you will make a very good one someday.

The other offered me support and guidance when I faced a hostile workplace. She allowed me a safe space to talk to get more clarity. As women who had experience navigating this agency, I appreciated and learned so much from both of them. In the next chapter of my professional career, I would make it my mission to help other women know their worth too. At the end of this road, I was climbing out of a box. I just had to pay attention to what opportunities came my way.

"See you at the Blue Martini, Meg!" my friend called out.

I answered back, "See you there!"

CHAPTER 21:

Awaken to Your True Calling

"As you navigate through the rest of your life, be open to collaboration. Other people and other people's ideas are often better than your own. Find a group of people who challenge and inspire you, spend a lot of time with them, and it will change your life."
—AMY POEHLER, comedian and Boston College graduate

End of August 2017

In numerology, 2017 was a one universal year that promised major changes, increased energy across the board on a worldwide scale, and new directions for many of us. Emboldened, no longer the victim, I followed the necessary path of transition. You would think the decision to make the move itself would be the hardest part. But I knew in reality that the follow-up, the becoming, would be the challenge. There is an energy that supports catapulting one into space, what NASA would refer to as the "escape velocity"—the final push needed to take a person home. Once you buckle up and jump in, fire up the engines, and let go, you will catapult into a better, more exciting, and magical life if you allow it. All the strategic planning in the world couldn't prepare me for the unfolding of the next part of my journey after my *big* move, but I jumped in.

True to his word, at the end of August, Dr. Habib connected me to the band tour assistant of Coldplay, who provided tickets to the concert with friends and family room access to the pre-show and the after-party. With a group of my friends who donated to Love Button, my daughter

Ava and I set out on a balmy and rainy August evening in Miami to experience Coldplay's A Head Full of Dreams Tour as it lit up Hard Rock Stadium. And the band did not disappoint; it was by far one of the greatest concerts I have ever been to. Flashing our Love Button Banners for all to see, with eleven others by my side, we sang "Yellow" at the top of our lungs and danced like there was no tomorrow. Described as a Technicolor feast for the eyes by the *Miami New Times*, we woke up as the party continued, accented by brightly colored confetti, vibrant lasers, glowing tempo-coordinated audience wristbands, and multicolored balloons.

At the end of the show, four of us took off to the after-party. It was nearly two in the morning by the time we arrived at the Confidante Hotel on Miami Beach. My friend and I were feeling a little bit guilty about keeping our kids out late on a school night. Convinced that this was a once-in-a-lifetime experience, we went in to see what the rest of the evening had in store. My daughter and I thanked the band tour assistant for our tickets and the fabulous time. The inside of the bar was packed, so we retreated for a bit outside on the terrace until we decided to call it a night. On our way out, we saw lead singer, Chris Martin, at the bar. When he started to walk away, my friend called out his name, and he stopped. When we had his attention, she said, "Hello, Chris, we want to introduce you to our girls."

He looked down and shook their hands.

I added, "It's so nice to meet you. I'm one of Dr. Habib's friends, and we enjoyed the fundraiser in May. We're all big fans. What an amazing and inspiring show."

"Hello, so nice to meet you—thank you for coming!"

My daughter said, "Oh, my God! I'm so amazed."

Chris said, "Why?"

"I'm just a little girl from a little school, and you're Coldplay—you're famous."

"You know what, I was like you once, a little boy with big dreams." And with that, he gave her his electric blue Love Button hat, said his goodbyes, and left. Ava lit up, and so did I. We are all little children with big dreams; the key is to not give up.

Still on cloud nine, the day after the concert I got a text from Dr. Habib's office in California. "Good morning, Sis! Here is something from your family." Displayed on my phone was a photo of Chris holding *The Magical Guide to Bliss*. I wanted him to have my book and there he was, book in hand.

I replied simply to Dr. Habib, "Thank you!"

September to October 2017

The high continued until restlessness and impatience set in and highlighted for me the challenges that come with transition. The pendulum of my emotions shifted daily from joy, excitement, and endless possibilities to sadness, disappointment, and anger. At first, I rebelled against routine. I woke up when I wanted to, got dressed if I felt like it. I balked at any type of schedule other than to walk and take care of my dogs. After I resigned, I moved nearly twenty years of boxes filled with stuff, books, and important papers into our dining room, where they waited to be dealt with. Each day that I didn't handle the mess, I grew increasingly overwhelmed by the sheer immensity of the task. My engines were burning out. I had my freedom now, but what was I going to do with it?

Toward the middle of September 2017, I felt stuck in the identity conundrum. I had played the role of government immigration attorney my entire career. Now I wanted nothing to do with any of it. Who was I now? As part of the coaching course, thank God, I could interact with my fellow peer coaches with some consistency. Otherwise, this extrovert would have been too isolated and very lost. I knew I wanted to finish the memoir I'd started years before, but I promised myself it needed a happy ending. At this point, I had no idea what that looked like. And I was *not* happy. In July, before I left the agency, I had made a new vision board. I grabbed it for reference. Loaded with so many great ideas, I knew that I had to start somewhere if I were serious about my goals as I'd set them out.

After coming to terms with the fact that I was going through another type of grieving process, this time because of a change I chose, I knew I needed to take meaningful steps to get organized. Who will I become without the titles I had acquired? I couldn't see my way through without making a dent in the clutter all around me. Because I didn't have an office space in my condominium, I couldn't accommodate all the stuff I'd brought home. With the help of one of my peer coaches, I started the process of setting out to weed through everything, shred documents, journal about what happened, and figure out my next move.

At the start of a new week, I woke up with a goal in mind to divide and conquer. I partitioned the room into five sections, each day tackling one. From the crack of dawn until late in the evening, I created two piles: keep what was necessary and move out the rest. Slowly, I could see my dining room table emerging. As I cleared each sector, I was no longer a candidate for the show *Hoarders*. Instead, I believed that my progress would even be heralded for display on the *Marie Kondo* show. With the help of my husband, I picked out an area in my bedroom for a desk and a bookshelf. After the week was done, I could see for the first time in a month how to navigate through.

Hiring a marketing company and graphics designer, I revamped the cover of *The Magical Guide to Bliss*, updated the bio, and republished it as a second edition, hoping to give it and my career as an author and speaker new energy. Now, having chosen to sail my own ship, hating the notion that I would have to go it all alone, I looked to other creative collaborators to help me finish the journey that had begun with a vision nearly seven years earlier. It was time to get my happy ending and figure out what my mother was trying to tell me with the vision of the lighthouse. I wanted to walk Paulo Coelho's *Pilgrimage* and get my message at the end of the world, also called Finisterre. So I called the only adventure traveler that I knew, Heidi, whom I'd met in 2015 at my first S.H.I.N.E. event, *Claim Your Tiara*.

In the midst of getting ready for our third S.H.I.N.E. in October, Dream, Believe, Create, I reached out to Heidi to invite her to present as a speaker.

"Heidi, do you want to speak at S.H.I.N.E. this year?"

"I would love to, when is it?"

"October—will you be around or wandering the globe?" I hoped against hope knowing that it was a possibility.

"I'll be in town, sign me up!

"Amazing!" I continued, "It's going to be amazing. I also have another idea that I think you might be interested in. Have you ever walked the spiritual pilgrimage to Santiago de Compostela in Northern Spain?"

"No, but I have always wanted to."

"Heidi," I excitedly shared with her my idea, "would you be interested in helping me set up a S.H.I.N.E. Adventure on El Camino? We can pitch it at S.H.I.N.E."

"Absolutely, wow I've never been, and I really have always wanted to go. What do you have in mind?" As we talked, we both got excited at the possibility of this happening.

"I want to walk a route to get to Santiago in a week, I'm not looking to rough it in hostels, I want to stay in nice hotels with private bath accommodations, and at the end we have to finish up at the lighthouse at Finisterre. Do you think this can be done?"

"Well, this is going to be wonderful. Let's see."

We spent the rest of the conversation discussing details. She said she had a contact she would reach out to and asked me to find out which dates in April would work for a nine-day journey: one day flying to Santiago, six days walking, one day to Finisterre, then a final day flying home. Once the details were ironed out, we would send out a marketing postcard to see who wanted to join us. It looked like this was really going to happen. I started to get excited. I was going to see the lighthouse. Thoughts make things. I had been chasing this vision since the day my mother died. Now that the foundation was set, we both sent out an invitation email to those we thought would be interested and waited to see who would make up the cast of characters for this magical journey.

On October 21, the night of our third S.H.I.N.E. Networking event, at the end of Heidi's presentation, we promoted the S.H.I.N.E. Adventure. And, on the following Monday, we already had 10 individuals signed up. At the outset, I had no idea how I was going to pull this idea off—now, I was excited that with help everything was coming together. I started to feel a little less terrified—like there would be movement forward and a payoff for taking that huge leap of faith starting over. Maybe I would get some closure at the lighthouse after-all. On that same Monday in the evening, I got a call from a former colleague who reminded me of a younger version of myself— I referred to her as my "mini-me." I personally hired and mentored her for years as a legal intern —was so excited when she was ultimately hired at DHS. Because we remained very close after I resigned, my former supervisor asked if she could deliver a package to me. I told her to come over—I was home.

When she arrived, she presented me with a wrapped item that looked to be the shape of a rather large picture frame. After we caught up a bit then said our goodbyes, I went upstairs to my condo and curiously opened it. Inside was the same piece of cardboard embossed with the DHS seal that my supervisor had at my farewell breakfast, only now it was signed with personal messages written by forty of my former colleagues and beautifully framed.

One message from a dear friend quoted Henry Ford—"Whether you think you can or can't, you're right." Then she set forth:

Thanks for the great Megnet, the great friendship, + the great times. You will continue to be spectacular at whatever you choose. Your charisma, intelligence and brilliant interpersonal skills will carry you through anything.

Another stated,

Good luck Meg—Butterfly lady. I know you will continue to provide inspiration to others as you follow your bliss.

As I read each note, I felt a sense of melancholy for my office and my old life. Mostly, I deeply missed my friends who I spent years with, getting to know and sharing our lives and the certainty of a routine and a place to go. When I got to what my former supervisor wrote, his words surprised me:

Dear Meg, You have been an indefatigable force of generosity and encouragement for so many, including over 300 grateful interns. We will miss you, but know that you are courageously pursuing your dreams and have no doubt they will be realized.

Then he quoted my words from my book, *The Magical Guide to Bliss*:

". . . and the mystery will unfold, enlightening you to serve exactly in the way you are meant to. MGB2B-10/2 Service Through Action."

As I read that, I felt all the pent-up anger that I had repressed for the past months rise up within me—until I let out a desperate cry and fell to the ground now fully letting it go and with that let the tears flow. As writing has been a part of my healing process, I decided to send an email to my former supervisor the next morning sharing with him what this gift meant to me:

The past almost three months I have had to process so much— most importantly the question, what do I have to show for the last 20 years of my professional career? And, I had to deal with so much anger because I kept asking the question did I stay too long? Yesterday, when the beautifully framed seal arrived with all the signatures of people that I have grown to know and love for the better part of the last 20 years, I finally understood—a plaque will never embody what I experienced at DHS. I had the privilege of working side by side with the best people along with the honor of inspiring students in their professional careers! And, you played a part there too—because truth be told, you were kind and understanding when the most traumatic experience of my life happened—I will always remember that, no matter what.

God closes one door and opens another —and I shall take with me all these lessons learned. While I will never have the distinction that I thought I wanted in the agency, I shall have it out in the world doing probably what is more aligned with my spirit and heart. This was the answer I was looking for. So I walk this part of my journey with a whole lot of faith because now I am making it up as I go along. Divinely inspired and guided by my little magical book too— all the wisdom my mother gave me is in there. So the mystery will unfold to serve exactly in the way that we are all meant to after all! You, my friend, will remain in my thoughts and prayers. Thank you for the seal- it has given me closure of this chapter. I can truly move on now.

He emailed me back:

Thank you for sharing your thoughts and feelings with me. You have touched me and many others over the years, and I will always think of you with fondness and affection. I think of you and your perennial "One Door Opens" hopefulness, and even keep your "Love" button with my reminders, next to my work station. I agree that, in the end, it is only our love of God, family, friends and the kindness shown to others that counts. It was my privilege to be with you during your difficult days, and to see you come back into the sunlight. I know it is your deep love that caused you to suffer so much with the loss of your mom. But, we know that love, like all of your most treasured memories of her, will endure. You and your sisters will remain her gift on this earth, just as Michael and Ava have been to you and Frank. In our faith we are called to believe this is not the end, but just a brief moment in time before we one day reunite. Your brother in Christ!

Reading this, I smiled from ear to ear. Grateful, it was time to see what was waiting for me. Taking with me what matters most—love and friendship, and the reminder my friend Luisa sent on a card, "Don't be afraid, just believe." (Mark 5:36b)

November 2017

The trip was booked, and sixteen pilgrims, a term used to describe one who journeys in foreign lands, showed up. Closing my eyes, I saw the lighthouse against a blue sky. I remembered the burst of white light that blinded me, and then heard her sweet, exhausted plea, "Let me go!"

Almost seven years ago, I thought I would never be able to handle a world without her in it. Almost seven years ago, I thought that anxiety, depression, and grief would hold me captive to a life filled with fear and unhappiness. Almost seven years ago, instead of giving up, I got the help I needed and faced my demons as I started walking out of the darkness. And now I had to prepare myself for a lot of actual walking. I really had no idea what I was in for.

I loved spinning. That was my favorite form of exercise. I loved dancing at Red Bike studios, lights turned down, club lights on, the Chainsmokers' "Waterbed" playing loudly. So much fun, and time passed quickly. I was aerobically fit, so what was a couple of miles walking a day. But as word got out that I was going on El Camino, everyone wanted to share their Camino survival story, from horrible blisters to exhaustion. I didn't want to hear any of it. I eschewed any and all research and figured I would face what I had to on the road itself. I was going to get closure at the lighthouse; this pilgrimage had a higher purpose for me.

Guided by wanderlust and whatever else drove each of us, in less than five months, our group would travel from Malaysia, Florida, Georgia, Illinois, Michigan, and Wisconsin to meet in Spain. This trip would mirror the last 111 km of Coelho's walk along the famous Camino de Santiago (St. James' Way) with travel days from April 13 until April 22 of 2018. We would end our S.H.I.N.E. finale at Finisterre, the oceanside town where the lighthouse I saw in my vision stood. Now I needed to figure out what I needed to do. Everything was set; I just had to get ready.

December 2017 through February 2018

On December 1, I celebrated my forty-eighth birthday at Blue Martini. Gathering my friends, we set out to spend the night dancing and drinking at a bar where salsa and lively music would launch my year of empowerment. I was feeling no pain, the champagne was flowing, and toward the end of the evening, as we were jumping and singing, my feet went one way and my back another. I felt a sharp stabbing pain on the left side of my body and nearly fell to the floor. The champagne and mixed drinks dulled the pain enough for me to get home in one piece. However, when the numbing effect of the alcohol wore off, I felt everything from the middle of my back, shooting down my left leg. The next day when my friend called to see how I was feeling, I said, "What happened last night? I feel like I pulled every muscle in my back. I'm getting old. My body is not cooperating with my spirit."

She answered, "Oh no! We definitely had a lot of fun. Happy, happy birthday. Rest up—I'll check on you later to see how you feel."

"Thank you so much." After I hung up, I got out of bed and winced forward in pain. I couldn't even stand up straight without a spasm. So much for getting ready to train and feeling empowered.

Over the next two months, instead of easing up, it got progressively worse. I started to worry that I had really hurt myself and would not be able to go to Spain. As each day passed, April swiftly approaching, I grew more and more anxious. Not even remotely convinced that I would be able to sit for the ten-hour flight to cross the Atlantic, how would I be able to walk El Camino as well? The only experience that I ever had hiking was when I went to camp in Clyde, North Carolina. I remembered that I could barely complete the one-day trail up to Chimney Rock. In less than two months, I would have to do a hike like that times six.

I was tight all over. Hoping to stretch enough to work out the pressure on my nerves, I tried using a rolling bar. Lowering myself to the floor in my bedroom, I placed the bar under the middle of my back. Rolling my body up and down putting pressure on the left side, I felt a stabbing pain and winced in agony.

"Oh no, oh no!" I cried.

"What happened, Meg?" Frank asked.

"I can't get up. I can't get up."

He bent down to grab my hand to move me to a sitting position. "Stop, stop. I can't move. Oh no! Oh no! What did I do?"

He went into the kitchen to get ice. Then, through the pain, after a few tries, he got me to my feet so I could lie on top of a yoga ball that sat in the corner of my room. I started to cry. At least before my brilliant attempt at release, I could move, albeit gingerly. Now I could not even get up off the floor by myself. It hurt to sit, stand, walk, or anything else that involved my back. "What am I going to do now?"

After a week of utter agony, I needed a plan, so I brought in the big guns. I started out with visits to my chiropractor, who also practiced a technique called Unified Therapy. Once a week, he worked on aligning my back while helping me to release my fear around this trip. Twice a week, I went to see my physical therapist; she assigned my case to one of her staff members who coincidentally had walked the Camino as a teenager. While giving me exercises to gain mobility, working on a mind-body-spirit angle, he also convinced me that I would be ready to go by the middle of April.

I worried out loud, "I can hardly sit, forget about walking."

"Meg, listen, I walked El Camino, and it's not as hard as you think."

"Really? I haven't even started to train."

"These exercises I'm giving you will help loosen your back. The body needs to stretch. If you commit to this, then you will be ready to go."

I stated, "I'm going to hold you to that."

He laughed. "Yep, that's my job, give you tools to help yourself. All of this—the massage, heat treatment, ice—will slowly help you regain movement."

Having successfully worked with Symmetry Physical Therapy before when I hurt my sacroiliac joint, I came back each time, needing to believe him. Finally, I went back to my acupuncturist and massage therapist every other week to help reduce the inflammation and release the knots and tension in my muscles. I had a plan. I may not be training like I'd planned, but I was giving my body tools to work through the pain I was experiencing. I felt I was improving somewhat, upbeat and optimistic. I was actually feeling excited and happy for the first time in a long while. That was until I turned on the television on Valentine's Day morning.

"Breaking News" screamed out in bold on all the local and national channels. Another deadly school shooting had occurred, this time way too close to home, in my sister Mary's neighborhood. Watching what was going on at a high school in Parkland, Florida, I cried as reporters announced that many students had perished. I fell on my knees praying for those families who were affected. Then I called Mary to find out if my nephews were out of harm's way. When she confirmed they were home with her, paralyzed with fear, I let my tears come, greatly saddened by what was unfolding both nearby and in the world.

February 28, 2018, The Love Button Delegation, Parkland, Florida

All major news channels reported that on February 14, 2018, a nineteen-year-old gunman had opened fire with a semiautomatic rifle at Marjory Stoneman Douglas High School in Parkland, Florida, killing seventeen people and wounding seventeen others. Parkland, about forty-five minutes away from Miami, was the next town over from where Mary lived. Her kids went to high school nearby. As the media covered the aftermath, the entire community locally and nationally was devastated. And that this horrific event happened on a day that was supposed to celebrate love on the planet did not make sense.

On February 28, two weeks later, Dr. Habib and Dr. Sherry traveled across the country from Los Angeles to meet up with a delegation of Love Button supporters in Parkland. We gathered together to spread the nonprofit organization's message of love in the midst of the tremendous sadness. Love Button mobilized in service to support a community healing and distributed thousands of Love Buttons to students, their families, and the community at large. As a Love Button Ambassador, I was a part of that group. Also a representative of Love Button, Chris Martin of Coldplay came in under the radar with the sole purpose of meeting with and offering solace to those affected.

I met up with Dr. Habib and Dr. Sherry before we all gathered at the Coral Springs Museum of Art, and I talked with them about my upcoming pilgrimage. Dr. Habib suggested that I dedicate a part of my walk in honor of the Parkland victims. He then offered Love Buttons so that, as an ambassador, I could hand them out to everyone I met along the way, elevating the energy of love.

"What a great idea. What a great way to honor them. How special."

"You can carry a button in honor of each one," he said.

"I will."

"When do you go?" he asked.

"Friday, April thirteenth. Italians say that thirteen is a lucky number. That's a good omen."

Having expressed her excitement, Dr. Sherry said, "After seeing the movie *The Way*, I want to walk it myself one day. I can't wait to hear all about it when you get back."

Before we left, our Love Button team formed a circle and held hands. Dr. Habib asked us to open our hearts to be of loving service to the community and to offer moments of peace in order for seeds of healing to take root. Dr. Steve Stone, executive director of the Memphis Friendship Foundation and self-described "sold-out Jesus follower," asked that the Holy Spirit work through all of us that day.

As a member of the sisterhood group founded by Denise called Sisters in Spirit of South Florida, the weekend before I'd volunteered to participate in a Girls' Empowerment Retreat with the Overtown Optimist Club. I brought a Love Button prayer flag and asked the girls who attended if they wanted to sign it, leaving messages of sympathy for those who lost their lives. After visiting and paying our respects to the seventeen at their makeshift memorials in a field nearby the school, I left the Love Button flag at the town's amphitheater near the place where one of seventeen four-foot-tall angels stood. We then traveled over to the museum together.

In line with the teachings in his book *The Clarity Cleanse*, Dr. Habib and Dr. Sherry started off the healing circle providing words of comfort and relief to the distressed families. Then the Marjory Stoneman Douglas drama students who founded Shine MSD moved all of us to tears when they offered an impromptu acapella version of their song "Shine," written by Andrea Peña and Sawyer Garrity. They dedicated their performance to the victims and survivors, promising that together they would shine their light and become something special. There was a moment where Dr. Habib asked all of us to silently move around the room and look into the eyes of another, practicing "soul gazing." There was a woman there whose name I didn't know, but I saw her and felt her intense sadness, and from my heart I cried with her without saying a word.

Why do we do what we do? I think connecting is why, so each of us knows that we are not going through all of this "alone." Because no one really is alone—it's just an illusion! There is faith in a humanity that sets aside reason and comes together stronger based in love. After leaving at the end of the day, I was still deeply affected by those who had lost so much. It seemed to me that when it comes to matters of the heart, when one person is affected, we all are impacted. So perhaps, if that is the case, in addition to walking in memory of my mother, I committed to honoring the lives of the Parkland victims. Maybe something that I experienced from this powerful day would impact my pilgrimage and revive my sense of spirit and my desire to walk in a positive way among the living again, in honor of those whose lives were lost. At least, that was my hope.

April 2018

By the time April rolled around, I had completed two full months of therapies. Three to four times during those weeks I would dutifully keep each appointment and do my follow-up exercises in hopes that I would be ready to go on April 13. I never even had a chance to complete one hike in preparation. To be honest, I didn't want to anyway. I resigned myself to the fact that whatever I did to prepare would have to suffice. It would be a baptism by fire. I committed to going on El Camino. I convinced others to join me. Already answering the call to adventure, I'd crossed the first threshold by quitting my job. I was sure this back issue must be some kind of test, an initial challenge along my hero's journey to see how much I really wanted to get to the other end. Long before I ever took the first step on the road itself, the pilgrimage had already begun.

We had plans to go see my nephew perform in Carnegie Hall in New York City the week before I was scheduled to leave. This would be a test flight to see if I could handle three hours on a plane. Sitting in the aisle seat on our flight to La Guardia, I did my best to get comfortable. When we arrived, my whole family gathered to celebrate his performance. The next day we went to St. Patrick's Cathedral, where my parents had celebrated the sacrament of marriage in 1965. My extended family showed up and took up two full rows. As was our tradition, my father started us off with a prayer of thanksgiving as he asked my mom to continue to watch over all of us. Then we lit candles in one of the many alcoves.

After the mass, I went up to one of the priests and asked, "Do you think you can bless me? I'm leaving next week for the northern part of Spain to walk El Camino."

He smiled and said, "Everyone has a Camino story. I have read so many accounts of transformational experiences there."

I smiled and said, "Yes, I need as many blessings as I can get to protect us all so that it's an amazing time of spiritual growth."

He placed his hand on my head. "God, watch and protect her and all who join with her so that they find what they are seeking, in the name of the Father, the Son, and the Holy Spirit."

Before he walked away, he turned to me and said, "Good luck and *Buen Camino*."

I smiled, "Thank you—you too."

Back in Miami, packing to go, upon Heidi's recommendation I ordered my walking sticks, got my hiking sneakers, bought two packs of brand-new cotton socks, purchased a mini backpack to carry with me during the day, and found a colorful windbreaker to keep me warm and dry. I also received a package from Dr. Habib and Dr. Sherry, with instructions not to open it until I got on the plane to Spain.

Still really nervous, I got excited visualizing how I would feel when I arrived at Finisterre, my final destination. I imagined that l would humbly kneel at the end with my mom's celestial body at my side, setting out a prayer of thanksgiving for everything that had shown up on this journey to give me hope and strength when I thought I couldn't go on. And there it will be, that lighthouse that she sent me in that vision seven years ago when her soul moved on. And Paulo, dear wise Paulo Coelho, my masculine spirit guide as I wrote my way out, he too would symbolically be there, for I had followed his lead, believed in myself, and earned my sword in the form of Love Buttons, now a warrior for love.

April 12, 2018, *The Seventh Anniversary of My Mother's Passing*

We are not here to grow comfortably numb. This is not why we have shown up at this time or this place in this world. A life so constrained by judgments or mores, we—I—can't do that anymore! Seven years ago, my mother left the physical plane. She would be joining me as I set out in two days on the adventure I sought to shake out of the doldrums. If that meant stepping out of my comfort zone for one moment, one hour, one season, I would do what I needed to do to uncover the answers that reside within and get my happy ending to this chapter.

Wake up to that truth. Wake up to the belief that this body is the vessel, the beautiful, perfect vessel whose energy attracts me to others, whose energy is the invitation to what I most truly want or desire, whose energy will bring me what I am willing and consciously setting out to find. I will put one foot in front of the other, mile by mile, and one memory to the next. Awake, alive, aroused—I will let the world permeate my very being, allowing my soul to blossom and, along with it, the dream that was born in me long ago.

I refuse to believe that the child within me is gone. I stand up against the notion that the dream has dissipated with her celestial body. I will not remain comfortably numb. That is not why I am here. That is not why I have shown up at this time. My life is no longer constrained by judgments or mores. It is love that I ultimately serve—for that I move on and out of the invisible cage doors—opening up my world to a new beginning each morning when I open my eyes to life. Ovid wrote, "Fortune and love favor the brave." Yes, I choose to be brave, and with that choice I will love and feel loved—no longer numb.

After discussing with my son why I chose to go on this trip and do something in the face of a world gone awry, I told him my mother would always say, "You fight evil with good." Then I wrote him this poem:

I will not stand by and watch things of hate just unfold.
You were born from glory and that story will be told.
To sit on a throne and look down throwing gold,
Will do none of us good for our souls won't be sold.

Instead I rise up for justice with others who are bold,
And speak truth to wrongs, we will not be so trolled.
And my wish for you child as you grow to be old,
Never take for granted your blessings,
For others gave life for love to take hold.

The following is an entry from my journal written on the eve of the pilgrimage:

Tomorrow, I leave for El Camino, with nothing blocking my way now. My mentor, Dr. Habib, texted me:

Go on the pilgrimage first. That walk will open up everything for you. . . . Your book, The Magical Guide to Bliss, is the manual for transformation.

I look forward to what I will discover on this pilgrimage. I am as ready as I ever will be: trust the process and hopefully transformation will follow. I will have my mom's purple butterfly with me the whole way and over eight hundred Love Buttons too. Like the song, sung by the late Doris Day, "Que Sera," "Whatever will be, will be." Mommy, I am open and willing to receive, keeping your legacy alive. And creating my own. When I close my eyes, you're still here, just a little beyond the veil. Your three little ones and soul mate are still making magic right where you left off, with you watching over us and keeping us safe. I am curious as to the blessings I know will come. Definitely not traditional, open to everything, my father calls me "spiritually eclectic," one of the best compliments I've ever gotten.

There comes a time when you come to that place where you have no idea what is next. When your dreams have been realized to a certain extent and you have reached a crossroads. There you need to start trusting your instincts. Start taking your own advice. Be smart—use the God-given brains and talents you were born with to get intentional. And for goodness sake, shut out all the naysaying that the world of Muggles and mere mortals are trying to dish out. You keep taking the next best step. You keep hoping that your faith will carry you through. You keep on moving forward. And show up as authentically *you*! I say a prayer of gratitude for this insight as I promise to carry and deliver the healing intentions entrusted to me by my friends and family at El Monte do Gozo, the Hill of Joy, the last stop before I get to the cathedral. I promise you I will never give up. In my guide, April is the month of transforming dreams into reality. I'm ready. I am about to live out the last chapter of this part of my journey.

CHAPTER 22:

Camino Di Amore—I Am the Way, the Truth, and the Light!

"They that sow in tears shall reap in joy. He that goes forth and weeps, bearing precious seed, shall doubtless come again with rejoicing, bringing his sheaves with him."
—PSALM 126:5-6, The Bible, King James Version

Miami to Madrid

All packed and ready to go, I kissed my black-and-white Shetland sheepdogs goodbye and went down to the lobby to wait for my husband, Frank, to come home and drive me to Miami International Airport to meet the others. Because our flight was in the evening, I spent most of the day getting myself together. I was afraid to go and put off packing as long as I could. Suddenly questioning what the hell I was doing, I dutifully ran down my checklist to make sure I didn't forget anything: passport, tickets, walking sticks, two pairs of shoes—sneakers and hiking—workout gear, lots of Salon Pas patches, Bio-freeze, Aleve, KT Tape, and an emergency kit filled with bandages, blister ointment, and other supplies. But unlike Coelho, who roughed it and slept under the stars overnight, I made sure that this adventure came with hotels and luggage transfers. With less than three hours to takeoff, if I'd forgotten anything, there wasn't much I could do about it now. As I nervously placed the Camino

Ways tags on my carry-on and main bag, I noticed that the zipper on the suitcase with my clothes was clearly defective.

"Oh no!" I gasped.

That was the last thing I needed to worry about, for my bag to explode with my essentials lost en route. Grateful to have an opportunity to correct this, as I ran into the elevator to return to my condo, I texted Frank to wait, then called him to be sure he would not get impatient.

"My bag is broken, gimme a second, I'll be right down!"

Organizing things on my bed for a quick transfer, I retreated into the storage unit we used as a pantry across from my apartment and pulled down an electric blue piece of luggage with the word peace in capital letters on the front and a giant peace sign.

"This is appropriate," I mumbled. "I'll look like a hippie with this peace sign. I always wanted to feel like a hippie."

I proceeded to return to my bedroom and, piece by piece, placed all my necessities back into the new bag. Laughing softly, I said, "So much for being a hippie with all these clothes and my makeup case along."

I closed it up, looked around my room to make sure I'd transferred everything, and rolled my luggage back to the elevator to return to the lobby. Smiling, I owned it: who am I kidding? I want the mythical freedom of being a so-called hippie, but I love being a diva. And in keeping with my diva theme, I placed the baggage tag that read "I Was Never Meant to Fly Coach" on the new bag. Seeing one of my many tiaras on top of the credenza, I thought to grab it as well.

"Nah, I got my invisible one close at hand."

"Meg, you're going to be late to your own funeral," my husband declared when he saw me come through the automatic front doors.

As he grabbed my stuff and put it in the trunk, I answered, "I hope so."

Yep, no matter what I tried to do, late again, just this time not running out to the bus with my shoes in my hands. My untimeliness drove Frank crazy—he timed his breathing by the movement of the hands on his watch. Lateness was a sign of my passive-aggressive rebellious streak held over from my youth. I often wondered how I could have married someone so rigid. I was grateful he'd agreed to take me to the airport and did not want to start a fight before I left. I put my seatbelt on in the front seat of the car and cut him off before he could even begin the expected lecture on tardiness. "I'm calling Denise!"

"Hey Lady D, you ready for this?"

Denise answered, "Hey! On my way—see you there!"

As we pulled into the departure area for American Airlines international flights, it was another busy day of travel. MIA was a chaotic place with people coming and going from all over the world. This airport was enormous, and I knew it could take a while to first get through security and then get on the monorail to the departure gate. As I willed Frank to drive faster, I thought, *I don't need additional stress, please move!* Ava, my daughter, cried out from the back seat, "I'm going to miss you so much, Mommy!"

"Oh, my poof, I love you—I'm going to miss you too!" Arriving curbside with time to spare, we all got out of the car and shared one last hug.

"Frank, you set up my international phone service, right?" *Please say* yes!

"Yes, I did."

OMG—exhale—it almost gave me a panic attack ruminating over all the worst-case scenarios that could happen to me: stuck in a forest, alone and miserable, hurt without any possibility of being rescued. Left behind by the other skilled hikers; at least with my phone by my side, I would have a chance at survival. One more check off my list; at least there are some things I can control. Nature unscripted, a hypochondriac's hell, scared the sh*t out of me. Clearly, this adventure trip would not be like walking around Epcot or Disney World visiting all the different countries in the World Showcase on a Saturday afternoon. I knew that. As a camper in the mountains of North Carolina and Tennessee for at least five summers during my formative years, I knew that the outdoors was filled with creatures, and that agitated me. Just thinking about it, I couldn't help but wonder, *Why am I doing this again?*

It was Paulo's mystical tale that brought me there. Oh, and her lighthouse, Mommy's lighthouse—how could I forget that? Sure, there could be thieves, scary diabolical thieves who would hide in the trees and jump out when I least expected it. Rabid dogs and other animals wandering the streets looking for food. Snakes, oh my God, what if I stepped on a poisonous snake and it bit me? I would have no idea what to do. And spiders and ticks, I detest those tiny creatures that would latch on your body until you realized way too late that they'd passed on Lyme disease and other disgusting infections. With these scenarios playing out in my head, you would never know I was going on a magical nine-day vacation. I felt more like I was about to begin the greatest crash test of my life, and if I failed, I would pay for my stupidity for the rest of my life. Then I remembered the words of my mentor, "Go on the pilgrimage first. That walk will open up everything for you." Breathe, Meg, keep smiling, you have your phone!

"Thank you for taking care of the kids and dogs while I'm gone. I'll call you tomorrow when I get in."

"Have a safe flight, we love you." Ava and Frank got back into the car and waved goodbye.

Then one of the baggage handlers approached me, "Ma'am, where are you going?"

I hate when they call me Ma'am. It makes me feel so old.

"I'm traveling to Madrid then Santiago, Spain."

"I can help you. Can I see your ticket and passport?" I gave him both. He looked at the documents and said, "I'll be right back." Then he disappeared.

About fifteen minutes went by, and I grew nervous thinking that he had been gone for an unusually long period of time. *Oh well, great, he stole my stuff, I guess I'm not going. Any excuse to get out of this*, I thought. Then I realized he had my passport. *Great, now I was a victim of a crime—he was going to sell my document, and I would be screwed. Stop, Meg, Stop!*

Reason taking over, I grabbed another skycap and asked him where the other guy had gone with my documents. He said, "Don't worry, trust the process!" Okay, duly noted, thanks universe—I get it, stop worrying and trust the process. Besides, what choice did I have now, I told everybody on social media and beyond I was going, I helped to organize a group of sixteen pilgrims, and it was my idea. I would look pretty stupid, especially since my message was you have to try, begin somewhere—ugh! I was haunted by practice what you preach.

Then I laughed out loud at a memory of a trip to Busch Gardens when my son was three. There was a ridiculous roller coaster called the SheiKra, the world's first, longest, tallest, and fastest dive coaster. As we stood at the bottom looking up, I gasped and declared that there was no way I was riding that thing. My son pulled my hand and exclaimed as loudly as he could the words I used over and over to encourage him, "Mommy, but you always say face your fears!" Screwed, I was screwed—I went, tried it, once, just once. I didn't want to give him ammunition to use against me for the rest of his childhood and adolescent years! And here I was hearing his voice, "Mommy, face your fears!" I had to set a good example for my kids. I do what I say I will do. So I'll do this once, just once. I didn't want to give myself any ammunition to use against me for the rest of my life.

Just seconds later, the original skycap returned. "All set through to Santiago—have a great time!" Breezing unusually quickly through security with TSA PreCheck, I arrived at the designated meeting spot and looked for my fellow travelers. I checked my watch and saw I had plenty of time. Approaching the bar at the Yard Bird restaurant across from our exit gate, I spotted my co-organizer, Heidi, and waved.

"Are you ready for this?" I asked.

"You bet!" she enthusiastically replied, as confident as I remembered her to be. We did not know each other well, but I knew her back story and that she had overcome some pretty big obstacles. I presumed the challenge of this trip paled in comparison to what she had gone through when her world was turned upside down after a thousand-pound tree limb fell from forty feet in the air and struck her, breaking her neck and rendering her unconscious. I noticed her well-worn backpack on the chair next to her and immediately felt very intimidated. She not only learned to walk again, but she had traveled all over the world hiking everywhere she went. Facing what happened, she didn't recoil in fear; she picked up the pieces and embraced adventure. She even said *Yes* to me and all the additional requests and accommodations that I needed. She probably would have preferred to rough it herself. I was so grateful.

I, on the other hand, was completely outside my comfort zone. *Oh God, what did I get myself into?* played over and over in my head. Yes, sure, it was an adventure, but I was more obsessed with the idea of closure; I needed a good ending to the last seven-year saga that started when my world was turned upside down after my mom died. Driven by a vision of something I hoped would change my life, change me, reprogram me, I would have to wait and see how this would unfold. The mysticism of this spiritual pilgrimage and Coelho's tale intrigued me, and Heidi's part as a co-conspirator, survivor, and warrior really got me curious too.

Heidi was the picture of the consummate hiker, fit and energized. She had hiked many trails before, returning from Arizona not even a month earlier. Meanwhile, I'd shown up completely inexperienced and ill-prepared. I laughed off my flaws while berating myself with comparisons. Preparing myself for the humiliation of being outed as a clear imposter, at least I knew with my phone I could call a taxi from the trail at any time. My role here was to inspire in other ways, so I'd prepared sixteen starter kits with pens and journals along with Love Buttons for each person. This was what I wanted to do with my newfound career. As competitive as my legal profession had been, I now wanted to collaborate in some way. That and not have to prove to anyone that I was worthy to be in the same room. For me, this Camino wasn't about who was going to finish first; it was all about finishing.

"Hey, ladies!" Denise arrived, looking as stylish as ever with her fancy, sparkly headband, playing with her brand-new camera. She was ready for this, the epitome of fun and confidence. With the mantra she declared, "Enjoy your view," and she clearly was ready to capture through the lens the beauty of the entire journey starting here. "Here we go!" She was the master photographer and documented events with fabulous photos better than anyone I knew.

"Let's get in our first selfie of the trip!" she announced.

I gave Heidi and Denise a Love Button, and we documented our first official moment of the trip to get us started. I loved Denise so much and was so happy that she signed up to go. Our adventures began in Malibu— here we were, on our way to Madrid, Spain. I loved her enthusiasm and the camaraderie we shared. Hers had been an important friendship and a piece of my puzzle as well. Better prepared than I, she had gone on a hike that previous November in Utah, so she had a feel for the outdoors and mountains already. Having spent hours after our cases getting to know each other well over the years, we were "sisters in spirit," and I knew I could turn to her for emotional support along the way. Besides, we had made a pact beforehand: "No woman left behind."

About fifteen minutes later, they called our group number to board AA Flight 68 scheduled to depart at seven o'clock. We were now a group of five as Vicky, arriving from Washington, DC, and her best friend Cristina joined us at the gate. The origin story of Vicky's involvement was interesting. I met her through her sister when she attended one of the church retreats that I served on. I used to email her my insights of the day to offer inspiration subsequent to that retreat. As I reached out to individuals who I thought may be interested in joining El Camino, my list of email addresses included her sister, but I'd sent the invitation to Vicky by mistake, as her email address was similar.

Vicky had wanted to walk El Camino the year before, but it didn't happen, so she put things into motion and reached out to her best friend who was all in. Then they both connected with three more close friends. So as synchronicity would have it, it was a fortunate misdirected email to Vicky that completed our group. The Miami contingency got on the plane and went our separate ways to locate our seats. I found mine on the aisle in the middle of the plane. A bit disappointed that I couldn't get an upgrade—we were packed in like sardines—I resolved to sleep during the ten-hour, hopefully uneventful, overnight flight there. I also resolved, *No turning back now.*

Then I remembered the package from Dr. Habib and Dr. Sherry and got excited. I reached under the seat in front of me and pulled out the box from my carry-on. Opening it up, I found two wrapped gifts and a card. I examined the card first. On the front stood a woman against a multicolored background, hands touching each other. It read:

If you give God everything
He will also give you everything.
Give to take.

Inside was a lovely note that said:

My Beloved Sister-
As you start your Journey—know that
We Love You.
We Honor You.
We Are with You.
We Adore You.
God Bless You.
As I sat in my meditation, these songs and this book came forth
for you to take on
your healing pilgrimage. Love, Light, and Clarity Ahead

I unwrapped the book first, *Love Never Dies: How to Reconnect and Make Peace with the Deceased* by Dr. Jamie Turndorf. The other package contained an iPod mini. I opened it up and plugged in the earbuds. As the plane took off, I smiled, feeling grateful and blessed for the gifts, buttons, and wishes of support from my friends. I pushed back my seat, opened the book to start reading, and let the music of the Gypsy Kings set out the soundtrack that would carry me off. Music always had a way of shifting me so I wasn't nervous anymore. I smiled when midway through Enya played, bringing me back to the first time I experienced hope when I met Dr. Eva at her clinic after my mom died.

Madrid to Santiago

April 14, we arrived in Madrid at nine thirty in the morning local time. The flight was long. I don't think any of us got any sleep. After traversing customs, we had some time before our connection to Santiago de Compostela, so we grabbed sandwiches, strong coffee, and water. Two more pilgrims in our group arrived at the gate to Santiago on Iberia Express Flight 3874. We were almost there. Promising friends and family to send live video, Denise and I stood at gate K66 in the Madrid Barajas International Airport and recorded ourselves, punch drunk and laughing. It was 4:50 a.m. Miami time.

I said, "Hey, everybody, we are here in Madrid."

Denise repeated, "Madrid."

"Yeah, I don't think anybody has slept. This is where we are," I said as I scanned the airport terminal.

I wrapped up, "Leaving for Santiago, we will see you over there."

Denise ended with, "See you in Santiago, bye."

I sat next to a beautiful Italian hairdresser from Milan, and we passed the hour excitedly exchanging stories. Creativity most definitely permeated every aspect of her life. She shared her Instagram posts of the incredible geometric shapes and colors she artistically crafted on her various models for her shows. Inspired by her works of art, I told her about my book and promised to keep in touch in hopes that our paths would cross again. With that, the plane touched down in Santiago.

Three more pilgrims in our group were waiting for us at the terminal's exit in Santiago along with our tour guide, Rita, who held an orange "Camino Ways" sign to get our attention. I was happy my bag arrived too. We rolled our luggage out to the bus that was waiting for us, and I put on my jacket over my sweater.

I finally got my international phone service set up and called Frank.

"We made it," I announced.

"Great, how did it go?"

"It was a long flight, half of the group is together, and we will meet the rest at our meet and greet for dinner tonight in Sarria, our first destination. It's a bit cold, but thank goodness not raining." Rainy season had hit Northern Spain for the majority of March, and the forecast predicted more of the same for April. I prayed to God that would not be the case.

"I'll call you tomorrow," I said.

"Great, have fun and get some rest."

Santiago to Sarria

En route to our hotel in Sarria from Santiago, we traveled the distance in a comfortable and spacious bus. It took a little over two hours to get to our hotel, Hotel Alfonso IX in Sarria, where we would begin walking the next morning. It baffled me that it was going to take us six days to walk what took us a little under two hours to drive. Exhausted from the nearly twenty hours of travel, I was looking forward to getting a good night's sleep and starting off fresh in the morning. As the bus sped along, its movement hypnotically rocked me back and forth as I took in the countryside on the way out of the city. The sites on the highway in this part of northern Spain contrasted greatly with what I remembered seeing on the Florida Turnpike heading north. Lush green fields, mountainous regions—it was truly captivating. When we got to the hotel, I headed directly upstairs so I could wash my face to refresh before the evening festivities. The room was very European, modern, and simple. I lay down on one of the twin beds and melted into the soft mattress. I wanted to fall asleep. But dinner was at seven thirty. It would be our first time all together as a group, and I didn't want to miss it.

I adjourned to the dining room, where I met up with Heidi and began to place the goodie bags I'd made on each chair, along with Post-it notes matching each of us with a Camino buddy. Rita, our tour guide, put a Camino passport at each seat as well. As each person arrived, I offered them temporary tattoos to place wherever they liked to get motivated for the trip. That is where I met the Malaysians, dear friends who were no strangers to hiking. Then the last of the seventeen arrived.

The hotel had arranged for a long table to be set. They served paella and potatoes, red and white wine, and we chatted happily as we went around the table sharing a little about ourselves and our intentions for the journey. It was clear that most were expert hikers, having told tales of conquering the journey to Mt. Everest base camp, multiple treks on the sixty-mile Avon Breast Cancer Crusade, and completion of the Kumano Kodo, the sister trail to El Camino. I laughed and thought I would probably not be seeing much of them tomorrow after we embarked for the day. Everyone had a reason for being there, some spiritual, some for the adventure. I had the next six days to see how our stories would intersect. While I felt a little more comfortable, I anxiously retreated upstairs knowing that without a good night's sleep, it would be even more of a challenge. When I got back to my room, I completed my first day's video journal, grabbed my purple butterfly covered with seventeen Love Buttons in memory of the Parkland victims, and lay in bed anticipating what lay ahead. I grabbed the "Camino de Santiago Facts" and "Tips to Get Ready" sheets. I supposed that now, the night before, it was time to read them:

1. *Camino de Santiago means Way of St. James.*
2. *The yellow scallop shells and yellow arrows mark the way to Santiago.* (Follow the yellow brick road.)
3. *The most famous Camino route is the Camino Frances or French Way starting in St. Jean Pied de Port.* (Yep, I am on the French Way.)
4. *The trail for St. Jean Pied de Port to Santiago is 800 km long and takes approximately five weeks to complete.* (Where Paulo started.)
5. *You need to walk at least 100 km to receive your Compostela certificate* (Check). *Sarria (111 km from Santiago) is the most popular starting point for walkers.* (So 111 km it is!)
6. *The pilgrim's passport (credencial) needs to be stamped at least twice a day if you are starting your Camino in Galicia* (Check).
7. *The 0 km of the Camino is actually not in Santiago but in Cape Finisterre, considered to be the "end of the world."* (Where her lighthouse is.)

Turning to "Tips to Get Ready," as I skimmed that list, I got discouraged and put it away. It suggested that you begin to prepare six months in advance with twenty-five to thirty-minute walks at least three or four times a week. I supposed it was too late for that. Wanting to share the excitement of the first night there with someone special and in the same time zone, I called my soul sister Teda who had moved to Madrid a year earlier. I missed her and was over the moon that I was able to arrange my flight to rendezvous with her on my way back. I knew that she understood my reasons for doing this, and that talking to her would calm me down.

"Teda! I made it here."

"Meggie, I'm so excited for you—are you ready?"

"God no! I have no idea what the hell I'm going to face tomorrow. Someone said it would be over sixteen miles walking. I have no earthly idea how I'm going to do that. I don't think that I have ever walked sixteen miles in one day before in my life."

"You're going to be okay. You can do it. Wow, I'm so proud of you."

"Really? I have no idea why." I laughed. "You should be doing this with me—meet me on the road."

"Not this time. Call me whenever you need me. You're going to do great, I know it."

I started to cry. "Do you think I'm crazy? I feel like I'm desperate to find something—I'm so tired of being desperate to find myself."

"Ah, Meggie, you're going to be okay, more than okay. Surrender to whatever you need to learn about yourself." She always knew what to say to me.

"I love you, Tedita."

"I love you too. Good night!"

I got up and arranged my clothes, shoes, and socks next to my backpack. I went to pull out the poles but decided to leave them in my suitcase. I did not want to carry too much. I still had no idea why I needed to them at all. I called downstairs for a wake-up call so that my bags would be ready for pickup at eight. I put two packs of Love Buttons in my backpack (I planned to give them all out tomorrow), made sure that I had everything I thought I would need, turned out the lights, and prayed, "Let this Camino di Amore show me the way, the truth, and the light." That's not too much to ask, right?

CHAPTER 23:

Tribe of Seekers— Weight, Lifted

"Life is a journey, not a destination."
—RALPH WALDO EMERSON, 1803–1882, American poet

I am a keeper of my dreams. I wake up and write down the messages received. When I woke up that morning at six o'clock, I smiled, fully aware that what I was about to begin had started out as a part of a vision. Seven years before, seeds of this journey were planted in my psyche with a lighthouse as I prayed for my mom. Before I could forget my dream, I grabbed my journal to capture the imagery of a cuckoo clock and a forest that came to me that night. Cuckoo clocks originated in the Black Forest in eighteenth-century Germany, a place where fairytales like Hansel and Gretel unfold. The pendulum-regulated clock strikes the hours with an automated cuckoo bird that comes out of a door in the middle: *coo-coo, coo-coo, coo-coo*. In a google search, I learned that clock imagery suggests a preoccupation with the passage of time or perhaps a fear of aging. The cuckoo clock itself represents the innocence of childhood, the enchantment of the "magic" of the happy bird that lives in the clock and visits to announce the hour. It can be seen as a bit mysterious rather than a serious timekeeper. Always running late, I definitely am not a serious keeper of time.

I wrote quickly to capture all the details.

I am in a dark forest. Just a glimmer of light lets me see the tall, majestic trees all around. The path feels rocky. I can't see my feet beneath me. The air feels thick as I hold my arms in front of me to help guide my way. There is no way around. I am making my way. I must go through. The mysterious cuckoo clock calls me in, I trust because it has been dark for too long. Then I start to question the journey, question my choices, and question myself. This place of unknowing, I hate it actually. To relinquish control, so uncomfortable. A wave of fear overtakes me as the wind blows through the denseness all around. There are no external guides here, I have to go within. Emotionally uncomfortable, there is no one to blame for this sadness. "Trust the process" is the whisper I hear through the leaves. I do not dare stop now, my life depends on it. Yet, like a young child who does not get her way, my desire to throw a temper tantrum is strong. To rage against what I perceive as injustice will not heal the wounds, yet it does give me temporary relief. My tears are what comfort my soul, for I am human, and the unknown frightens me so. To make sense out of what has gone before, my curiosity turns to anger then back to curiosity again. What if I accept that I am supposed to be here in this place—not seeing the path before me quite clearly, needing to leave behind what no longer serves me. Knowing that each step forward has purpose and meaning, for they say everything is as it should be.

Another crazy dream captured. I liked to think that something was going on that I couldn't see. Forces at work, weaving the magic around me to help me. I was so ready to dust myself off and wipe away my tears, so tired of being sad for so long. I hoped that if I got through the next six days, I could begin anew. Something tells me that this is the way. For I am walking toward the life of my dreams, right? To give my trip added purpose, I decided to dedicate each day in gratitude for someone I loved. The first day, I dedicated this walk to my work colleagues and friends.

As I got dressed, I pinned the purple butterfly to my backpack. I would love to tell my mom about this trip. Symbolically she was right there with me, and I still had to pay attention for signs from her. She helped me bring to life my guide to bliss. Perhaps here, in those moments of quiet when my doubts reemerge, she could help me lay new tracks that would convince me that I am good enough. With the goal to finish 111 km of El Camino to get my certificate in Santiago, I was determined to earn whatever awaited me at Finisterre—perhaps, along the way, abandon all "shoulds" and dance. Allow the enchantment of that happy cuckoo bird in my dream to overtake the darkness.

Looking around to make sure I had everything, I grabbed my suitcase, rolled it out of the room, and waited for the elevator so I could place it downstairs with the others. Dressed in yoga pants and a long-sleeved top, choosing my well-worn running shoes over my brand-new hikers, and topping it all off with my electric blue Columbia windbreaker to keep me dry and warm, I put my makeup on so at least I would look good. I marched off the elevator and followed the others waiting for instructions.

Sarria to Portomarin

"Good morning everyone! Buen Camino." I could hear the traditional greeting as everyone gathered at eight o'clock outside of the hotel for photos before we started the first day of the pilgrimage. Rita, our tour guide, reminded us to get our first passport stamp from the hotel concierge before we left.

"Okay, everyone," she began, "today we are off to Portomarin. I sent the highlights to look out for on the way to the *WhatsApp* link. Heidi will be with the faster walkers in the front, and I'll be the sweeper in the back."

She continued, "The whole hike is about twenty-two kilometers. Tonight we will all meet at Hotel Ferramiento in Portomarin for a family style dinner again. Don't forget to get your stamps in your passport. Buen Camino, everyone!"

We took a photo as a group outside the hotel holding the Love Button flag. Then we were off. We all crossed over the bridge and followed the first yellow arrow on our path that would lead us up eight flights of stairs to the top of the city. Before I started the climb, I noticed a mural of the Merlin of El Camino on the wall to my right. He was wearing John Lennon style glasses, a hat, and a cape, and he carried a shepherd's staff like the pilgrims described in Paulo's *The Pilgrimage*. From the staff hung a small water gourd as well. His name was Zapatones, and he had lived a short life from 1954 until 2015 as one of the magical characters of Compostela, the field of stars. I got excited. On this hero's journey, I had found a magical Merlin sign.

Without further delay, Denise and I started the climb, laughing all the way up. We were not starting out slowly. At the top, there stood an iron cross overlooking the city of Sarria. At its side stood a mosaic of its coat of arms. On our way out of the city, we passed a large stone fortress called the Magdalena Monastery and decided to go in. Greeted by a lovely, older Spanish gentleman dressed in plain clothes who was the priest in charge, I walked into a windswept courtyard filled with unmanicured pink and red rose bushes. After introductions, Padre Antonio de Santiago de Barbadelo told us that the monastery was originally founded in the twelfth century by Italian monks who wanted to set up a hospital for the pilgrims. The Augustinians took over in the thirteenth century. Now he was a member of the Mercedarians, officially known as the Royal, Celestial, and Military Order of Our Lady of Mercy and the Redemption of Captives, who had taken over in 1218. He told me that the monks took a vow to give up their lives for anyone in danger of losing their faith. I felt that was me so many different times over the last seven years.

There was something about that monastery; once again an electricity and energy overcame me that brought me to tears. When I set my butterfly on the dais, the light came through from the stained-glass window of St. Anthony, patron saint of lost things, above the altar. As children, we often called upon him. He made me smile. I said, "Help me find myself, St. Anthony." Before we left, we thanked Padre Antonio, signed the visitor ledger, got our stamp, and exchanged buttons. Mine said "Love," his "Mercy." Leaving the monastery, we returned to this century back on El Camino, but the feeling remained that I was walking in the shoes of someone who lived in another time.

Vicky and two others were by my side. Seeing how difficult it was for me to climb up the hills, Vicky kindly offered me one of her poles.

"Thank you. I stupidly left mine in my suitcase. Not much good they will do for me there. Amateur move. I'll give it back to you later on, I promise."

She answered, "No problem."

I would soon learn that Vicky loved the trees. She was fascinated by them, and her enthusiasm was contagious. I started to pay attention. She would stop at each one and take photos, pointing out how intricate they were. We passed by farmland blanketed by tiny yellow poppies, both rural and lush. Crossing over a twelfth-century stone bridge named Aspera, painted by nature with green moss, we watched the Celeiro River flow quickly underneath. As the babbling brook on the other side greeted us, we felt like we were walking in a fairytale. As we entered the forest for the first time, surrounded by overgrowth, a majestic sycamore stood in three parts. Using my imagination, I could make out the figure of a pointy-nosed witch on the right and the shape of a squawking hen on the left. Perhaps at one time dilapidated, after weeks of heavy rain, new growth was peeking out around its long branches.

Along with the color yellow on the arrows, this particular part of the road reminded me of Dorothy's adventure through the dark, magical forest when she first encountered the Tin Man. It would not surprise me if the trees came alive and started to throw apples at us. Vicky's best friend showed up after we climbed our first dirt hill that led to an old working stone fountain. Oak and chestnut trees lined the road. Her best friend too had a great camera to take photos and a keen eye for the beauty of the landscape all around us. With my iPhone to capture memories, I was happy others were prepared with better photo equipment that could do things justice.

About two hours into our day, I needed a shot of espresso. I saw arrows pointing to a restaurant called Casa Barbadelo, and when I finally arrived, I grabbed two more waters, a coffee, and a scallop shell, the first iconic symbol I purchased on El Camino. Not only was the scallop shell and yellow arrow used to find your way along the trail, it was physical proof that you had taken the journey and completed the pilgrimage to

Santiago. In medieval times, the shell was used to drink water from the well. On my way out, I loaded up with six more small bottles of water and tied the shell to my backpack as a symbol of where I intended to go.

Outside the bar, there was a lovely fountain with a statue on top. I couldn't tell who it was, but it was covered with strings, bracelets, crosses, and rocks left behind by pilgrims who passed by. I added a Love Button to the facade. And before we took off, a beautiful dog greeted me. Definitely a herding dog, she looked like my Shetland sheepdog Leonardo. She was all black with a streak of white, not rabid as I, at the outset of this journey, had feared. And away we went. This time Denise went ahead with two others and Vicky, her best friend Cristina, and Rita stayed with me.

While the skies were overcast, I was hoping that the rain would not come. As we walked along the road, I spent the rest of the day getting to know the three of them better. As lovers of music along with great conversation, we started to sing. Having seen the Broadway show *Jesus Christ Superstar* presented as a TV special earlier that week, I had been listening to the song Mary Magdalene sings to Jesus, "Everything's Alright," the whole week before. Suggesting that we listen to it now, I found it on my Apple playlist, played it on my speaker phone loud enough for everyone to hear, and sang along as we walked through Vicky's magical forest on El Camino.

After an hour passed, I walked alone now for the first time. I really paid attention as I passed by the small hamlets on the flat road. The simplicity of this rural area in Spain amazed me. We had already passed sheep, goats, cows, and German shepherds with their owners dressed in traditional smocks. The building foundations were made of old stone, recently updated to a more modern look. In many respects, time stood still on the road. Wanting to enjoy the music along with being outdoors, I put my earbuds in and took out the iPod mini that Dr. Habib and Dr. Sherry had sent to keep me going along the way.

Happily lost in daydreams as the rumba flamenco style music of the Gypsy Kings played, I imagined that I was a world class adventurer. Excited to be walking alone, taking it all in, it wasn't until I came upon a fork in the road that I wished one of my fellow pilgrims were there to show me the way. It looked like the yellow arrow directed me to go two different ways. Gazing to the left and right, seeing no one, I chose the path up a dirt hill, still singing out loud the lyrics to "Bamboleo," unconcerned if anyone heard me. I waved at the cows on the right side of the road and smiled at the sheep on the left. After about twenty minutes bouncing along on this path, feeling so accomplished and free, I thought I heard someone yelling my name from behind. I lowered the volume of the music and listened. Again, I heard my name. Curious, I turned around and did not see anyone. Oh great, I'm making things up now. About to continue up the hill, I clearly heard someone frantically screaming:

"Meg, *stop!*"

"Meg, stop? What?" I stood still and took out my earbuds.

"Meg—*stop!* You're going the wrong way." That time, I turned around and saw a young woman who looked like our guide, Rita, running up the hill waving to get my attention.

"Rita, is that you?"

She approached closer and closer and said, "Yes! Stop—you went the wrong way. We saw you turn up the hill and figured you would backtrack once you didn't see anyone on the road. But you kept going and you were dancing and singing."

Embarrassed, I apologized profusely over and over.

"I'm so sorry—how did that happen? I followed the arrow." I turned around and followed her back down.

As we returned to the main road together, Rita, out of breath, remembered that I wanted to write about my time on El Camino and laughed. "I just think you want drama for your story!"

"Great, brilliant, do not need that kind of drama. I won't be listening to any more music." *Saying that out loud made me sad. Without music, how am I going to have any fun? Oh well—my feet hurt already, I'm ready to be done—can't afford to get lost—that'll do me no good.* I remember when we were going on vacation, harassing my parents. *How many more minutes to get there?* Day one and I was tired after five hours of walking—five more days of this—Crap!

As we approached the last couple of miles before stopping for lunch, I made sure to follow one of my friends at all times. I didn't want to make this harder on myself or anyone else, for that matter. I felt bad that I'd been enjoying being lost in the moment. A little ashamed, I no longer cared about my surroundings but wanted to get to the next stop. Everyone became quiet; we had already walked almost 11 km and were tired. We wanted to get to Bar Morgade to get off our feet and take a rest before it started to rain. When we turned the corner toward a long winding road up another hill, the last thing we wanted to do was stop. An elderly gentleman approached mumbling something at me and Vicky. When we didn't pay attention, he came out further and got in the middle of the road to block our way. *He must be a hundred years old,* I thought. He stood there looking at us for a response. While I did not want to stop, I was curious as to what he wanted.

"Come...." (There followed something unintelligible in heavy Castilian Spanish.) He refused to let us pass and gestured for us to go behind him to what appeared to be a very old fortress.

"What did he say, Vicky?"

"He wants us to follow him. What do you want to do?"

I replied, "When someone stops on the road and tells you to follow, unless it's dark and scary, you go."

He guided us to the stone building down the hill. It was a church called Santiago de Barbadelo, a jewel of Galician Romanesque, one of the few Romanesque towers remaining in Spain. The older man told us that he was the priest in charge and that the building had been constructed at the same time as the Cathedral of St. James. It was breathtakingly beautiful. Pink, red, and yellow roses adorned the stone walls surrounding the church. After we passed through the north doors and its animal decorated columns, we saw the altar with its old wooden pews in the small church. Under a gold thurible, a metal censer suspended by chains in which incense is burned, fresh roses and greenery lay at the foot of the altar. Saint Anthony stood holding Baby Jesus as Virgin Mary prayed above. The fresh air felt cool on my face. We never would have seen it if he had not stopped us, and now we were grateful. We knelt to say a prayer, thanked him, signed the guest ledger, received a stamp in our passport, and left. As luck would have it, it didn't start to sprinkle until we arrived at the bar for lunch. Then Mother Nature unleashed the rain when we got inside. At that point, we had logged over 12 km and needed a break.

Refueled, recaffeinated, and relaxed, it was time for us to go. We had another 10 km to Portomarin. If we wanted to get there before dark, we needed to move a bit faster. The novelty of the road had already worn off. Now walking in the rain, we were tired and wet. Heading out of the hamlet into the forest to see what we could see, the trees covered us overhead. But a cold wetness started to permeate my running shoes. I looked down to find my new nemesis—mushy, dark brown, crappy *mud*. Actually, it was like quicksand. I figured out a new reason why one would walk with poles. The whole road was covered with it, and you had to use the sticks to figure out the shallow and deep parts and negotiate your footing accordingly. My socks were wet and sloshing around inside my shoes. *Gross.* I had an extra pair of socks in my pack, but there was nowhere to stop, so we continued on, climbing up on the side banks to miss the river that was flowing along our path. About an hour into this, I felt the skin on the side of my big toe pulsating.

All tales of horror on the Camino begin with, "Be careful not to get blisters on your feet!" That seems to be the death knell of the pilgrim. *Oh, God!* I began my internal monologue: *On the first day—really? Blisters! I'm such an amateur! I have no business being here—overweight, ill-prepared, shoved out of a career, what am I doing in life? Old, I look terrible—and now, on the first day, I'm afraid to look at my feet!* Let the berating begin. If I heard anyone talk to someone like this, I would have called them an asshole. But what to do when you're the one beating up on yourself? Knowing this wasn't going to help me at all, I wished I had my music to drown it out. *Take a deep breath, Meg, keep moving forward. Some spiritual pilgrimage this is turning out to be! I now feel worse than when I began.*

At this point in the day, the seventeen had separated into three groups. The fast walkers at the front guided by Heidi, the middle group, and the slower ones at the back guided by our sweeper Rita. Needless to say, I was with Rita. By the time we reached 97 km, we'd caught up with Denise after she broke away from the middle of the pack. We were all starting to hurt a little more and were going more slowly.

Approaching a bar to get more water, I noticed that hanging from a window above, there was a black witch with a creepy white face. She was perched on her broom on the terrace outside what appeared to be a bedroom window. Knowing Rita was an expert in the area, I inquired, "What's that, Rita?"

"Galicia is thought to be a magical place. The ancient pagan heritage of the Celtic tradition still influences many parts of this land. In fact, you will see many witches like that along El Camino. They refer to them as *meiga*."

"Did you say magic?" My ears perked up, my interest renewed. "Tell me more."

"Christianity built many monuments to cover the pagan ones, but the locations and their energy, if you believe in that, are still the same. It's a Galician word that means witch or wise woman."

I have always been a storyteller and will always be a storyteller. It is one thing that throughout my life holds true. When I say it, write it, draw it, sing it, or am in the company of it, this is the *I am* that empowers me to live the life of my dreams, telling the most amazing story of my once around on this planet. In that vein, I love a good story too. Before I left on this trip, I watched the entire series of *Outlander* on Starz and loved the Celtic folklore and magical storytelling that originates with myths and legends of the standing stones and magical people. Trained for the last twenty years in court to get to the bottom of the story, I was excited that it found me here and wanted to know more about this, so I googled it and discovered some interesting tidbits to show magic still abounds here:

Galicia has always been known as a haunt for witches. In 1572, an inquisitor referred to its inhabitants as "full of superstitions with little respect for Christianity." In 1610, dramatist Tirso de Molina wrote, "Galicia produces witches as easily as turnips." Maria Solina is one of Galicia's most famous witches. Born in the fishing town of Cangas in 1551, according to legend, she raised a female army to stop an attack by the Turkish fleet. Many consider Galicia to be the seventh Celtic nation. There are countless ring forts, witches, and bagpipes found all across the land. (Taken from listverse.com)

Then I looked up the history of miracles on the pilgrimage:

And pilgrims have traveled El Camino de Santiago through Galicia for over 1,000 years. After Jesus died, St. James traveled to the Iberian Peninsula to evangelize. In AD 44, after returning to Jerusalem, he was beheaded. Legend holds that James's corpse was placed in a boat, which floated to Galicia. In the ninth century, a hermit had a vision of St. James's burial site. Miracles were attributed to the site, and it rapidly became a popular pilgrimage destination. Here the supernatural and the divine are often interlinked. The holy pilgrimage was actually appropriated by the Catholic church from a pagan pilgrimage to (what they believed was) the end of the world. Long before King Alfonso II took a hike from Asturias to pay homage to the relics of St. James, pagan pilgrims would journey across northern Spain to complete a born-again ritual. They would finish at Finisterre (which literally means "the end of the world"), burn their dirty clothes, and witness the sun sink into the infinite sea off La Costa de Morte (the Coast of Death). This journey symbolized the pilgrim's death and rebirth. (taken from the Urban Travel Blog.com)

Renewed with an additional purpose on this journey, it would be my "born-again" ritual. I could do this. Five more days. I purchased a magnet that showed 97 km over the yellow scallop shell and looked at Denise. "This is when we made the decision to finish what we started. No looking back now. I'm going to remember this mile marker."

"Okay," Denise agreed. "Let's get this over with—gotta finish today. I'm exhausted and in pain. Had no idea what I was getting myself into." We both laughed.

About two hours later, after stopping briefly at Peter Pank Bar for refreshments, we headed to the top of the mountain overlooking Portomarin. Our final destination for the day, Hotel Ferramiento was over the bridge across Rio Mino, or so we thought. When we got to the other side, a stone staircase was waiting for us and I laughed out loud, "Are you kidding me!"

"Well let's do this," Denise said.

With each step, we all felt a growing sense of accomplishment, like Rocky as he ran up the steps in Philadelphia. I can tell you we most definitely didn't run. Looking at the Health app on my phone, Denise and I took a moment to celebrate the 16.7 miles—42,066 steps and 41 floors—we had traversed, and this was just the first day. We had five more to go.

In the hotel, I pulled off my soaking wet sneakers and socks and dusted off the dried, caked on mud from the bottom of my pants. And there I saw for the first time the status of my feet, two blisters forming on the right and left foot near my big toe. If that were not enough, a burning sensation was coming from an unidentified red, angry rash that had broken out all over both feet and legs up to where my socks covered them. *Oh God, I have gangrene,* the hypochondriac in me declared.

After taking a shower, I put my flip-flops on and joined the others for dinner, celebrating that we all made it through the first day. Once again, wine flowed to accompany salmon and delicious vegetables. I was noticeably worried and asked anyone who had any expertise with hiking what the rash was and if there was anything I could do to about it.

One of the seasoned hikers asked, "Are your socks new?"

"Yes," I answered.

"Did you wash them before you came on the trip?"

"No, was I supposed to? I never wash my new clothes."

"You could be allergic to the material. It happens sometimes. That is why you should have washed your new socks beforehand."

I answered, "All my socks are new, and I didn't wash any of them before I left. There you go!" *Amateur move number one hundred. At least it wasn't some horrid disease from the mud in the forest.*

After dinner, we went back to our rooms. I arranged my items, getting ready for the next day. This time, I was taking the walking sticks and would try a different pair of socks. I grabbed my KT tape and blister Band-Aids and wrapped my feet for the night. Then I recorded my second entry of the video journal. Trying to be as upbeat as possible, I recalled the two Frenchmen I'd met earlier that morning, which felt like a lifetime ago. One was a retired professor who had joined his colleague from work to finish the second part of the Camino this year. The other one worked with the French government. As we talked about the state of the world, my disgust with the direction of the United States' politics, and issues with the effect of climate change on the environment, I smiled. They reminded me of DHS, especially my friend who was the office champion of sustainability. She was doing her part in educating all of us to save our environment for future generations. It was clear that under the new administration, her efforts were not well received, but she persisted anyway. I dedicated my day to my smart and forward-thinking former work colleagues back home. Very tired, I grabbed my pillow to get more comfortable. Then it dawned on me that for the first time in a while, I felt no back pain. The walking had actually helped. Before I closed my eyes, I said a prayer: "God, thank you for healing my back; now please work on my feet."

Portomarin to Palas de Rei

April 16. The alarm went off at six, and I woke up dreading the fact that we would be walking the same distance, if not more, than yesterday. *Why was I doing this again?* My legs ached all over. I felt muscles I had not known even existed the day before. I begrudgingly got dressed and packed up my things to go. *No one forced you to do this, Meg. This was your idea. Suck it up. What's one more day?*

Everyone had already congregated below. The hotel had set up a continental breakfast spread: cheese, bread, juices, everything you would need to get started. I put my suitcases with the others, grabbed some food and coffee, and waddled over to Denise who was sitting by the window with a great view of River Mino, under which lay the ancient city of Portomarin.

"It's so pretty. I guess this is all I am going to see of these cities. If we get in at eight every night, I'm going to be too tired to go sightseeing. How are you doing today?"

"Yep, I'm feeling this. My roomie had me put Vaseline all over my feet last night to protect against any blisters today."

At that point Heidi joined the both of us. "How are you both doing?" she asked.

"I'm in pain and already have some blisters. I had no idea," I said.

"Some decided to take a cab to the halfway point, and we are going to meet them there. Do you want to go with them?" she asked.

I answered, "No thanks. I'm going to walk this whole thing, but it's harder than I thought it would be."

Heidi replied, "Yep, since you've not done this before, you're probably the ones who will have the hardest time."

I said defensively, "I think we are the only ones who are going to be honest and admit that we're having a hard time. I'm sure everyone is feeling this!" And we all laughed.

It was a cold morning. I was grateful, preferring to walk in the cold rather than the heat. I hoped that it would not rain. I couldn't stand the mud. I felt lucky that yesterday it only sprinkled on us at the end. Heading down the hill away from Portomarin, I noticed the mist lingering over the river to the left. It felt foreboding. I also noticed that more pilgrims showed up today. At the bottom of the hill, the group took another photo and off they went. Denise looked at me,

"Rita said that there was another big hill coming up. Did Heidi say some took a taxi?"

"Yep, she did. I thought you heard her ask us if we wanted to join them. You're going to walk this with me, right?"

"Well I guess so; they already left."

Trying to convince myself, I said, "We can do this!"

"I'm dreading those hills, but here goes," Denise replied.

And right from the start, we navigated a steep incline for what seemed like forever, about four hours in duration. Halfway, she looked at me like she wanted to kill me and said, "We got this, right?" I smiled. I hoped so. I was hurting too.

When we were finally back on the flat road and parallel to the highway, El Camino got really busy. No longer peaceful, groups of people appeared along with cars zipping past us. Because I wanted to start giving out more Love Buttons, I moved ahead alone to start talking to other pilgrims. Today, I promised my magical friend that I would walk for her son who was going through a challenging time. As synchronicity would have it, I met a mother and her daughter from Colombia who had embarked on this adventure together to get closer because it had been a rough year.

When I handed them buttons, the daughter, about eighteen years old, replied, *"Chata de amor."* [Love Button in Spanish.] "Thank you!"

"How cool that you're walking with your mom."

"Yes, I promised her I would before I left for college. We seemed to have grown apart this last year."

I said, "This is quite a way to bond. Have you done anything like this before?"

"No, this is the first time. My mom is amazing. She's kept up for the last 100 kilometers."

"Spending that much time together, I guess you get a better appreciation."

"Yes, you do."

I said, "Good luck, my friends, Buen Camino!" And they walked on.

"Buen Camino" is all that I heard all morning from every pilgrim I passed.

We finally got to Gonzar, the first bathroom and coffee stop after 8 km. Grateful that I hadn't needed to use the "Camino natural bathroom" yet, and hoping not to have to, I got in line. I also got my monthly visitor. No wonder I was in such a crappy mood and beyond emotional; it wasn't just this crazy notion to walk close to 77 miles in six days. I popped a few Aleve to minimize the pain from the cramps and from my legs. *At least,* I thought, *I was prepared for that.* Moody as hell, I tried to minimize my bad attitude once my Camino amigos joined me. *Why take it out on everyone else?*

"Denise, I got a table for us over there! I'll watch your stuff if you need to go to the bathroom." Rita was right behind her.

"What's next?" I asked.

"Well there is a pretty big hill on the way to the hamlet of Castromaior, it's a Celtic settlement surrounded by ruins." Another good thing about being the slowest with the sweeper was that we got all the good information.

A young man with a gorgeous dalmatian-like dog showed up at the bar.

"Hey, puppy." Then I addressed his owner, "You really walk the whole way with him?"

He nodded.

"Wow, I don't think my dog Leo would make it past the first hill."

"You ready to go, Meg?" Denise asked after she captured some amazing photos of the dog.

"Sure, let's do it!"

It was almost one thirty when my phone rang. Surprised, I answered it.

"Go, Mommy, go! Go, Mommy, go! Go, Mommy, go!"

"Ava?"

"Hi, Mommy, it's Ava and Daddy!"

"Hi, guys, where are you? What time is it over there?"

"Hey, Meggie," Frank answered. "We told you we would cheer you on—so here is your daily call. On our way to school. How are you doing?"

Frank had changed his tune. After being less than enthusiastic the first day, I'd asked him to be supportive, and this kind of call was exactly what I needed.

"Smiling ear to ear. We're walking near the highway today, and I remember this from the movie *The Way*."

"Hey, Frank," Denise announced over the speakerphone. "Yep, Lady D, Rita, and I are together. It's going to be a long one, so keep us in your prayers please!!"

"You got it, you ladies, got this. We'll talk later, Meg—love you!" He hung up.

We stopped at Castromaior, the over two-thousand-year-old ruined walls and pathways of an ancient Roman town. Rita explained how this was a perfect example of the historical sights on El Camino. She pointed out the old fountain at the bottom of the farmhouse, its timeless, rustic beauty. I appreciated what she had to say, nodded to thank her, but was not in the mood.

About two hours later, we were at a crossroads, about to walk over the main highway, and for some reason the number on the yellow scallop shell mile marker along the way looked like it was going up, not down. It was supposed to go down, closer and closer to 0 km.

"Rita, did you see that? What the hell! How can that be?"

"I don't get it," Rita replied. *Don't yell at Rita, she had nothing to do with this. Can we just get there already? Put me out of my misery.*

I felt like this was as perfect a time as any to do a Facebook Live and throw a public temper tantrum for all the social media world to see:

"Hey, Facebook friends. Look where we are! In the middle of nowhere in Spain. I'm here with Denise and Rita. Say hello, ladies. It's the second day on El Camino, and it appears that the mile markers are magically going up, not down. Like a cruel joke, the universe is playing with us, I'm about to lose my mind!!"

I panned around. We were literally standing in the middle of a fork in the road, the arrows pointing ahead, the sun beating down on us, not a cloud in the sky. I looked down at my phone, and one of my soul sisters had sent me a note on messenger:

"You know how much I love and respect you. I'm proud of you for being so brave to embark on this journey. This is from the universe so don't shoot the messenger: YOU'RE ON A SPIRITUAL JOURNEY, PUT YOUR PHONE AWAY!!!"

I read it aloud, and we all started to laugh, knowing she was right. I wrote back, *"Yep, got it! Doing what I can to get through this!"*

She wrote back, *"You GOT THIS."* Called out and embarrassed, I turned to Rita and Denise and said, "Okay—no more tantrum. I'm sorry, let's go!"

Through the various hamlets, we were greeted by a herd of cattle that almost knocked us off the road, passed by Hospital de la Cruz, through Ventas de Naron, a medieval village where in 820 AD there was a fierce battle between the Christians and the Moors, and finally reached El Crucero de Lameiros, the cross of Lameiros. Rita explained that the cross was built in 1670 to represent Jesus's life from birth to death through the images, with the Blessed Mother holding his body at the end. On its base, we saw the symbols representing the death and suffering of Jesus Christ: a pair of tongs, a crown of thorns, and a skull. At that point, we had walked 15 km. Realizing that we were only halfway there, I asked if I could sit down and placed a Love Button on top of the base. My mother would have loved Rita for all the historical knowledge she brought to me. I laughed and remembered how passionate my mother had been about history, even when I showed no interest.

I remembered one summer when my parents took us to France on vacation. While traveling the countryside in the tour bus, my sisters and I were so tired that we decided not to get off the bus to see the Château de Chenonceau, so we stayed behind without telling my parents. To my mother, and probably anyone else who cared about history, Chenonceau is not to be missed. An impressive architectural mix of late Gothic and early Renaissance, the château spans the River Cher in the Indre-et-Loire department of the Loire Valley in France. When my mother looked back to see if we were paying attention and none of us were there, she took off running back through the forest to the bus. I remember looking out the window and saw what appeared to be a distraught, crazy person coming right for us. Realizing it was my mother, I told my sisters to look. She got on the bus and pulled all of us out, yelling and crying all the way back. We all stood in front of the famous three arches and took a photo as a family.

Every time I go to the French pavilion at Epcot in Walt Disney World, I see the movie *Impressions of France,* and there stands Chenonceau. I think of my mom and laugh to myself, for the story will stay with me forever. If I were not with Rita, I probably would have missed all the history on El Camino so far, my head looking down, focused on getting the walk done. As I admired the cross, I thought that my mother made sure that would not happen; she was right there educating me.

The rest of the day we were open to learning about the different historic spots on El Camino. In Ligonde, at 76 km, we entered this very important village in medieval times. We passed by Casa Campelo, a typical rustic Galician house in the village that housed an organization called Fuente del Peregrino, or Pilgrim's Fountain. It was founded in 1999 to show all pilgrims who passed the unconditional love of God through acts of service and hospitality. We met a German man who volunteered his time to offer a place to stay for anyone who passed. He greeted us, offered us refreshments, and invited us inside. We asked if we could use the facilities and then made a donation and thanked him for his kindness. While inside, I saw a pamphlet that provided a spiritual look at the pilgrims' symbols in a succinct fashion. I asked if I could keep it as a memento, and he said yes. I sat down on one of the old wooden chairs in the house to rest my legs and take a better look at it. Reading through, it offered the following insights about the yellow arrow, the backpack, the Band-Aid, the walking stick, and the scallop shell:

> *__The Yellow Arrow__. The arrow shows the Camino path. If it weren't for this, many times we would not know where to go. Whenever we find it again, we are reassured that we are on the right track. How do we feel when we can't find the arrows? What a huge help that someone came before us to mark the way! Our life is like the Camino. Sometimes we feel lost and frustrated when we can't find the way or signs to reassure us. What arrows do you follow? Who or what do you look to in life to point the way?*
>
> *__Backpack__. When we are at home it didn't seem to matter what we put in our backpack. Now that we have to carry it, we realize how much everything weighs and how much each thing counts. We also recognize how many things we can truly do without. On the Camino of life, we all carry a backpack. Sometimes we add things, then we have to carry it, and finally we reach the point that it is too much to carry. What can you take out of your backpack today to make your trip lighter? What excessive baggage are you carrying in your life?*
>
> *__Band-Aid__. Blisters, wounds, sprains. Nobody is free from the pain on the Camino. Sooner or later our body pays the price, and we have to take a slower pace or even stop. Strangely, the Camino wouldn't be the same without pain. Because of pain, we realize how difficult the Camino is, and when we finish each day's walk, we become a different person from who we were when we started. On the Camino of life similar things happen to us which we must learn to deal with. How do you face the pains of life? Do you have "life wounds" which you need to deal with?*
>
> *__Walking Stick__. Every pilgrim needs help to keep walking, especially when we have walked a long while. The Camino allows*

us the privilege of meeting true travel companions. Think about the special people on the Camino who help or encourage us when we want to give up. Their life stories and conversations inspire us as well. This is one of the many great life lessons that the Camino offers us. Who are the people who serve as "walking sticks" in your life journey? What would it look like for you to be a "walking stick" for others?

<u>Scallop Shell</u>. Years ago, every pilgrim who walked and reached Santiago received a special manuscript and scallop shell to hang on their back or hat. This symbol represented the changed life which they experienced as they walked on the Camino, and that they were now returning home as a different person. The shell, if you look at it from above, looks like a hand. This symbolizes the good works that Jesus did for humankind. Whoever wore the shell wanted to express publicly their desire to live by this lifestyle of serving and loving the rest of humanity. What changes have you experienced on the Camino? What steps do you need to take to be a true pilgrim in life?

(Information taken from pamphlet courtesy of La Fuente del Peregrino)

Looking over at Denise, I thought how funny that we had found ourselves together on these profound, almost unimaginable adventures over the past two years, first in California at a celebrity's house party and now walking El Camino in Spain. As we walked, Denise and I shared more of our life story.

I stated, "I can't believe I am doing this. I would never imagine in a million years that this is where I would be at this point in my life. You know, I thought I was never going to be happy again after my mom died—I truly thought Frank wanted to leave me too. It was such a strange experience. No one ever could explain grief to me—I don't think that anyone can ever prepare you for it either. But, when it came down to deciding to live or just fade away, I chose to fight my way back. Ultimately, there was no way I was going to give up. Friends like you really helped me through it. I am forever grateful. I always looked forward to seeing you in your courtroom."

"Yes, it has been quite a journey," she stated and smiled.

"And, now I'm starting my whole career all over—yep lots of leaps of faith."

So day by day, I forged ahead doing what I could to heal from the pain of many losses. After picking myself up and getting the help I needed, I decided to challenge myself and ended up on this pilgrimage. We all go through physical and emotional pain, but suffering is optional. Saying "yes" to this experience meant I didn't want to suffer anymore.

"I am so curious as to what awaits at Finesterre—gotta make it through the next four days."

Rita called out, "Ready? Next stop through Lestedo to Palas de Rei."

We both reluctantly stood up, and I said, "Let's go."

More sheep, more gravel, more downhill and uphill. I was really tired and ready to be there already. This part of El Camino felt like it was never going to end. My blisters had blisters now. Even changing socks halfway, I felt the rawness of my skin in my hiking boots. Looking at the rash climbing higher on my leg, I got worried that something really bad was going on in my shoes. I resolved that I would get to the outskirts of Palas de Rei and call a cab then.

"Can we do that? Can we call a taxi when we get to town?"

"What?" Rita said.

"I mean, we will have arrived there. Completed our obligation for the day, right? Please." I moaned.

Denise replied, "There is no way I'm going to stop until I get to where everyone else stopped. We are going the whole way—no questions, no cabs, that's it."

Then she looked at me with her million-dollar smile. And I shook my head, knowing she was right. As the pamphlet said, Denise encouraged me when I wanted to do nothing but call it a day. She was my symbolic walking stick, although, at that moment, I wanted to hit her with a real one.

"Fine, okay, fine! Buen Camino," I said sarcastically and pouted.

At the side of the road was a memorial. "Oh, look, look there, a notice in memory of some guy who died on El Camino. That's great, I am going to die here. Would it be worth it?"

Happy that nobody paid attention to my comment, we kept walking. We finally crossed the city line into Palas de Rei. We had another thirty minutes of agony to get to the middle of town. I couldn't feel my legs anymore, and my feet were on fire.

Coming down the long gravel road that took us to the end, excited and exhausted, I took a video to capture that incredible moment in time:

So here we are coming up on the end of day two, and it was literally almost 18 miles. Walking into town square at Palas de Rei or something like that. Cause right now I'm so tired that I'm not sure what I'm saying. So, yeah, I can't believe we made it, day two, everyone said it was 13 miles, but it was eighteen, whatever. We are here. The road and I will part and meet again tomorrow. But we took the challenge, and we made it. Thank God!

It was getting dark, almost seven o'clock. We'd walked eleven hours. Now we headed for town hall, where everyone else was finishing the day off. As we approached, we saw fellow pilgrims from our group exiting the church after mass, walking toward us, and clapping. We arrived in the city to a bold welcoming of love, and it felt wonderful.

"You made it!" they cheered.

"We made it!" we cried.

Hugs all around, they walked up the hill to grab a taxi to take them to the hotel. I looked at Denise and said, "Don't you dare get in that cab before we make it to town hall."

She smiled. Walking down the hill, we arrived at the center of town and entered the church as the rest of the patrons were leaving. Walking right in, Denise and I went to different sections, dropped our gear, and collapsed. I felt the weight of the world slip off my shoulders, fell to my knees, and cried tears of gratitude and disbelief for a full five minutes.

Gathering what strength remained, I lit a candle under St. Anthony for my family, my mom, and my friend's son, and I hoped that today's walk helped him get past some big hurdles as well. I signed the church's ledger and got the final stamp of the day in my passport. After I greeted the priest and thanked him with a Love Button, he guided me to some baskets at the front of the altar. Asking which language I spoke, he pointed me toward the English basket and told to me to take a message. I did and read it:

For we are God's workmanship, created in Christ Jesus to do good works, which God prepared in advance for us to do. (Eph.2:10)

It was the perfect message for me. I smiled and thanked him. Denise and I walked out of the church. Now in Palas de Rei after collapsing from exhaustion on the church bench—letting the tears flow, releasing so much pain and sorrow, and at the same time such a sense of accomplishment having persevered—I felt like this was a turning point for me. Outside, the church bells were ringing in celebration, music to my ears marking this moment in time.

We grabbed a taxi to take us up to Parada das Bestas guest house. After two days of walking, I felt like a VIP riding up there. When we got to the hotel, we were greeted by gorgeous black and white border collies that looked like my dogs. I got my suitcase, went to my room, and recorded a video to send to my husband, dad, and sisters. Through tears I said:

Hey—I made it through today. This is the hardest thing I have ever done. I mean I never in a million years thought I would ever get through this. I had no idea what to expect. My feet are killing me. Even with my blisters, I walked 35 miles in two days. I'm crying because I can't believe I finished it, didn't think I would finish it. These are kind of happy tears if you can believe it. It was a long day. What doesn't kill you makes you stronger, right? I'm very emotional. If this walk didn't break me, not much can. At least I don't give up—I don't quit. I have four more days, and I have no idea how that is going to happen. Please pray for me. I love you all.

Even after doing the video, I couldn't stop crying. My feet looked like two huge sausages, with broken blisters and a worsening rash. I sent a text to Dr. Habib, and he replied that I should bathe both feet with coconut oil and drink mint tea. It was worth a shot. After I showered, I joined the rest of my group at dinner. As we walked in, they greeted Denise and me with applause. I started to cry again. Even though I was emotionally spent, I just couldn't stop the flow of tears.

Looking at the Health app on my phone, I took a moment to take notice of the 17.9 miles—44,412 steps and 6 floors—we traversed. Outside my room, there was a working fireplace. It felt good to sit on the couch, getting warmed up. Another member of my group was out there too. She showed me some of the beautiful photos she captured that day.

"Wow, those are amazing, Cristina," I said, jealous at not really getting a chance to take in the beauty of it all.

"Tomorrow's walk is shorter, right?" I said optimistically.

"I think so. We're supposed to get in a lot earlier."

"Thank goodness! You don't happen to have coconut oil with you?"

"No, not coconut oil."

"Well, I guess I'll get some tomorrow. Good night, my friend."

"Good night!"

Before I went to sleep, I wrote to my soul sister who messaged me earlier that day: *"Got to Palas de Rei and bawled. Sat in the church and bawled and am still crying."*

She rejoiced with me: *"FREE AT LAST! I feel a lot of Mother Mary energy around you. This is your HEALING."*

I was relieved, but I knew there was more ahead. We still had four more days to go.

CHAPTER 24:

Nevertheless, She Persisted

"Nevertheless, she persisted."
—**SEN. MITCH MCCONNELL**'s rude retort in an attempt to
silence Sen. Elizabeth Warren on the floor of the Senate.
Instead it has become a feminist movement slogan.

Palas de Rei to Melide

At seven in the morning, we waited outside the guest house for the taxis
that would take us back to the center of town. Rita announced, "Today
is going to be an easy and beautiful walk, only 15 kilometers. If you get
to Melide first, be sure to eat some delicious octopus and call the accommodations to pick you up when you're done. Heidi is up front, and I'll
be at the back. The weather looks great. Enjoy."

Today I was with Vicky, Denise, Rita, and two more. Following with
her daily themes, Denise wore her red, long-sleeved shirt completely
covered with hearts.

"It's all about self-love today," I pointed out.

"Yep, all about self-love!" Denise replied.

Sporting my black LOVE cap, I was into this theme too. We took
photos in front of the stone statue of two traditionally dressed pilgrims
pointing the way to El Camino and headed out of Palas de Rei.

I felt playful this morning. Taking more photos with my friends, I
started to pay attention to the little things along the way. As we passed
a house called Casa Villanova, I sent the photo to Mary who graduated

from Villanova University. I saw a white car on the left side of the road whose license plate boasted my name. Standing and pointing proudly to the word "MEG," taking it as a sign I was on the right path, I took another photo. First stop, I got a stamp in my passport at Parroquia San Xulian Do Camino, a beautiful Romanesque church named for the patron saint of travelers. Inside, I lit a candle, dedicating my walk to all the healers back home who helped me get this far.

At one thirty, Frank and Ava called. "Go, Mommy, go! Go, Mommy, go! How are you doing?"

"So much better today."

"Awesome, you got this. We love you!"

"I love you too."

We walked through the enchanted forests. The day before, Rita told me that there was a little medicine shop in the first hamlet. There it was, Artesinia Castillo de Lobo, the Wolf's Castle. In the shop, the owner pointed out a *bolsa medicinal*, a medicine bag. A local medicine woman had made the pretty, sparkly bag to place under your pillow at night to help you on your spiritual path. This place made me think of one of my magical healers who helped me in Miami, so I bought her the medicine bag. I remember her telling me before I left for Spain, "You may be going with others, but ultimately this journey is an individual one. Remember that. This is about finding your own way."

Continuing on, it felt like we were walking through a fairytale land. Cobblestone roads led up to an old medieval bridge crossing over the river and past the mud. It was really peaceful. Passing livestock all around, I noticed that the mile markers had a lot of inspirational graffiti such as, "You were made for greatness" and "Love wins." I liked these reminders. Prior to crossing over the last bridge before the village of Leboreiro, I saw someone had placed a Love Button on a white rain boot. I was happy to see that another person in my group was leaving a trail of breadcrumbs for me, and that we were going the right way.

We met at the restaurant called A Garnacha in Melide, a pulperia where they sell octopus, Galicia's most classic dish. While I was more interested in washing my clothes than eating octopus, I looked for a taxi to travel up to Casa Teillor with those who had already finished lunch. There, the rooms were gorgeous villa-like lofts. When I asked whether they offered a cleaning service, the owner took my clothes to wash them herself for minimal cost. It was still early, only a little before five. Looking at the Health app on my phone, I saw it had been an easy 10.5-mile walk—26,626 steps and 4 floors. Tonight, I was going to enjoy a shower and a nap for the first time since arriving in Spain. When I got up, I felt refreshed. With renewed energy, I was actually going to engage in tonight's evening festivities for the first time since we began the Camino. I could not wait.

Just before dinner, we gathered at the grain storage to wait for the owner to open up the dining hall and deliver our food. In this open-air facility, we were able to sit on the cement benches and watch the brilliant orange-yellow sun set over the small town. This whole evening felt like a return to medieval times. With the exception of the modern apartments, Casa Teillor offered an opportunity to experience what the authentic Galician rural life was like, a beautiful quiet compound in the countryside. Boon, one of the Malaysians, encouraged us to read Gokan-no-ge, the "Five Reflections" from the Zen tradition to bless the food before we ate:

> *First, let us reflect on our own work and the effort of those who brought us the food.*
>
> *Second, let us be aware of the quality of our deeds as we receive this meal.*
>
> *Third, what is the most essential is the practice of mindfulness, which helps us to transcend greed, anger, and delusion.*
>
> *Fourth, we appreciate this food that sustains the good health of our body and mind.*
>
> *Fifth, be thankful for all and eat with gratitude.*

The seventeen of us spent the evening drinking and singing acapella campfire songs starting with "She'll Be Coming Around the Mountain." Denise and I sent out a video to document that we were at the halfway point on our pilgrimage.

Denise began jubilantly, "Hey, it's Denise and Meg."

"Yes, we are still Denise and Meg. A little battered," I replied and laughed. "April 17, we finished 10.7—hike and walk. We did it."

She said, "Three days. We are over the halfway point."

I added, "We made it over 61 kilometers, so far, and we need to get to 100—pray for us. We laughed, we cried, rolling hills, and we are still smiling."

And Denise concluded, "We are still smiling. So remember, conquer your fears, look for your life challenges, just do it, and this too shall pass. Today's message from Denise and Meg is self-love. Enjoy your view."

Today was a good day. I had clean clothes, soaked my legs in Epsom salts, and got coconut oil to massage my feet. The rash was getting better, and I felt like I had a new lease on life. We had 50 km left. Still a long way, but I started to actually believe that I had this.

Melide to Arzua

To prepare myself for day four, I went to bed early. At three o'clock, I was wakened by my phone ringing. It was the concierge at my condo back in Miami. Forgetting the time difference, and never having known a time where a three a.m. call meant good news, my first thought was that something horrible had happened. So much for a good night's sleep.

I said, "Hello—is everything okay?"

"Yes, ma'am. Jimmy John's Subs is here with a food delivery, can I send them up?"

"Are you kidding me?" I laughed. "Please call my son via the land-line, it's three in the morning where I am in Spain."

"I'm so sorry. Will do."

I had not talked to my son, Michael, all week. I guess this was his fifteen-year-old way of letting me know he was still there and thinking about me.

I texted him, "Your food is on its way up. I love you, Mikey."

I tried unsuccessfully to go back to sleep. Alone in this huge rustic villa, it felt a little haunted. Wooden shingles covered the windows, and when the wind blew, the noise reminded me of a scene out of a scary movie. My imagination ran wild. I definitely watched way too many horror movies as a kid, thanks to my dad. This reminded me of the film *Halloween* when Michael appeared out of thin air. My thoughts were going crazy now. I grabbed my journal to write, and a small book fell out. It was the small pocket book I'd brought because my friend's mom recommended it—*As a Man Thinketh* by James Allen. I opened it up and read it.

Allen declared that the effect of thought on circumstances was profound. "A man's mind may be likened to a garden, which may be intelligently cultivated or allowed to run wild; but whether cultivated or neglected, it must and will, bring forth. If no useful seeds are put into it, then an abundance of useless weed seeds will fall therein and will continue to produce their kind." I did have a history of planting useless weed seeds. Whether gifted to me or adopted as my own, I took note of this and made a promise to consciously plant good thoughts. I read some more and dozed off.

At seven o'clock, I woke once again and met everyone in front at eight. Diligently wrapping my blisters, still gross, I readied myself for the 15 km ahead of us. It was another beautiful morning, cool under a clear blue sky. We photographed a gorgeous sunrise over the vista below. Heidi announced that she would be walking in the back, and Rita took the lead today.

Our first stop was Santa Maria de Melide church, not even 1 km down the road. Classified as a national monument, a gem of Melide's Romanesque style, Vicky pointed out St. Anthony on the right and Our Lady of Sorrows, its patron saint, in front. Today I dedicated my walk to spreading love with the Love Button Global Movement. After I loaded up my group with a ton of Love Buttons, the faster hikers took off.

When we got to the split point to veer right uphill, a huge sign in the middle drew our attention to two mile markers, one for bicycles and the other for hikers. Uncertain, we turned toward the path to the right. At route marker 49,577, I saw a Love Button on top, smiled, and knew we were going the right way. We started the steep uphill climb toward Boente. We were on our way to Arzua, Cheese City.

Rita said that Arzua had a number of legends associated with the city and its oak trees.

I googled one called "the legend of the pilgrim":

There was a passage of a hungry pilgrim through the town of A Coruna. When he knocked on the door of a bakery where they had just warmed up the bread, the lady of the premises replied that they did not attend to thieves, that if he wanted bread, he would have to pay for it. The poor man on the pilgrimage knocked on another bakery in the village, where he was given more fraternal assistance, offering bread from last week, since the day was still baking. In a moment of carelessness, the pilgrim disappeared mysteriously without a trace, and at the time of taking the bread out of the oven, the buns of the first bakery had turned to stone, while those of the hospitable bakery had turned to gold. (taken from vivcamino.com)

Then I read about the famous cheese of Arzua. They even have an annual Cheese Festival in its honor. Accompanied by folkloric festivities, people from near and far would come and delight in eating Arzua's cheese.

Together with four others in our group, Vicky said, "I guess we will be eating cheese today!"

I was glad to be with these ladies on this route lined with beautiful oak trees acting as a natural canopy. Once we left the forest, Alicia and I noticed that there were more tiny butterflies and small finches hovering around us.

Alicia said, "That is how my mother shows up for me since she passed away. She's a beautiful little finch."

I replied, "Really? What a beautiful and colorful little songbird. My mother shows up as a butterfly."

She said, "I know. I remember you telling your story. You know, I have loved you and your mom from the first time I heard you talk about her at the Emmaus retreat where we first met. I even googled her."

I replied, "Really? That is so amazing!"

"Luckily, I found a photo of her, so I could put a face to the beautiful person you adored. I adored my mother, Mery, too. It was so hard when she got sick. I remember that she was a fighter. She loved life so much."

"Alicia, you definitely are a lot like your mother: smart, full of life, and a bright white smile that lights up every room you enter. I always wanted to get to know you better. Didn't know I had to go on a 77-mile torture hike to do so. Life is so funny, right?"

She laughed, "Yep, life is so funny that way. All of us walking the same Camino, yet encountering different characters. Each life a unique unfolding, so blessed to live it to the fullest."

I nodded in agreement, "Look, there is another finch and butterfly, I think our moms are watching over us to tell us that they are proud of us."

"Yes, they are!" We both smiled.

As we entered another hamlet, there were traditionally dressed women selling tourist mementos at the outskirts. We watched them approach the pilgrims in front of us, haggling for sales. The young one cajoled the pilgrim with trinkets, bracelets, and the like.

Alicia looked at me, "I think she's a pickpocket. Did you see her hands were hiding under the shirts?"

"Oh my, I think you're right."

"Yeah, I put the Love Button in her hand so she couldn't steal from us."

"Way to go, Alicia!"

Check not being pickpocketed off the list of possible disasters.

On the way up the next hill, we saw a wall labeled Comida Para El Alma, Food for Thought. The fence was lined with orange and yellow cards that contained inspirational thoughts. I read the first one:

There is fast food but there is no fast wisdom. We can only under-stand new ideas when we are ready for them.

How appropriate. Seven years ago, I would not have been ready for any of this. Whatever wisdom we gained certainly did not come fast. After reading the rest of the cards lined up against the fence, we saw a table covered with stones. For a small donation, you could take a "sorrow stone" and leave it wherever you like, symbolically leaving sadness behind you. Traditionally, pilgrims would leave sorrow stones at Cruz de Ferro, the Iron Cross located in the Leon mountains outside of Astorga. I bought two, one to take to El Monte do Gozo, Mountain of Joy, and the other to gift to my soul sister Teda when we met in Madrid at the end.

At one o'clock, I got my daily check-in call from Frank and Ava. It was the highlight of my day. No sweeter words than, "Go, Mommy, go!"

We crossed the medieval bridge over the River Iso, 11 km into our walk. We had another uphill climb awaiting, but until then, the sightseeing in Ribadiso was magical. Some took advantage of the cool water and soaked their feet. I was too afraid to take off my shoes, worried that it would do more harm than good.

When we arrived in Arzua, Vicky and I caught up with three more of our group at Café Louie. We sat down and ordered a huge dish of Arzua's cheese. The cheese was soft like muenster and just salty enough. Building up a decent thirst, we washed it down with the restaurant's delicious signature sangria.

Plenty full and a little tipsy, before we got ready to call a taxi, we wanted to stop at the nearest pharmacy. After I grabbed my backpack and walking sticks, I turned around to make sure we were all together. Then without looking, I went to step off the curb and landed on the edge of a storm drain cover. I lost my balance for a moment, and my right ankle turned on its side and twisted. I tried to put my weight on it and winced in pain.

"Vicky, I think I did something to my ankle."

She replied, "Oh no. Well, we are going to the pharmacy anyway. You can get something for it. Then we can take a cab and get ice at the hotel."

"Thank you." I wiped the tears from my eyes, wondering why everything I do has to be so dramatic. I was actually enjoying myself, and now this. I hobbled with Vicky over to the pharmacy across the street. One of the other pilgrims went in and bought Voltaren gel, an anti-inflammatory. Then we found a chair to sit and wait for the taxi we called to take us to the hotel.

We arrived at Casa Brandariz to drop off those staying there and waited for transportation to take us down the hill. Our group was staying at two separate locations. It was such a beautiful place. There was a bell tower located beside the main cobblestone building. We stayed at Casa Corredoira, a chalet of rooms alongside a granary and working farm. Roosters were running all over the place. The manager grabbed a traditional pilgrim's hat, cape, walking stick, and gourd so we could all play dress-up in front of the old building across the way. Laughing playfully as we dressed the part, parading across the small enclave, it was lovely.

After checking into my room, I took off my shoes to inspect the damage. On top of the rash and blisters, my right ankle was really swollen. I wondered if it would be smart to walk on a sprained ankle. I looked down at the words on my T-shirt before I changed: *Nevertheless, She Persisted.* "Okay, Mary Jo," I said, looking at her purple butterfly, "we will find a way." Checking the Health app on my phone, I saw I had walked 9.7 miles—25,495 steps and 26 floors. Two days left.

Arzua to Amenal

Thursday, April 19. At dawn, the roosters were up and had no intention of going back to sleep. I groaned and placed the pillow over my head. Having showered the night before, I tried to put as little weight as possible on my right side, but my ankle hurt a lot more. I got dressed as quickly as I could and asked my friend for the anti-inflammatory ointment she'd bought for her shin splints. When I was ready to go, I sat outside my room with my suitcase playing with the owner's two gorgeous dalmatians, Blanca and Africa. I temporarily forgot any pain. Tonight, my daughter Ava would be performing as Horace in the Miami Children's Theater Junior edition of *101 Dalmatians*. The synchronicity was not lost on me.

Today, I dedicated my walk to Amenal in memory of the seventeen Parkland victims. Knowing that we had 23 km to walk, I tied up my hikers extra tight to give my right side added support and popped a couple of Aleve. There was no way around the pain, but I had come here for a purpose. Onward.

I started off the day walking with the same crew. The rest walked way too quickly. While it had been difficult to keep up with them before, now I gave up. Before we got to the first stop, I was surprised to see two of the faster hikers sitting on the side of the road, one of whom was my Camino buddy. I tried to catch up with them, but they got up and continued before they saw me. I was sad not to be able to get to know them during the day. While we shared some of our stories in the evening, they hiked at a rapid pace, so talking during the day was out of the question.

The road was really crowded that day. As we drew closer and closer to Santiago, I imagined that it would be. After a stop at Casa Calzada, everyone went at their own pace. I found myself walking the path alone for the first time since day one. I wanted to put my music on but hesitated. Listening to the sounds of nature would have to be enough. Passing by the little brooks and rural farmhouses, I noticed a lot of dandelions, little yellow butterflies, and calla lilies, the flowers that had been in my wedding bouquet. Today, there were lots of high school kids on the road.

About thirty minutes up the road, I approached a group of fifty kids on a field trip from a school called Compañia Maria in Salamanca. Most of them walked in pairs or groups, laughing and talking. I thought about my best friend, Alicia, my soul sister from high school, the first contemporary who contemplated spirituality with me. I longed for those times when we went to the beach on weekends and talked about our dreams. Smiling, I reflected that she was the only person who ever went on long walks with me. When I go back to Orlando over the holidays, we walk 5 miles around Lake Adair to catch up on lost time. It was nice to think about her here, as she always loved me for who I was.

Around noon, I was walking through an isolated area surrounded by forest. I was all alone and starting to worry. I thought if I got mugged, I could not even run for help because of my ankle. Grateful to spot another person on the road ahead of me, I walked as fast as I could to catch up. I could tell it was one of the boys from the school. I had given him a Love Button earlier that day. As I got closer to him, I saw him swing his backpack to the front of his body and hold it to his chest tightly. *Oh, my God,* I thought, *this kid is scared of me.*

I laughed and said in Spanish, "Don't worry, I'm not going to rob you."

He laughed, and I introduced myself. "I'm Meg."

He smiled and replied, "I'm Dany."

"I saw you earlier with other students. Where are you all from?"

"Salamanca. And you?"

"I'm from Miami. Are you here on a student trip?"

"Yes, my ninth-grade class retreat." I thought, *This kid is the same age as my son.* "And you?"

"I'm with a group too. Not sure where everyone is. I guess it's kind of a retreat."

For the next 3 miles, we walked side by side in conversation. The coach/mentor in me took over. I asked him what he liked to do, what he wanted to be, what made him come alive. He told me the story of a teenager who loved to play video games, was pretty much a loner, and a child of divorced parents. He seemed insecure and acknowledged he didn't think that he would accomplish much in life.

I said, "Dany, it's way too early for you to give up on the rest of your life. You've only just begun. I have a fifteen-year-old son too, I remember how hard it is to be a teen."

He answered, "Yeah, my parents don't get me much."

"Yeah, we forget what it's like to be your age. We want the best for you; we just don't have a lot of time or patience. You know, Dany, you really are such an incredible kid. I'm so happy to have met you on the road. Thank you for walking with me."

He smiled. "You're welcome."

"Besides, at least there were two of us to fight off anyone who could harm us."

He laughed.

As we approached the highway where I needed to cross over to meet my group, Dany waved at a group of kids by the picnic bench up ahead. They waved back.

"I guess I'll leave you here." I grabbed a bunch of Love Buttons, having already explained what they were about and handed them to Dany. "Now you're a Love Ambassador too."

He introduced me to his friends. Then I gave him a hug. "See you all in Santiago. Buen Camino!"

He waved and said, "Buen Camino!"

Today was the first day I saw kids on El Camino. Today, I walked for Parkland school victims. Amazing synchronicity.

About to cross the street, I got my daily call from Frank and Ava, "Go, Mommy, go! Go, Mommy, go! Go, Mommy, go!"

"Hi. I just met a really cool kid today. Reminded me of Michael. It was really nice to walk with him. Those teenage years are so tough. What I would do if I could go back knowing what I know now. Forget that, I wouldn't go back for a million bucks. How are you guys?"

"Great, but we miss you. How are you?"

"I'm almost done, tomorrow is the last day, thank God. I sprained my ankle yesterday on a storm drain cover. Not the smartest thing to do with 25 miles left. I wrapped it up and am hoping for the best. One thing after another."

"Sorry to hear that. Do what you can do. You only have one more day. We love you."

On the other side, 15.5 km down, I met Heidi with two others who were inside having lunch at a restaurant in O Empalme. I waited there until Rita arrived with Denise to finish off the walk. Some were going to wait for a taxi to take them the rest of the way. While tempted, I decided not to. I committed to finishing the whole thing. Less than 5 miles left to go, I would take advantage of this break to get my second wind. I could do this. Not even thirty minutes later, I saw Denise walking my way with a huge smile on her face. I started applauding and got up to greet her.

"To God be the glory, my friend." I was so proud of her.

"Trust the process." She laughed. "Amen, sister!"

"Look at her rocking it, 10 miles—day five!"

"I listened to you and trusted the process."

"So proud of you."

"Amen," Denise said, throwing her arms up in the air. We gave each other the biggest embrace ever. Having the requisite distance to complete 100 km tomorrow, Denise decided to take a taxi the rest of the way.

Rita looked at me, "Are you going to go with her?"

I answered, "No, but are you okay to walk the rest of the way, Rita?"

"Sure, let me get Denise taken care of, get some water, and we'll go."

"Thank you so much. Five miles doesn't seem that far right now, I can't imagine not doing it."

Denise got in the cab. Rita turned to pay for her drink at the bar, then looked at me and said, "Let's go!"

What a beautiful walk to Amenal we had together! It was the loveliest part on El Camino thus far. For the last five days, I'd questioned if I could do this, felt the pain in my feet and legs, and berated myself for showing up in less-than-ideal condition. Now, in the home stretch, I could feel the finish line so close. The two of us walked through the magical forest talking about our dreams and aspirations. Her adult life was just beginning. We enjoyed the simple things the rest of the way. She shared with me her favorite tree, a massive, lovely oak covered in bright green moss in the middle of the forest path. A mother was following close behind as her little girl ran down the road, playing with her dog. An older gentleman was returning home after a long day of work. I couldn't help but think how everything had gotten so complicated over the last twenty years with kids, careers, and invaded by the "shoulds." Here, we were walking along, and it was truly peaceful.

Walking with Rita, I remembered my younger self and wondered what I would have done differently if I could go back knowing what I know now. I got married at thirty. My mom was still alive, I liked my job, I loved my colleagues. I was in great shape, excited about the future. I didn't feel beaten down by the world. How quickly time passes! I envied Rita's innocence. Traveling this path in silence, I recalled how fearless I used to be, excited to travel the world and take on new challenges. At nearly fifty, with two children, almost two decades married, I yearned to fall in love with life. I wanted Rita's carefree nature to rub off on me. I wanted to tell her to hold on to her light, especially when life throws unsettling curveballs.

An hour and a half later, we crossed the highway to Hotel Parrillada, Amenal. Celebrating, we both toasted the end of this hike and the beginning of the evening with a glass of wine while we waited for transportation to our sleeping quarters. Seeing everything through the eyes of thirty-year-old me, I was grateful for those last few miles. My journey seemed to have gotten a bit too sad and my light a little dull over the years. I told Rita not to worry too much as to how things unfold; as long as she kept looking for the good in this world, that is what she would find. Then Rita shared with me one of my favorite stories:

A traveler came upon a gatekeeper at the outskirts of town,
   "What sort of people live here?" he asked.
   "What were the people like where you've come from?"
replied the gatekeeper.
   "They were terrible. I'm happy to leave and start anew."
   "Well, I'm afraid that you'll find the same people here,"
replied the gatekeeper.
   Disappointed, the traveler left.
   Another person approached the gatekeeper and asked the
same question.
   "What were the people like where you've come from?"
replied the gatekeeper again.
   "They were amazing."
   "Wonderful," said the gatekeeper. "You'll find the same
kind of people here."

This parable reminded me that I always find what I'm looking for. Only one more day to Santiago. I prayed that I would find a stronger, more confident version of myself when this journey came to an end. Right now, I felt tired. I was struggling to stay optimistic about my future. My ego took a pretty big hit when I left government service. Yet that little voice within begged me not to quit. *Don't stop walking, don't give up on yourself, and like my father said, don't let the bastards get you down.* I looked at the silver bracelet on my wrist that I had worn since I resigned. It said, *"She believed she could, so she did."* I took it off and offered it to Rita.

"What's this?"

"I want to give you this bracelet to remember me!"

"Wow, thank you, Meg." She smiled as she read the words out loud.

I added, "I just never want you to give up on the beauty of your dreams. I am so grateful that you are helping me realize one of mine."

"I promise I will do my best." She smiled and put on the bracelet.

I hoped it would be a talisman of inspiration for her, a reminder to us both as we navigate the next twenty years and beyond. I still believed that magic was waiting for me in life; I just needed to keep going. While frustrated that this couldn't be easier, I knew there had to be a reason.

When I got to the Hotel Mujino da Pena in O Pino, I grabbed my *Magical Guide to Bliss* for the first time on the trip to read the insight of the day. For April 19, it said, *"Run quickly so you can fly."* The quote came from a poem from Hafiz, the fourteenth-century Persian poet. It read:

Run, my dear,
From anything
That may not strengthen
Your precious budding wings.

On the bottom of the page, the Magical Key to Bliss read: *Pay attention to conversations today and lean toward those that strengthen you.* Between Dany and Rita, today had been filled with conversations that strengthened my budding butterfly wings. At dinner, Heidi stood to give a toast, holding her red wine, offering a few final words before the big day:

"This trip would not have been possible without each and every one of you. It took every single one of you to make this happen. . . . The Camino is all about relationships, who you meet along the way. Salud!"

Looking at the Health app on my phone, I was amazed. I had walked 15 miles—37,509 steps and 5 floors. My final video journal tonight was a reminder for me:

This is it, I'm so glad it's almost over. My foot is swollen, and I'm exhausted. I'm ready for closure. My mother would not want me to cry about her and what happened and all the bad memories. She would want me to celebrate. She said, "Let me go!" I think that also means let this bad stuff go, like all the toxic stuff in my life right now, let it go. I met a lot of really great people, I was walking with the kids today. Met Dany. Just one more day, I'm tired of beating myself up and picking out my flaws. I'm going to finish what I started—I'm finding my way!

Tomorrow, we were walking to Santiago—the final day.

CHAPTER 25:

Catedral de Santiago de Compostela and the Lighthouse—Making Peace with Pain

"No eye has seen, nor ear has heard, no mind has conceived, what God has prepared for those who love. . . ."
—1 CORINTHIANS 2:9, THE BIBLE, King James Version

Amenal to Santiago de Compostela

Friday, April 20. My alarm went off at seven. The night before, as I rummaged through my emergency kit for an anti-inflammatory to help reduce the swelling, I'd found a vial of holy oil alongside my rose quartz heart stone. Last year, my friend Eva brought it back after she visited the statue of Infant Jesus of Prague at the Discalced Carmelite Church of Our Lady Victorious in Malá Strana, Prague. The story goes, in 1637 when Father Cyrillus found the statue in disrepair, while he was praying, he heard voices say:

> *Have pity on me, and I will have pity on you. Give me my hands, and I will give you peace. The more you honor me, the more I will bless you.*

And ever since, those who visit the statue document miraculous claims. Reading the words on the vial out loud as if it were a magical incantation, *Graciosus Jesulus Pragensis*, I bathed my feet with the entire bottle of oil, hoping for my own miracle to get me to where I needed to go.

The next morning, eight hours after application, I pulled off the covers and looked down at my feet. My ankle was actually worse. Disappointed, but instead of feeling sorry for myself, I carefully wrapped both feet with KT tape and added Rita's ankle brace for additional support. "I need to get through one more day," I muttered. I closed my eyes and begged, "Please let something wonderful happen today."

The owner of the hotel, a kindly older gentleman with gentle eyes, noticed that I was struggling to bring my luggage downstairs and offered to help. Following him, holding on to the railing, I arrived at the reception and placed my walking sticks and backpack against the wall. As I sat on the bench waiting for the taxis to return us to our starting point, the owner of the hotel asked in Spanish, "Can I offer you something that could help your ankle?"

"Oh please, yes, thank you!" I replied.

"You're not the first pilgrim who needs help with feet and you won't be the last." I laughed to hear him call me a pilgrim. Before this trip, I always associated the word pilgrim with Thanksgiving and the Puritans who roughed it when they came to the New World in the 1600s. That was definitely not me. Gratefully, I accepted and applied the medicine underneath my sock and brace. It immediately cooled the area, and the pain subsided a bit.

I looked at him and said, "Thank you!"

He smiled. "You're welcome." When the taxi arrived, he said, "Don't forget your stamp."

I shook his hand. "You're very kind."

"Buen Camino!" He smiled as we got in the cab.

I called back, "Buen Camino!"

Today was the last day.

We joined the rest of our group at Hotel Parrillada Amenal. Everyone was in a great mood and ready to finish what we'd started. After taking a final picture at the beginning of the road, I made my way to my Camino buddy to wish her the best. "Let's do this!" I said with a huge smile.

"Amen, let's do this," she replied.

Setting my sights on the first big stop, el Monte do Gozo, Mountain of Joy, approximately 11 km away, I bit the bullet and took off. After only thirty minutes on the road, I was in agony and could not hold back tears, as my ankle was throbbing. I was thinking, *How am I going to finish this?* I was in no mood to talk to anyone. I wanted to be by myself, and I was miserable. I started to doubt that I would make it to the final destination. I muttered under my breath, "You stupid girl—how are you going to give up now?" After walking every step of over 100 km, I had to find a way.

I started humming the tune, then singing out loud the song Mary Magdalene sang to calm Jesus in *Jesus Christ Superstar*: "Everything's all right, yes, everything's fine." I felt better. Then it dawned on me, I needed my music. I missed my music. I lived for my music. It was what I had been missing on the Camino since that first day. Music!

I made a playlist for all the big events. Every year, I set a theme and matched the songs. My sister Aimee too. Music was in our genetic code. Before I left for Spain, I'd asked friends and family to send me suggestions of great songs for the mixed playlist that I created for this pilgrimage I called El Camino 2018—real original. After day one, I'd put my earbuds away, afraid of getting lost again. *Not today!* Today, I needed the magic of my music to take me the rest of the way. I needed to move to an actual beat, dancing to my own soundtrack.

Like a good movie comes alive with the sound of an orchestral accompaniment, I inserted my earbuds, clicked on the first song on my playlist, and off I went. "We Own It" by 2 Chainz and Wiz Khalifa from *The Fast & Furious 6* rang out—starting with the rap intro—then the bass—*boom boom-pow, boom boom-pow, boom boom-pow.* I started to pretend that the musical artists were talking directly to me as I danced on the road, pushing ahead. A second wind accompanied that determined beat; I pounded on my walking sticks, moved my head up and down, and sang the refrain loudly, alive with purpose and not a care in the world. I was sure that those around me thought I was having a seizure. I started to believe those lyrics I heard. This is the biggest day of my life. Everything rode on today. This was what I had chosen. Not giving up would define so much for me. How could I not try? I'm going for it. No more stress. No regrets. I decided to own it.

From "This is Me" from *The Greatest Showman* to "Smoke Clears" by Andy Grammer. From "Cheap Thrills" by Sia to "People C'mon" by Delta Spirit. From "Warriors" by Imagine Dragon to "Take Me Home" by Chainsmokers. From "Higher Ground" by Daniel McGahan to "Poem of Atoms" by Salar Aghili. From "Mi Gente" by Gente de Zona to "Got the Feeling" by Syn Cole. From "Charlie Brown" by Coldplay finishing up with "El Camino" by Gypsy Kings, for the next 6 miles, I let these songs inspire me, and I tried to forget the pain.

Arriving at a bar called Camping right before the beginning of a long uphill climb, hearing Olivia Newton John's "Let's Get Physical," one of my colleague Richard's God-winks, I knew he was cheering me on as I finished my own journey of Los Tres Magos. On the hard-paved asphalt of the highway up through the town of San Marcos, sun beating down on us, not a cloud in the sky, Vicky joined me as we quietly walked together up a very long and steep hill. I broke the silence as we neared what looked like a park.

"I can't wait to see our first view of the three spires of the Cathedral of St. James."

She nodded. "This could be where El Monte do Gozo is. I think we have to walk up the stairs over there."

As we ascended the cement steps, I imagined it would look magical like the Emerald City when Dorothy and her gang drew near. I don't know why I expected that feeling—the gray street most certainly did not look like the yellow brick road. I did smile as a cool breeze hit me at the top of the hill. I looked over at Vicky and asked, "What's that?"

Before us stood a modern-day monument left behind after Pope John Paul II celebrated mass here in 1989. A strange-looking modern structure portrayed the Pope's visit and the pilgrimage of Saint Francis of Assisi in the thirteenth century.

"Let's go check it out," she replied. Grateful for her company, I was happy not to be experiencing this alone. Walking around the four-sided base of the sculpture, I found a spot to sit down. Then I dropped my backpack and sticks so I could pull out the envelope filled with letters of intentions, the sorrow stone, and Megan Murphy's Kindness Rock that I'd carried with me from home, setting out the message, "Check your ego and focus on your soul." I first placed the letters at the base of the monument and then covered them with various stones scattered around. On top of them, I put the Kindness Rock.

"Okay, focus on my soul," I repeated. "May joy replace the painful memories for all of us." My made-up ritual was suddenly interrupted by two gorgeous golden retrievers. They came bounding around the bend with their owners both sporting Love Buttons on their collar. I smiled.

Closer to the path leading down to Santiago, eucalyptus trees lined the road. There was a crowd gathering around an old horse and buggy decorated with colorful ribbons and strings. Looking down from the hill, I could barely see the top of the cathedral because it was cloudy and overcast. I was expecting to feel a huge sense of relief knowing that the end of this Camino was near, but it still seemed far away. Swatting away huge bumblebees, hoping not to get stung, I saw Rita, today's sweeper, and called out her name to get her attention. Making eye contact, she smiled and waved at Vicky and me. "Are you both ready to finish?" I nodded and asked, "Rita, How much more do we have to go?"

"About an hour more of walking left."

"Another hour—Rita, nooooo!" I was hoping she would say just a hop, skip, and a jump away. I wanted to cry out in joy like the pilgrims before me. But when she said one more hour, I wanted to throw a temper tantrum. "C'mon, you're kidding me!" I replied.

"Well, we still have to go down a street called Rua de San Pedro, that will be at 14 kilometers. Then about 3 kilometers more into the Praza do Obradoiro, the main square of Santiago de Compostela old town."

"Okay, let's finish this." I was really tired, and my feet were throbbing. I laughed it off, "What's one more hour anyway?"

We began our descent down the steep grassy hill away from the Mountain of Joy, walking toward the neck of the road with the other pilgrims. Today, I dedicated the final part of El Camino to my father. This past year, both of us faced real challenges that had us navigating our career paths in entirely new directions. After serving Orlando in a group for over forty-four years, he was brave enough to open his own cardiology practice. When I left DHS after nearly twenty years, I started my own business as an entrepreneur. We were each charting new territory. If he could start again, so could I. Today, I would celebrate that spirit of never say die. Noceros don't quit!

Finally, we made it through Rua de San Pedro and reached the entrance to the city. I kept looking to see if the cathedral was nearby. *Just keep swimming.* The others sent text messages that they had safely arrived at the bar in Porta de Carino in Santiago over thirty minutes earlier. I was in the last group again, but I didn't care, I just wanted to get there.

When my phone rang, I answered it.

"Go, Mommy, go! Go, Mommy go!" they cried out.

"Hi, Frank and Ava!"

"How are you doing?" Frank asked.

"Pretty beaten up! Both ankles are swollen and blisters on my feet. We are in the city but no cathedral in sight. I thought that when I crossed the city line, I would see it. I've been walking and I don't see it anywhere. You want a laugh?"

"Okay," he replied.

"I don't even know what the cathedral looks like—I never even saw a photo before I left. I really had no idea what I was getting ready for. So much for being prepared!" We laughed together.

"You got this, Meggie," he said. "We love you. We're rooting for you!"

"I'm excited to get it done. I don't know how I'm still walking, my ankle hurts so much. I'm going to finish this!"

He replied, "C'mon Meg, you got this. This is your last day—you're almost there. Can't wait to hear from you when you're done."

"Oh, God. That sounds really good at this point. I really do appreciate the call. I'll call you when I get there. I feel like it should be right around the corner. I gotta find this place. I love you both!"

"We love you too!"

Now at its outskirts, Vicky and I happily took a photo in front of the sign that read in big colorful letters "SANTIAGO DE COMPOSTELA." As we entered the city, we could see it was definitely not a hamlet. Pilgrims were mixed in with the hustle and bustle of everyday working people. As we crossed the busy streets, I started to doubt that this journey would ever end. I kept looking for a church spire but saw nothing. That's when I met a pilgrim named Diana. She approached us and introduced herself.

"This is the last day of a five-week, 600-kilometer Camino," she explained. "After 450, I pulled my hamstring. I almost quit, but I had already gone so far."

"Wow, what did you do?" I asked.

"I stopped and stayed at a hostel for a week to see if it would heal enough to continue," she replied. "I just didn't want to give up, so I started up again."

I said, "While I have not walked nearly the distance, I twisted my ankle on day four and kept going too. I came to finish it, and that's what I'm going to do."

"Yeah, every morning for the last two weeks I woke up wanting to quit but kept going. Even this morning, knowing it was my last day, I questioned if I could make it."

With a renewed purpose, I looked at her, "There's no way you're not going to make it to the cathedral after 600 kilometers. We're going to do this together, so let's go."

I needed the added push. Talking to her for the next thirty minutes, time passed quickly as we shared our stories. Originally from Texas and disillusioned with her life, she moved to Germany to teach English and to find herself. I told her that I was on El Camino to do the same thing, find myself after years of questioning my career and life. Both of us had a lot to gain by finishing this, I wasn't going to let myself or her down.

When we arrived at the bar, Denise came out to greet me with a big hug. "What's everyone doing?" I asked, "I didn't realize they were stopping to eat lunch?"

Denise replied, "I think everyone is about to pay the check."

Diana had already crossed the street and was waiting for me. I knew they wanted to go into the square together, but my feet were throbbing in pain. Physically, I could not wait. I set aside my "disease to please" others and made the decision to go on. This was my journey, and I had to be true to my path. I needed to own it, to prove to myself that I could do it.

I told Denise, "I have to finish this; tell them I'm going to go."

I crossed the street and joined Diana. Paulina, a Camino amigo from my group came too. In its interior now, the three of us walked through the city not sure where to go. There were no yellow scallop shells with arrows to guide the way. When Paulina asked for directions, a local showed us the path that led to the main square. As we crossed under the large stone archway that led into the plaza, we heard bagpipes ceremoniously announcing our arrival. I felt the anticipation and excitement build. As we reached 0 km in the Praza do Obradoiro, Diana and I cried and hugged each other, grateful we got each other there. Waving goodbye, Paulina and I continued in silence past the closed, scaffolded main entrance of St. James Cathedral looking for a way to get into the church. Turning the corner to the right, we saw a steep set of stairs lead up to another entryway.

"Pau, I have no idea how I'm going to make it up to the top on this foot."

She answered, "Yeah, I'm hurting too. Let's go over there to the left. I think I see another way up."

We walked to the side of the stairs and saw a ramp that was previously hidden from our view. We smiled at each other as if we discovered gold.

"Much easier this way—thank God Paulina!" She turned and smiled from ear to ear.

When we made it to the top, our backpacks were checked by a security guard, as a street performer sang "Hallelujah" by Leonard Cohen in the background. I gave the security guard a Love Button—in exchange, he gave me a prayer card of Saint James, the saint whose remains were buried in the cathedral. On the front of the card was a photo of the saint's face. On the back, in Spanish, there was a statement written by Pope John Paul II when he was a pilgrim arriving in Compostela on September 11, 1982. It was translated into English as follows:

Vigor del Camino— Energy of the Camino

The Camino of Santiago created a vigorous spiritual and cultural stream of fruitful exchanges between the towns of Europe. But what the pilgrims were really looking for with their humble and penitent attitude, was that testimony of faith that seemed to ooze from the Compostela stones from which the Saint's Basilica was built.

Juan Pablo II, Pilgrim in Compostela 9.XI.1982

I nodded—walking by faith brought me here. Feeling like something was missing in my life, I was yearning to discover a deeper sense of my purpose—find out clues as to what I am supposed to do here on this Earth. Perhaps I would learn something more as long as I was open to the messages from ghosts of pilgrim's past—like this one from John Paul II. Who knows? Seeking still and awakened to possibility, as long as I continued to trust the process, I am certain that keeping the faith will guide me home again with new understanding.

Initially, the inside of the church was dark and cold. However, when we stood in front of the altar, we were finally embraced by light and warmth. Facing the dazzling Baroque display surrounded by a shiny gold facade, I was in awe at the majesty before us. I felt my mom's presence all around. In fact, Paulina, who shared with me on the road that she was living with the same breast cancer diagnosis as my mother, reminded me a lot of my mom's fierce strength, determination, but most of all her incredible faith. My mom never complained to me about her illness. She just prayed without ceasing until the very end. Her entire life story was a testimony of faith in something greater than herself.

When we sat down, dropped our gear beside the pew, and fell to our knees, I dropped my head, letting the emotion of that moment take hold. I looked over at Paulina, glad I was not alone—grateful she was there with me in this holy place. I allowed myself to smile through the tears. And my doubts vanished. I had finished what I started and was so grateful.

I prayed, "Mommy, it's beautiful here. You should be here with me in person. I miss you so much. Tomorrow I'm off to the lighthouse. What will I find there?"

Suddenly, a large group of school children appeared across the aisle and broke the silence. The guard looked over and motioned for them to be quiet. As a former teacher of young kids, Paulina looked at me and whispered, "Good luck to him. There are too many. It's not going to happen." I laughed with her, then looked up and saw Alex, her brother and another fellow Camino amigo join us smiling jubilantly from ear to ear.

Excited now to share my accomplishment and ready to celebrate, I texted my husband Frank, my dad, and my sisters, "I made it to the cathedral in Santiago!"

My dad replied, "Hallelujah! This is the beginning, Meg. I'm proud of you. Your spiritual awakening has just begun. Lots of blessings will come from this."

I replied, "I hope so."

On my Health app, I walked 11.1 miles—27, 888 steps and 38 floors—today on a badly sprained ankle. I made it. I truly felt relieved that all would be well. I had overcome so much to get there. When we joined the others to take a group photo in the middle of the Praza do Obradoiro in front of the cathedral, the same musician was playing a rendition of "What a Wonderful World" by Louis Armstrong, the song I chose for the father–daughter dance at my wedding reception. I said to myself as I listened to the words of the song, *"Oh, Dad, it's a wonderful world."*

In my room at the Hotel San Francisco, a beautifully restored convent, I had an appointment with a massage therapist named Petrea (the feminine version of the name Petrus, Coelho's guide in *The Pilgrimage*). She looked at my foot to assess the damage and determine whether I should go to the emergency clinic.

"It's pretty swollen but not broken. You may have pulled something too. This happens a lot with El Camino. I'll give you a strong anti-inflammatory gel to apply. Ice it and stay off of it as much as possible."

I answered, "Thank you." Relieved, I did my best to let go of my anxiety and tried to relax and enjoy the massage.

Grateful for my walking sticks, I used them to get to mass in the cathedral later that day. At the evening Pilgrim's Mass, the priest read the list of pilgrims who had been received in the Pilgrim's Office in the last twenty-four hours, their nationalities, and where they started their pilgrimage. I sat with the Miami crew and greeted other pilgrims we met along the way. At the end of the celebration, there was a *Botafumeiro* ("censer" in Galician) ceremony, one of the most famous and popular symbols of the Cathedral of Santiago de Compostela. After my friends explained it to me briefly, I googled it:

It is a large thurible that hangs by means of a system of pulleys from the main dome of the cathedral and swings toward the side naves. It weighs 53 kg and measures 1.50 metres; it hangs from a height of 20 metres and can pick up great speed . . . The purpose of this great censer is to symbolize the true attitude of the believer. In the same way that the smoke from the incense rises to the top of the temple's naves, so must the prayers of the pilgrims rise to reach the heart of God. (taken from catedralsantiago.es)

It was impressive flying from side to side over the pilgrims, leaving a trail of smoke and the fragrance of incense. After the mass concluded, I joined Alicia to light a candle at the relics of St. James. Then we climbed the small staircase behind the altar, waiting our turn to embrace his statue.

Alicia said, "Lean in and hug him."

I did. I placed my arms around his shiny gold shoulders and announced, "Thank you for leading us safely here."

Returning to the hotel, Heidi handed me my Pilgrim Passport and with it, the "Compostela" Pilgrim Certificate for El Camino. It was beautiful, written in Latin, *Duam Margaritam Nocero*, issued by the church on April 20, 2018, as proof that I walked 111 km to Santiago de Compostela. Some believed that walking to Santiago and getting the "Compostela" meant that they had secured a VIP ticket to show St. Peter at heaven's gates. I spread out the Pilgrim Passport on my bed and reviewed each stamp that reminded me of every place and the people that I met over the last week. Taking two Aleve, lying on my bed with ice on my ankle and leg, I read my Facebook posts. My friend Ana said, "I have been following your journey and am proud of you, my friend."

Before I turned off the light to get some sleep for Finisterre, I wanted to be sure to capture everything that happened that day in my journal:

Almost to the end—both ankles swollen—blisters on both feet— in the city, but no cathedral in sight. Wondering if I sat down, would I be able to get up? Met Diana, who reminded me not to quit! With my friend—we walked on. We heard bagpipes play, a beggar on the side, we passed the Square where it says 0 kilometers—scaffolding covered the main entrance. This was not what I expected. My friend and I moved on to find another entrance— Diana left. Walking in, the cathedral was beautiful. I sat down, put my head in my hands and cried —just cried. I did it, now I have ice on my feet and lying here not really knowing if I'll be able to walk tomorrow—not sure how to feel. I could have given up —there were many moments I thought I would—I wanted to so badly! Now time to see the beauty of Finisterre—I've earned it.

Eyes have not seen the goodness that awaits. Ears have not heard the blessings that are on the way. My mind conceived a vision of the most beautiful lighthouse on April 12, 2011. Tomorrow, I would finally get to see what was waiting there for me.

Santiago to Finisterre

Saturday, April 21. Day trip to Finisterre: To the End of the World.

Sitting with Denise at breakfast, I confided in her, "I don't think I'll be able to walk the distance to meet the bus because of my ankle. Will you take a cab with me?"

"Yeah, sure I will."

Arriving at Calle da Senra 14, we waited to meet our new tour guide and travel up the Costa da Morte, the Coast of Death. Our itinerary set out visits to the towns of Ponte Maceira, Muros, Ezaro, Muxia, and Finisterre.

Denise said, "You know from that bus, I'm going to enjoy the view."

"Absolutely, going along the ocean. This is the view I've been waiting for."

The Costa da Morte was given its name because of the large number of shipwrecks along its rocky shore. Today, we would get to see fishing villages, lighthouses, medieval bridges, mills, and waterfalls. I moved to the back of the bus to a row where I had room to elevate my right leg. This would be the last adventure together on this trip for our group of seventeen.

At our first stop, Ponte Maceira, the guide told us that it was famous for its mills and the fourteenth-century medieval bridge over the River Tambre. Choosing to stay on the bus, I recorded a video instead:

All on our way to Finisterre, feeling a little bit more relaxed today. I'm trusting the process like the guy at the airport said to me the first day. And I'm going to leave my little butterfly at Finisterre. And with it, I hope to leave sadness behind and bring more light and love into my life. I'll get more clarity, so I won't be clouded by things that I'm afraid of.

At the next stop, I tried to walk toward the forty-meter waterfall of Ezaro. Unsuccessful, I sat on a bench near the parking lot and took in the beauty of its magnificence and power, the only waterfall in Europe that flowed directly into the sea. I did enjoy the gorgeous windmills as we traveled along the coast. When we got to the fishing village of Muros, a designated Historic–Artistic Monumental Site, I got off the bus and had to take photos with Denise portside. It was such a quaint little coastal town. Fishing boats were lined up one after the other on the side of the dock. We sat on a bench next to a statue of a bronze anchor and enjoyed the cool weather as a light breeze caressed our faces.

"How about this for enjoying the good life?" I asked her.

"It's beautiful here," she replied.

"Are you glad you came?"

"Yes," Denise laughed, "I'll be back. Next time I'm bringing the boys."

"They would love this." I nodded. "I'm one and done. I find it crazy enough to walk more than 70 miles to find a lighthouse I saw in a vision. I wonder if I made it all up. Wanted to hold on to my mom, yearning for something special—a final message from her. What if nothing is waiting there for me after all of this?" I looked at my foot. "And I did permanent damage?"

Denise nodded, "This adventure has been eye-opening. Lots of things to be proud of."

"One more selfie, and then let's go see what's waiting at Finisterre?" I asked.

"Absolutely! Let's do it—it's gorgeous." We both smiled and headed back to the bus.

Next stop was Finisterre. Organizing myself, I took my mother's butterfly off my backpack, unhooked all but four of the Love Buttons—these represented my father, my two sisters, and me—and wrote on one side:

Your legacy continues with your tribe—Poppie, Mary, Meg, Aimee.

And on the other:

For Mary Jo Nocero. In Memory of the Most Beautiful Butterfly!

As we drove closer, I was getting more excited. We arrived before lunchtime. The guide explained that this was considered to be the end of the ancient world. The lighthouse had been constructed in 1853 at the tip of Cape Finesterre. It stands as a reminder of the numerous marine battles that occurred between the French and the English and the numerous shipwrecks that rest at the bottom of the Atlantic Ocean. She advised that we look for the bronze boot that marked the end of the journey. She added that this is where the pilgrims would come and burn their belongings to pay homage to the old ritual and make a clean start. Then she gave us one hour to look around.

Holding my purple butterfly tight, I slowly got off the bus and turned toward the road that led to the lighthouse. Walking toward it alone, I took a deep breath as I waddled past the last mile marker post decorated with the yellow scallop shell on El Camino—0,00 km. Feeling a cool breeze off the Atlantic Ocean, I walked the last few yards determined to discover why I was so obsessed to get here, hoping something magical was waiting for me.

Standing in front of a two-story white structure that blocked the tower with the bright light at the top, I went to open the door underneath the words FARO DE FINISTERRE. It was locked. Disappointed, I walked away still looking to get closer. On a stone tablet in front, surrounded by what looked like yellow daisies, I saw a bronze plaque with the words "DE CAP DE CREUS A CABO FISTERRE 1998." Not understanding its meaning, I looked to the left, and there was a cement staircase that led up to a cliff overlooking the ocean. I grabbed onto the flimsy railing and carefully climbed up to the top, walking out onto the big boulder covered by more bright greenery and flowers. As there was nothing there to protect me from falling, I was careful to stay away from the edge but close enough to get a better view. To the left, there it was, the same lighthouse I'd seen in my vision, here at what was believed to be the end of the world where only a thin veil separated heaven and earth.

Taking it all in, believing she could hear me clearly, I whispered, "Mommy, why did you bring me here?"

Denise's laughter reverberated behind me, and I turned around. Right in front of me, I had my answer. There on a tall, four-sided thin white pole next to the cement stairs, I read the following: *May Peace Prevail on Earth.* Smiling, feeling an electric sensation run throughout my body leading to goosebumps on both forearms, I sat down on the cement slab right beside it and said those words out loud: "May peace prevail." Peace found me here, what I was seeking was seeking me—it was even on the side of my suitcase in big letters. As I let the message sink in, I closed my eyes and felt my mother say again, "Let me go!" For the last seven years, I had mourned her loss. I felt so much guilt and pain about her suffering. Seven years ago, she found her peace, and now it was my turn.

Looking at my purple butterfly, I finally understood. "This is where I will leave you. Maybe now we will both fly free."

I bent both sides of the butterfly, got up, and reached up to the top of the pole, anchoring it there.

"I hope the wind carries you away."

Sitting down again, I let the tears fall. Denise and my fellow pilgrims sat by my side and hugged me. Letting go of the butterfly, I released the pain I carried over the last forty-eight years: from being bullied as a child, never fitting in, the disappointments at my job and career, the sadness of losing my mom, grieving the loss, never feeling I'm enough, shame and my failures, and the physical pain I encountered in body and soul.

"I am going to do my best, Mom, I promise."

Remembering what my dad said about me as a baby, that I was always smiling—so happy. I wanted to feel like that again, for me and the rest of my family. That was my mission, to make peace with my pain so I could be truly happy again. Denise and I recorded a video journal marking both an end and a beginning:

"Hi, it's April 21, and we are in Finisterre, at the end of the earth."

I chimed in, "Day seven of a seven-year journey for me, seven days walking for both of us, and 77 miles."

Denise continued, "I'm going to pan a little bit so you can see the view, the ocean below, and you can hear the water. You can see the lighthouse and the sign with the butterfly for Meg, peace on earth."

I looked up. "That butterfly—I've been traveling with it. She's right up there, she's right there, my mom. Telling us it's time to bring peace so we can shine our light."

Denise concurred, "The message today is shine our light and keep the peace."

I said, "That beautiful lighthouse—be the light for other people so they can find their way. We have to walk each other home with love. Denise has love all over her today."

Denise laughed. "It has been an awesome journey, spectacular. A lifetime of memories, unbelievable the journey and challenge. Meg, I'm so glad you followed your spirit."

Taking in the view and the landscape one more time before we made our way back to the bus, miraculously, I felt lighter. I had done what I'd come here to do. And, just like pilgrims of the past, it was time to make a clean start. Listening to the whispers of the wind, I heard my mother say, "I told you that you could count on grace to get you through. I am so proud of you."

On our way home, the bus passed more wind turbines on the hills near the highway as the sun set. It reminded me of the windmills in *Man of La Mancha* and its protagonist, Don Quixote, who was always "tilting at windmills," attacking imaginary enemies. I laughed at the symbolism and hoped to not waste my energy doing the same. I'm going to realize my own impossible dreams, don't need anyone's permission to do so. I just need to be true to myself. Anything else is exhausting. Tonight, I'll celebrate the last night in the company of good friends.

Back in the restaurant courtyard of Hotel San Francisco, we spent the evening laughing and reminiscing over the last seven days that brought together seventeen strangers who were now leaving as forever friends. Then my group, led by Heidi, toasted my mother:

"Thank you, Mary Jo, for showing Meg the vision that brought us all together here. It was a Buen Camino!"

Before I returned to my room, I stopped in the courtyard of the Hotel San Francisco and recorded a last video journal:

Day seven is over. I just want to say thank you for everything. It is done—it's done. I feel peace. All my love. See you in the United States. We are going home.

Back in my room, reading my messages on social media, I found my friend Teresa had sent me something her father told her before he died:

"La vida es un camino, no un destino. Disfruta el andar." [Life is a path, not a destination. Enjoy when walking.]

She added, "Sometimes the truth is staring us in the face, and we fail to see it. So glad you realized happiness lives. Dorothy said it best, 'There's no place like home!' Fly home soon, shiny butterfly!"

I smiled and replied, "Thank you, I'm ready."

The next morning, before we left for the airport, we waited in the lobby for our transportation to arrive. It was still dark outside and very early. Because the dining room was not open, the hotel provided each of us with a breakfast bag for the road. Grateful, I took it and sat down to check my boarding passes, take an inventory of my luggage, and gather my thoughts. Everyone around me looked tired, as some had been out celebrating until the early morning. I did feel a pang of jealousy; I was so worried about getting through these last days that I was too exhausted to really celebrate anything.

I looked up and saw that Heidi was handing out something.

When she got to me, I asked, "What's this?"

Heidi replied, "It's an El Camino postcard. Write your name and address on the front and a note about our El Camino experience. When you're done, return the card to me so I can mail it out at the airport."

"What an amazing idea, thank you so much."

I loved this kind of exercise. Timely captured thoughts, delivered exactly when I need to be reminded most. On the front, it boasted a map of the entire route of Camino Frances, the French Way, from Saint Jean Pied de Port ending with Santiago de Compostela. Right above the path, it displayed all the symbols of our journey: walking sticks, gourds and shells, *cruz espada* (Santiago cross), stamps in the passport, mile markers identified by the yellow arrow and seashell, and statue of Santiago. On the back, I wrote:

4/22/18
Meg,
It's just the beginning. Make your peace with your past and fall in love w/ your life. Everything is more than all right. It's all about love—then there will be peace if we start from there. Trust the process. I love you.
Meg and Mary Jo

As I finished filling out my card, Boon sat next to me, and I smiled. "Where are you off to next?" I asked.

"All of my crew are staying in Madrid for a few days before we head back to Malaysia."

I laughed. "Only for a minute, right? Until you take off on your next rocking adventure?" Knowing the truth of those words, he laughed too.

Then he shared with me, "You know, you and Denise really amazed me. Having hiked quite a bit, I knew it wasn't going to be easy. I didn't know whether you were going to be able to finish. But you both did. You both surprised me and showed me the power of the human spirit. I'm very impressed."

"Well," I said, smiling, "thank you. The one thing I regret is that I missed a lot of the fun. Next trip, I'll be sure to celebrate."

We saw headlights pull up in front of the hotel. It was our transportation to the airport. It was time to say goodbye. Today, I would get to see my friend Teda at the airport in Madrid, and then I would leave for home.

Denise stood next to me as we waited to get on the minibus. I smiled at her and said, "Today, somehow it's gotta be an easy travel day. Maybe we can get upgraded. It's going to be a long flight. I hope we can get VIP treatment. In fact—let's manifest this."

"You think?" she replied.

"Why not? We show up acting like VIPs, then people will treat us like VIPs."

"All right, sign me up!"

Flying Home

Arriving at the Madrid–Barajas airport, Denise and I had a six-hour lay-over before our next flight to Miami. I let Denise know that I was going to meet up with my friend Teda outside the terminal and asked if she wanted to join us.

"No thanks; I'm going to go find our next gate. I don't think it's close. This airport is huge. I want to relax a bit."

"Okay, I'll see you there then. Save me a seat."

After she mentioned the airport's size, I realized I had no idea how far I had to walk and grew concerned. I could barely walk; I knew there was no way I could run if I were cutting things close. I wanted to give myself at least two hours beforehand because I was on a wait list to upgrade my ticket to business class. But there was no way I was going to miss seeing one of my closest friends after a year apart.

When I finally left the secured area and arrived at the coffee bar called Éspression Lavazza, our rendezvous site, I sat in a location where I would be easily visible. I put my carry-on next to the table, put my foot up in an attempt to minimize any inflammation, and waited. After about thirty minutes, I heard Teda's voice.

"Meggie!" I stood up excitedly and turned around.

We hugged, and I said, "It is so good to see you, and what a trip I had. This is the perfect ending. Our very own soul talk."

"I'm so proud of you. You amaze me. How was it?"

"I wish you had come with me. It was an experience that, while I know it has huge meaning for me, I'm definitely not doing it again."

"I'll go eventually—who knows when?"

I pulled out the rock with the cross of St. James and gave it to her.

"This is what you leave on El Camino along with your sorrows and pain. Take it with you when you do go."

We lost track of time and spent the next few hours catching up. Then I looked at my watch and jumped up.

I said nervously, "I have to go. I have no idea where the next terminal is. If it's far, I'm definitely screwed."

"Don't worry Meg, I have an idea. I think that there's a service here for people who need wheelchair assistance."

I wasn't sure what she was talking about, but I got up and followed her. Teda walked up to a young man standing in front of a kiosk that had a yellow sign that read in Spanish PMR—*personas con movilidad reducida* (persons with reduced mobility.) Teda asked in Spanish if I could get assistance to my departure gate.

I grabbed her. "Are you sure this is okay? I feel funny asking."

"It's free. That's what the service is for."

The young man then proceeded to take my ticket and passport, went to his computer, and then returned.

"Vamos—let's go!" He handed me everything and a voucher and invited me to sit in the wheelchair.

I hugged Teda and laughed. "Thank you so much. I miss you already. I can't believe this; definitely VIP!"

I had to go through security again to return to the terminals. The young man moved to the front of the line, handed my documents to the agent, and told me to go through the metal detector. He met me on the other side. Instead of going through the airport, we entered a tunnel that led to a shuttle outside a corridor. The driver took my carry-on and helped me get on board. He drove me past the airplanes on the tarmac to a terminal approximately fifteen minutes away. When we arrived, another young man was waiting with a wheelchair to take me to the gate.

Arriving, I saw Denise. She looked at me and smiled.

"VIP is right—how did you get an escort in a wheelchair?" she asked.

"That was all Teda's idea—thank God." I took a deep breath, relieved. "There was no way I would have made it otherwise."

"That was a far walk too. Took me about an hour to find where I was going."

"Know what I have?"

"What?"

"A voucher for you and me to board the plane before the rest of the people—I told you VIP."

"Awesome!"

On the plane ride home, in a dream state, *I saw my mother sitting next to me as healthy as could be. All was well in my world. All made sense. I held her hand tightly. Then I saw my young children come to the* door; I knew those big brown eyes well. I bent down and gently lifted their gaze to the sky where together we saw the most brilliant sunrise colored by hues of red, yellow, pink, green, purple, orange, and blue. I turned to look at my mother, knowing that if I left her, I couldn't come back. I grabbed my children's hands, looked at her, smiled, and waved goodbye. She placed her hand at her heart center to remind me that I did not have to go far to find her there.

I woke up, inspired, and wrote:

El Camino di Amore

Who am I? Just another soul walking on this road.
Who am I? Doing my best to bring a little more love and find a story to be told.
Who am I? Looking to you my friend for the key to be free.
Who am I? Taking back my power to show up authentically.
Who am I? To each of us as we find the other as we roam.
Who am I? Eternally grateful to each one of you for each day you are walking me home!
Who am I? I am magical, I am passion, I am all I am meant to be.
Who am I? I am the road, El Camino, for now you are all a part of me!
For when I let go, I remind my feet—time to dance,
The pain goes away, with Love, El Amore, peace is finally given a chance!
Love wins! Buen Camino

Arriving in Miami, I waited for Denise so we could leave the plane together.

"Did you sleep?" I asked.

"A little. I'm happy to be home," she replied.

"Me too. Another adventure complete. Now to process everything that happened."

We both laughed rather wearily.

After we collected our bags, Frank met us curbside. I greeted him with a big hug and kiss.

"Let me get your bags," he said after hugging Denise.

After placing them in the back of his SUV, he got in the car and asked, "Ladies, how'd it go?"

"Amazing," Denise answered.

"Yes, amazing," I agreed.

He started the car. "So last year Malibu, this year Madrid. Where to next?"

I said, "Maui by the ocean for me."

Denise answered, "We shall see!"

Gazing out the car window as we left the airport, armed with all the wisdom gained, I remembered what Alicia, my fellow pilgrim, said when we arrived in Santiago de Compostela. "You'll never be able to experience true happiness if you're constantly looking for it. Usually it's right there in front of you the whole time—you don't have to go anywhere."

And she was right, I can find true happiness and bliss each day when I count my blessings all around me, embracing the magic where I am. Or, as Denise says, just enjoying the view. It only took me forty-eight years, struggling against and then trusting the process, feeling shame, seeking approval, letting it go, quitting my job, choosing another path, traveling to Northern Spain, walking 111 km to find a lighthouse so I could embrace life, knowing that there is no one else that I would rather be than me. Leaving the cocoon, I set out on a new journey. Strengthening my budding wings, I get to be free if I so choose. Excited to see what my future holds, I'm ready to shine; the sky is the limit. Now I do believe:

I am a Beautiful Butterfly, La Bella Farfalla—it's time to manifest the life of my dreams!

Epilogue

"However dark the night, however dim our hopes, the light will always follow the darkness."
—LOUIS ZAMPERINI, American World War II veteran, 1917–2014

August 2018: A Day with Lady Liberty

On another extremely hot and humid day in August, while the weather was very similar to that life-altering day ten years earlier when I learned of my mother's diagnosis, I knew the events of this day would unfold very differently. As I sat up in my bed to welcome a beautiful Miami sunrise over Biscayne Bay, I was excited. About ten days earlier, my artist friend Hector emailed me that he had received his appointment letter to appear at Miami's US Citizenship and Immigration Services to become a citizen of the United States of America. Today was the big day, and he had invited me to attend.

Leaving my house, I realized that this would be my first naturalization ceremony. Today, I would not be sitting in a courtroom asking questions on cross that would challenge the applicant's story. Today, I would not witness disappointment on the faces of those who were ordered removed from the United States. Today, I would welcome my friend and many more from all over the world, as fellow Americans who would take the oath of allegiance.

I pulled up to the front of the immigration building, parked, took a deep breath, and looked in the rearview mirror to make sure my makeup had not melted off. I smiled, noticing the glitter I'd sprinkled over the bright pink shadow on my eyelids and consciously reapplied my red lipstick, making sure it stayed in the lines. I got out of my SUV, pulled down and smoothed out my black dress, and took another deep breath to build up my confidence. It had been a year since I'd resigned as an immigration prosecutor. Today I showed up at this federal building, head held high. To complete my outfit, I put on a pair of my favorite black heels, even though it was still hard to walk despite four months of therapy. Immediately as I stepped out onto the concrete, I felt the oppressive midday heat come up through the pavement. I was certain it would be much cooler inside.

After going through security, I saw Hector's provocative painting of a sexy woman covered by the American flag, entitled "The American Dream," over by the left wall. The speaker's podium stood in the middle, and on it was the seal of the Department of Homeland Security. Above, an American flag was adorned by two decorative crescent swatches of red, white, and blue. But my attention immediately focused upon the small replica of the Statue of Liberty that stood in front.

Seeing the statue, I couldn't help but smile as I was reminded how the theme of freedom had played a huge part in my life over the past year. In fact, in June, my sisters, my dad, and I had traveled to New York to celebrate our seventh annual trip together that we fondly called Poppiepalooza, a play off the slang term referring to an exaggerated event. This year, we visited Brooklyn, the Statue of Liberty, and Ellis Island and discovered more about this nation's immigrant story.

With our tour guide, among many famous landmarks in Brooklyn, we visited Greenwood Cemetery, a Revolutionary War historic site. There, we learned about the Irish American Charles Higgins's Altar to Liberty. His altar showcased a statue of the strong, fearless woman Minerva, the Roman goddess of arts and war, standing at Brooklyn's highest point and gazing down. Her left arm saluted and her eyes were locked upon her twin, the Statue of Liberty, who stood tall 3.5 miles away in the New York Harbor. Our guide called it one of the coolest statues on Planet Earth. Standing next to it on the hill, I was moved as tiny yellow butterflies flew all around on a gorgeous, sunny summer day.

The next day, we traveled to see where my great-grandfather entered the United States at Castle Garden, followed by a tour of Ellis Island, the gateway and busiest inspection station for over twelve million immigrants between 1892 and 1954. Among the highlights, I entered the Grand Hall where after a long, arduous journey by sea, the many ghosts of the past waited their turn to discover if they would be admitted to start their new life. Outside, on the memorial wall, surrounded by beautiful yellow and purple flowers, families honored their legacies in the garden near the water. I was proud to see the last names of my family (Santangelo, Rao, Nocero, Simone, Scanlon, and Cuomo) listed among the many immigrants who came through escaping religious persecution, political strife, and unemployment, seeking family connections, or lured by adventure, all looking to be a part of the fabric of this country.

And we had a chance to get reacquainted with Lady Liberty herself, a gift given by the French in 1884. This piece of art symbolized democracy and served to welcome those who had arrived through Ellis Island. It still stands as a symbol of liberty and a beacon of hope for the world. As I walked around the platform near her feet, I looked up to see her holding the flame of freedom high, moved as she beckoned to the highest part of each of us. Then, reading the iconic poem written by Emma Lazarus inscribed on her base, I could almost hear the words spoken aloud: "Give me your tired, your poor, your huddled masses yearning to breathe free," Emma had written. "I lift my lamp beside the golden door." I was grateful that my Italian American relatives had taken that journey to come to America in search of opportunity, hope for a better life, and a chance to fulfill their potential in a way that would inspire most dreamers.

Back in Miami, the officiant called out each individual to stand once their country was named. People from Colombia, Venezuela, Cuba, Italy, France, and Azerbaijan all stood together, each holding a small American flag, ready to take on the great responsibility of upholding the rule of law and the torch of freedom themselves. And after the oath was administered, the master of ceremonies encouraged everyone to stand, sing, and celebrate as they played country singer Lee Greenwood's song, "God Bless the USA."

Waving and singing along, I had a flashback to the festivities of my wedding celebration almost nineteen years earlier: all my friends and family waving American flags at our reception in the grand ballroom of the Italian-themed Portofino Hotel in Orlando, Florida, dancing along with the band as they played patriotic melodies that included this song. There I saw my mother, waving the flag, smiling at me, and celebrating.

My heart sunk a little as I remembered how happy I was, feeling so beautiful and young and elegantly dressed to the nines in my silk satin strapless wedding gown complemented by my tiara that lay perfectly atop my long jet-black hair. My mother looked equally stunning and full of life in her elegant red spaghetti-strapped formal gown with sequins sewn on the bodice. How I yearned to go back in time. We were all glowing as we marched around the dance floor, drunk on both the excitement of the day and the fine Italian wine. And at the end of the night, when the music stopped, I remembered hugging my mother ever so tightly, thanking her for everything, as I, like all these new Americans, began a new chapter.

After the ceremony was over, I congratulated Hector and his family and left. As I started my car, I waited a moment to process all that happened over the last seven years that ended with my spiritual pilgrimage on El Camino. I was proud of my story; I promised to continue to write well and edit often. As I still gather the keys that will unlock secret treasures, I continue to walk forward on this journey with an open mind and an open heart, embracing my creative side. My healing will continue. As my father said, "As long as you wake up and make peace with the pain as a blessing, not a curse, the reason for this spiritual pilgrimage will continue to come to light." Certainly, my beautiful relationship with my tribe is a gift that I hold dear.

My mother left me a message on my voicemail in February of 2011. It is the last recording I have of her voice. She said, "Hello, my Meggie, I'm looking for you wherever you are." I know she is. Since she passed, she has come to me in my dreams. In one of the first after she died, *my mother and I were sitting at the kitchen table, the place where we spent hours talking. She looked so young, as if she were about thirty. She was wearing one of her favorite light blue nightgowns. She looked at me and said, "Well I guess the chemo didn't work."*

Feeling incredibly lost, I asked, "What do we do now?"

She said, "I guess we have to move forward."

El Camino continues as each sunrise greets a new day. Now I get to choose what I care about and what brings me joy, and to do my best to make a difference living out my own legacy. And when I face more challenges or need inspiration on my hero's journey, I'll grab my *Magical Guide to Bliss* off the shelf and share whatever insight is offered. Whether the theme is January's carpe diem or February's love. Whether I seek deeper meaning as March offers profound wisdom or take an adventure as April transforms dreams into reality. Whether I explore May as I further resurrect my creativity or really embrace joy in June. Whether I celebrate freedom in July or friendships in August. Or whether I bask in September's sweet inspiration or empower myself with October's service, only to end the year with gratitude in November and awe-inspiring magic and miracles in December. My *Magical Guide* has helped me release fears, set intentions, become the observer to the unfolding all around, get excited to continue to tell all about it, and embrace a beautiful human story—one marked by passion, perseverance, a loving family, good friends, tears, turmoil, courage, love, and laughter.

December 2020: Choose Faith over Fear

Walking through the darkness, never giving up looking for the light, breaking free—no more closets or cocoons for me. Now that the metamorphosis is complete, I know the only way forward is to choose faith as a companion over fear.

One of the best definitions of faith I've discovered came from the Bible at Hebrews 11:1: "Now faith is the assurance of things hoped for, the conviction of things not seen." Faith gave me the ability to know my strengths and talents when others pigeonholed me as ordinary. And my father once said, "Don't count out the seemingly ordinary because that is where sparks of the extraordinary begin." Faith empowered me to believe in possibility where external circumstances proved challenging. And, after almost losing my faith when my mom died, I managed to hold on and push through even when I felt like I wanted to die; even when the ringing in my head from the tinnitus would not stop. When I chose to fight on, I promised when I emerged from my cocoon, I would share my transformation through grief in hopes that I could help someone else who was experiencing a similar challenge.

At the beginning of 2020, who knew that I would need to rely heavily on my faith when the pandemic began and the world turned upside down? In January, when no one knew what was coming, I conducted my first interview of Season Three on my "Manifesting with Meg: Conversations with Extraordinary People" podcast. It ended with this inspirational call to action by a former teacher: "I encourage you to seize the day, not only seize it but seize it with gusto." And, at that time, who knew how important these words would be to help navigate what would follow?

This year, I had many opportunities to seize the day by taking all the lessons learned since my mother passed away and putting all the wisdom to good use. Having just started my fifth decade, I certainly felt a fire under me to get things finished. I spent the majority of the year decluttering my emotional and physical surroundings. I purged a lot of unnecessary baggage I was still carrying around that no longer served me. And, luckily, I had the support of many close confidantes to help as well. When I made the choice to shift and embraced the forward momentum, I felt like nothing could stop me from completing my goals as long as I focused on possibility—not even a pandemic.

As I explained before, at the end of every year for as long as I can remember, I meet up with my oldest and dearest friend Alicia on Christmas Eve morning at around five thirty to walk 5 miles around her neighborhood and catch up. She lives near my childhood home, so when I visit my dad for the holidays, one of the best gifts is to spend time with her. While we were still dealing with the limitations of the pandemic, following the health and safety protocols, we set our plans to follow through with our ritual while taking additional precautions. This year, we changed up our routine and met up on Christmas Day morning at nine instead. Pulling up into her driveway, I put on my butterfly-decorated face mask, cleaned my hands with pumpkin-scented sanitizer, and grabbed my heavy red shawl to stay warm.

Looking at the cracked skin on my hands from excessive washing to prevent the spread of the virus over the past eleven months, I whispered, "I need to use heavier cream."

I got out of my SUV and excitedly walked up the pathway to her house and rang the bell. When she opened the door, I belted out, "So good to see you. Are you ready to go? I so need this."

I bent down to pet her golden retriever who was equally excited to go on our walk.

I continued, "Feels a bit like a clarity or closure walk this year—pretty sure I need a little of both."

Alicia responded, "Yeah, you know it! Kinda glad we're changing up our pattern and walking today instead of yesterday. Don't want to ever repeat this year again."

"There are a lot of things I don't want to repeat anymore. How is it that in my fifties, I'm still dealing with bad habits and old issues? I get triggered and I'm right back to that little girl who felt like she wasn't good enough. I'm so done."

"At least you have the awareness, right? Thank goodness for that. Let's go." We laughed. She put the leash on her dog, and we walked down to the sidewalk and turned left.

And there on that quiet street, we began our walk. Admiring the holiday lawn decor and lights, Alicia, a veterinarian, pointed above to the telephone line where a large bird was perched.

"Look, there's a hawk. That's a good omen for us, a messenger of higher vision and intuition."

"Much better than the vultures I passed on our way over to your house." I laughed.

"Yeah, you're not kidding."

After about an hour, we crossed over the busy main road and continued walking through a new part of the College Park neighborhood that led to Lake Adair. As we got closer to the water, the wind picked up quite a bit, and the temperature dropped. With the sun's warmth on my face, I felt the contrast of the cool breeze as it hit the exposed skin on my neck, hands, and ankles.

I announced, "That feels so good. I'm definitely awake."

She replied, "How about what's going on in the world?"

"I'm excited. Lots of hope and possibility for new beginnings. I told you the rule of law would save us!"

"Let's hope so. We have to make it through January still!"

"I really do have faith that all will work out. What is the alternative? By the way—I love Rumi's quote 'Live life as though everything is rigged in your favor.' I gotta go with that! Especially now."

I looked over at Alicia and smiled. Friends for over forty years—our deep conversations around spirituality, dreams, and shared struggles sustained me. I was genuinely happy to be in her company.

We continued to talk about our life choices, lessons learned, and how far we've come in life. But most importantly, we talked about how we were done with criticism and judgment and looked forward to the future. I shared with Alicia that I had a dream the first night at my dad's house: *A female figure was trying to force me to look into a mirror and point out my flaws. I turned away from her and yelled out, "No more!"* I knew that this was a sign that I just wasn't going to believe the lies I told myself anymore. I had to let shame go. I am enough. I had to believe that because I've had enough.

On New Year's Eve, I went to lunch with my good friend and former colleague Richard for a belated birthday celebration. Ten years after our original pact of Los Tres Magos, we commented how different both of our lives were professionally and wondered what gifts January 6, 2021, would bring. Then, he handed me a beautiful yellow orchid and a card. On the outside of the card, it read "At 50." On the inside of the card, he wrote, "Dearest Meg, Happy 50th! Can you believe ten years ago we were at Miraval Spa walking labyrinths? Seems like yesterday. Love you, Richie."

I smiled, remembering that incredible trip for my fortieth birthday with Rich and my older sister Mary. Another activity that was inspired by Oprah who showcased it on her show, the three of us spent four days at this incredible destination spa in Tucson, Arizona, where we did some self-exploration in the desert and had new experiences like the Grammy award winner Tony Redhouse's "Drumming" class.

I laughed, "Rich, my God! Miraval was that long ago? After this past year, I could use a spa retreat like yesterday. Once we can, we'll set one up soon!"

"Yes!"

Then I laughed again, "Oh, and by the way, I just turned fifty-one."

"How did I miss that?"

"Rich, you're making me younger. I'll take the do-over. That's the best gift ever!"

Saying our goodbyes and wishing each other a happy and healthy new year, I felt so grateful once again for family and friends like this. I know how important these relationships have been and are as I keep moving forward on this journey to bliss. These connections are the precious gifts in my life that I never want to go without, for they have given me the most amazing memories and experiences. I couldn't have imagined a better reminder as to what is important in life, what kept me going when I thought I could not, and what I cherish as this difficult and unusual year comes to a close.

I end my story as I began, with inspiration. My mother once said, "When you allow your past wounds to heal and release the pain, you can help the world to heal." So I happily share my story, surrendering to it exactly as it unfolded, hoping it helps to inspire just one of you to wake up to the wonderful possibilities in your life. As for the tinnitus, a diagnosis that nearly did me in, I am grateful for it now. It woke me up to examine my life. Forever both a student and a lawyer, I am moved by the Greek philosopher Socrates who famously uttered the words, "The unexamined life is not worth living." Trusting the process, knowing that life will still have its ups and downs, I choose to move forward with a confidence that only comes from conscious awareness that everything has a purpose. Remembering that love is a decision, my family continues to do our best to support each other's dreams—knowing that no one is perfect and we are all works in progress. I'm grateful that I'm even closer to my father and sisters. Having survived the last ten years without my mother physically here, finding my footing again as I start this new chapter, I sat down and this time wrote a poem in honor of my mom:

May Peace Prevail on Earth

....

*I walked to the end of the world to find your lighthouse at Finisterre,
and what did I see?*
A message was there between Earth and the veil to eternity.
A tall post with words in various languages on this hill by the sea—
A written wish to the universe filled with hope and possibility.
"MAY PEACE PREVAIL ON EARTH," it read very succinctly,
I sat with both feet on the ground and really felt you there loving me.
It starts now, I thought—Calm the storms within to be free.
Let me learn this and let it mold my destiny.
There are many ways to die—it starts spiritually.
A voice not heard, injustices allowed and people who only think of the "me"!
*You taught me to look to enlightened ones —Jesus, Mother Theresa and
Gandhi—*
*Those powerful words set out, love one another and be the change you
wish to see.*
Who am I to become? You always said we are created from divinity.
Anger can wake you up—but don't let it hold you in captivity.
*I will do my best to shine, founded in love, joy, and peace—a fragrant
potpourri.*
*I can invite others to join me—wounds start to heal out in the open for
a better reality.*
Bowing my head, I see you still and I hope you are proud of me.
*You were always a voice for good and actions sound, I follow in the
footsteps of your legacy.*
Knowing I am enough—you'd want all of us to be happy.
No regrets, keep stress at bay so I can enjoy the world and its beauty.
As I start this new chapter, I know you are there watching over me.
Call me Butterfly—I am awake and I know this will set me free.

Dear Butterflies, I know my story may not be exactly like yours. While the circumstances are different, I am pretty certain that the underlying themes around the human condition are not. And I know what calls you to question who you are, why you are here, and why you go through what you do is specific to your experience and journey. This is what makes you unique and special. This is why the world needs you to wake up and come alive to the beauty of your dreams, choosing to take action and live intentionally with bliss and happiness as your goal. We've got this, and I'll be right there with you, striving to love unconditionally—ready to serve. I am looking back now and thanking God that I am in a much better place. It would have been too sad to have given up or gone through life asleep. There's so much magic in this beautiful world. If we can wake up to it by connecting with others from a place of love, this experiment called America will succeed and we'll be well on our way to bliss.

Knowing how he inspired me throughout the past ten years to never give up, I asked my dad for a final quote to leave me with at the end of this story of transformation and butterflies. He turned to his book called *Movie Quotes for All Occasions: Unforgettable Lines for Life's Biggest Moments* by Joe Scheibli and chose this:

"Life's a Garden. Dig it."
—**JOE DIRT**

So simple—there you go! Awaken, be intentional, get excited, tell your story, and dig it. Butterflies, I know we're ready. I believe in you!

NOW IT'S TIME FOR ALL OF US TO FLY!

Acknowledgments

To my father, Michael a.k.a. the Poppie, I am so grateful to learn with you what it means to be consciously alive. To Frank, my children, Michael and Ava, and my dogs, Leo and Luciana, I owe you all the greatest gratitude for helping me not to give up. To Mary Scanlon and Aimee Nocero, and their families: Tim, Patrick, Ryan, Rodney, Hunter, and Chase. Mommy is proud of each of us. I thank my extended family, specifically Betty, Pat, Eileen, Charles, Lori, Coco Padilla, the Simones, and the Mantillas.

To my cousin Margaret Santangelo, you believed in me and guided me along the editorial process helping to bring my story to light. To Wendy Shanker and Devan Sipher, for your incredible initial guidance. To David Landau, you gave of your time generously to edit this manuscript. To Pat Santangelo, I am eternally grateful for your love, support and incredible edits to my book. To Jennifer Leveau, Paul Lane, Tom Ayze, Rico Sogocio, Mike Spatola, and Simone Gers for your insights. My Bellas, Team S.H.I.N.E., Sisters in Spirit, Emmaus, Tanya Mikaela and my Butterfly Circle, Jennifer Diliz and Thrive Girl Thrive families, together we do rise. To Alicia Eliscu (Payton & Cadence), Lisa Lommerin, Teda Melero, Berta Medina-Garcia, Michele Barrett, Grace Hawley, Wendy Allen, Giseli Lemay, Norma & Pau De Regil, Richard Jurgens, Michele Drucker, Kevin Creegan, Gary Shendell, Corin Sands, Barbara Charris, Andrew Deutsch, Liam Beliveau, Karyn Todd, Linda and Karen Dalton, Jessica Quesada, Janet Woods, Pam Grout, and my soul sisters and brothers and butterflies, your friendships mean the world to me. Specifically, for my soul sister Denise Lane for saying yes to walking this journey with me embracing self-love.

To Jill Slaughter, Jessica Ciosek, and the Algonkian 18, I am grateful to be in the company of the best storytellers. To Reading Between the

Wines, for our shared love of books. Especially for my sixteen Camino Amigos—Heidi Siefkas, Denise Lane, Rita Sarmiento, Ana Victoria Rivas-Vasquez, Cristina O'Naghten, Alex Gutierrez, Alicia Carrazana, Paulina Gutierrez-Tawil, Jeanne Koss, Debbie Sullivan, Kristie Dickinson, Guan Bee Lim, LK Loh, Boonler Somchit, Chan Lai Ngoh, and Tan Jooi Chong—you all gave me the opportunity to write a beautiful ending. I will forever be grateful. For my DHS/ICE colleagues, Luisa Santiago, Kellie Santos-DeJesus, Jill Swartz, Phil d'Adesky, Judge Horn, and the Miami Immigration Court, ECU, the Divine Five, Catrina Pavlik-Keenan, Randee Lehrer, and the IPEC July 2017 class, you helped me start over. For my mother's caregivers, Shannon Cronk, Placido Buniao, and Dina Alcius, you blessed all of us. For Amy Butler, thank you for the beauty you brought to my life. For Hector Prado, thank you for my beautiful butterfly painting. To Christine Crabtree, for introducing me to the wisdom of Paulo Coelho. For Paulo Coelho and Liz Gilbert, the author guides on my hero's journey. For Oprah and George Burns, your photos are amazing. Chelsea Hettrick, for your support. Jose Bandes, Ismael Cala, and CNN, grateful for the opportunity. Eva Paglialonga, Cecilia Shaw, Paul Canali, Stan Sowinski, Natalia Sikaczowski, Olga Reyes, and Maite Albuerne, you are incredible healers. For Dr. Habib Sadeghi and Dr. Sherry Sami, you shared love with a stranger, now soul family. For Chris Martin and Coldplay, thank you for your music. For Red Bike Studios' amazing instructors. For Dr. Jessica Mosley, for encouraging me to unapologetically show up authentically. And for Lawrence Newberg and Jon Saxx, you brought me music, pure imagination, and endless possibilities. For She Writes Press (SWP) publisher Brooke Warner, the SWP team, and the authors in the SWP 2021 Cohort. For my amazing cartographer, Mike Morgenfeld. For the PR by the Book team, thank you for helping this butterfly fly higher. To everyone else who is a part of my past, present, and future story. And for the old stationary bike in the gym at Brickell Key II.

Finally, thank you, Mom, Mary Jo, for the gift of *life*, the example of *love*, and the reminder to *laugh*, focusing on having no regrets. I know you are our angel, our beautiful butterfly, and will continue to watch over us and our families each step of the way.

Photo Journal

Miss Mary Jo Santangelo, New York Cherry Blossom Princess

Meg Nocero and Fred circa 1979

Perhaps you sent a lovely card,
or sat upon a chair.
Perhaps you sent us beautiful flowers.
If so, we saw them there.
Perhaps you spoke the kindest words
that any friend could say.
Perhaps you were not there at all,
just thought of us that day.
Whatever you did to console our hearts,
We thank you so much, whatever your part.

The Family of Mary Jo Nocero

Nocero/Simone Wedding, February 19, 2000   In Remembrance of Mary Jo, April 12, 2011

Susan G. Komen Breast Cancer Walk, October 2011—Orlando & Miami, Fl.

Mary Jo Nocero Women's
Tennis Scholarship
Presentation at Trinity
Preparatory School,
October 2011

(left) Liz Gilbert at Miami Book Fair 2013; (middle) Dr. Wayne Dyer at Hayhouse Writing Workshop 2014; (right) Dr. Oz at NOIAW Awards 2014

Oprah Winfrey & Mari Viña-Rodriguez at
Oprah's Life You Want Weekend in Miami, Fl., 2014,
Photo Credit George Burns

With Denise Lane, Frank Simone,
Dr. Sherry Sami & Dr. Habib Sadeghi at Love Button
Global Movement Event in Malibu, California 2017

(left) With Richard Jurgens at a Career Recruitment, Photo Credit Sharon Bogard;
(right) The Intern Butterflies on my office door

Day 1 of El Camino at Sarria: L to R: Debbie Sullivan, Jeanne Koss, Vicky Rivas-Vasquez, Meg, Denise Lane, Tan Jooi Chong, LK Loh, Guan Bee Lim, Cristina O'Naghten, Kristie Dickinson,Heidi Siefkas, Boonler Somchit, Chan Lai Ngoh, Alex Gutierrez, Paulina Gutierrez-Tawil, Alicia Carrazana, Rita Sarmiento

17 Camino Amigos at the "Catedral de Santiago de Compostela" with Pilgrim Passport and Certificate

The Lighthouse at Finesterre, April 21, 2018

Simone Family: Frank, Meg, Ava, Michael,
Luciana and Leo, Photo Credit: Maria Brito

(left) S.H.I.N.E.: Amy Butler, Lisa Rosen, Tina Ashley, Pam Grout, Denise Lane, & Karyn
Todd Essence Festival 2019; (middle) Delene "Dr. Mom" Musielak & Dr. Jessica
"MizCEO" Mosley; (right) S.H.I.N.E. Love 2019, DJ Lawrence Newberg and Jon Saxx

(first) Lisa Lommerin at Omega Institute, September 2015;
(second) Teda Melero, May 2017- right before she moved to Spain;
(third and fourth) Dr. Alicia Eliscu, H.S. May 1987, November 2020

Meg Nocero 2019, Photo Credit Michelle Citrin

With Artist Hector Prado at S.H.I.N.E. Networking Event in 2017, Photo Credit World Red Eye

Original Cover Design by Artist Hector Prado

About the Author

Meg Nocero, Esq., is a former federal prosecutor, inspirational speaker, certified empowerment coach, and award-winning author of *The Magical Guide to Bliss: Daily Keys to Unlock Your Dreams, Spirit, and Inner Bliss* and a book of affirmations called *Sparkle & Shine, 108 M.A.N.T.R.A.s to Brighten Your Day and Lighten Your Way*. She holds a BA in Spanish with a concentration in Italian from Boston College, an MA in International Affairs from the University of Miami, and a JD from St. Thomas University School of Law. She is a member of the Florida Bar and serves on the Wellness Committee of the American Immigration Lawyers Association.

She holds certifications from the Federal Law Enforcement Training Center, the DHS/ICE Mentoring Program, the Institute for Professional Excellence in Coaching, the International Coaching Federation, The Happiness Studies Academy, Yale's The Science of Well-Being, David Allen's Getting Things Done—the Art of Stress-Free Productivity, and Stephen Covey's FOCUS: Your Highest Priorities on Time Management.

After she was brought on stage in Miami with Oprah Winfrey in 2014, she was inspired to manifest the life of her dreams and founded Butterflies & Bliss LLC as well as S.H.I.N.E. Networking Inc. that provides educational scholarships to young innovative leaders and is a Love Button Global Movement Ambassador. She appeared on CNN Español with Ismael Cala and hosts a YouTube/podcast show *Manifesting with Meg: Conversations with Extraordinary People.* She has delivered a TEDx talk entitled "Wake Up! How to Create a Better Story for a Happier Village" and has been interviewed for online media including MSNBC, CBS, the Boston Herald, and the Chicago Tribune. She also participated on the "Improve Your Mind, Body, Soul, and Even Your Wallet" panel at BookConline 2020.

Meg is also a contributing author for *Amy Butler's Blossom: Create Love—Express Beauty—Be Kind,* for *Thrive Girl Thrive, A Woman's Guide for Abundant Mental, Emotional, and Spiritual Wellbeing,* and *The Price of Greatness: Powerful Stories of Overcoming Tests, Trials & Adversity in the Pursuit of a Dream.* She was named a finalist in the Inspirational and Motivational Nonfiction Categories for the 2017 and 2020 Next Generation Indie Book Awards and the eleventh Annual National Indie Excellence Awards; she won the 2019 Independent Press Award for Motivational Books; and she was named a Notable Top 100 Indie Authors in the Shelf Unbound Best Indie Books, a Gold Level-One Recipient for the Mom's Choice Award in 2020, a 2021 finalist in the Book Excellence Awards and a Quarterfinalist in the 2021 Book Life Prize Nonfiction Contest.

For inquiries email megnocero@mac.com;
Connect on social media @MegNocero

Author photo © Michelle Citrin www.michellecitrinstudios.com

SELECTED TITLES FROM SHE WRITES PRESS

She Writes Press is an independent publishing company founded to serve women writers everywhere. Visit us at www.shewritespress.com.

Motherlines: Letters of Love, Longing, and Liberation by Patricia Reis. $16.95, 978-1-63152-121-8. In her midlife search for meaning, and longing for maternal connection, Patricia Reis encounters uncommon women who inspire her journey and discovers an unlikely confidante in her aunt, a free-spirited Franciscan nun.

Don't Leave Yet: How My Mother's Alzheimer's Opened My Heart by Constance Hanstedt. $16.95, 978-1-63152-952-8. The chronicle of Hanstedt's journey toward independence, self-assurance, and connectedness as she cares for her mother, who is rapidly losing her own identity to the early stage of Alzheimer's.

Godmother: An Unexpected Journey, Perfect Timing, and Small Miracles by Odile Atthalin. $16.95, 978-1-63152-172-0. After thirty years of traveling the world, Odile Atthalin—a French intellectual from a well-to-do family in Paris—ends up in Berkeley, CA, where synchronicities abound and ultimately give her everything she has been looking for, including the gift of becoming a godmother.

Her Beautiful Brain: A Memoir by Ann Hedreen. $16.95, 978-1-93831-492-6. The heartbreaking story of a daughter's experiences as her beautiful, brainy mother begins to lose her mind to an unforgiving disease: Alzheimer's.

At the Narrow Waist of the World: A Memoir by Marlena Maduro Baraf. $16.95, 978-1-63152-588-9. In this lush and vivid coming-of-age memoir about a mother's mental illness and the healing power of a loving Jewish and Hispanic extended family, young Marlena must pull away from her mother, leave her Panama home, and navigate the transition to an American world.

Note to Self: A Seven-Step Path to Gratitude and Growth by Laurie Buchanan. $16.95, 978-1-63152-113-3. Transforming intention into action, *Note to Self* equips you to shed your baggage, bridging the gap between where you are and where you want to be—body, mind, and spirit—and empowering you to step into joy-filled living *now!*